# The Information Please Kids' Almanac

For information about permission to reproduce
selections from this book, write to Permissions,
Houghton Mifflin Company, 215 Park Avenue
South, New York, New York 10003

CIP data is available.
ISBN 0-395-64737-1 (cl)
ISBN 0-395-58801-4 (pa)

Information Please is a registered trademark of
Houghton Mifflin Company.

Printed in the United States of America

Design by Catharyn Tivy

BP 10 9 8 7 6 5 4 3 2 1

# The Information Please® Kids'Almanac

*Alice Siegel and*
*Margo McLoone Basta*

Houghton Mifflin Company
Boston • New York • London
1992

*For my daughters, Catherine and Elizabeth,*
*who are my heart and soul.*
                    *— Margo McLoone Basta*

*This book is dedicated to my husband,*
*George, and my three sons, Andrew, Howard*
*and James.*          *— Alice Siegel*

## ACKNOWLEDGMENTS

We would like to thank the following
people for their help and support. Thanks
to Vivienne S. Jaffe, a great editor and
collaborator; Jane Dystel, who had the
idea; Steve Lewers, who put it all together;
Marnie Patterson, who held it all together;
Jane Letus, who typed and retyped with
patience and intelligence; Joann Sackett,
the best children's librarian; Buffy Barlow,
for all her help; Arthur Semioli, N.Y.P.D.,
and Luise Erdmann, the thoughtful lady
from Cambridge. Additional thanks to
Debbie Feldman for her input and support,
to Doug Basta for his ideas and suggestions,
and to William Basta for his patience.

*Margo McLoone Basta*
*Alice Siegel*

# Contents

# Animals

*From Aardvarks to Zebras*

FROM THE SINGLE-CELLED protozoan to the highly complex and intelligent human being, there are more than a *billion* kinds of animals on earth. Animals inhabit every inch

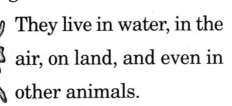

of our planet, from the coldest Arctic region to the hottest desert. They live in water, in the air, on land, and even in other animals.

## ANIMAL TYPES

Because there are so many animals, scientists have grouped them into categories so that they can be studied more easily. Remember, however, that there are always exceptions to any rule. The living world is a place where rules are hard to make! Here is a simplified breakdown.

*Amphibians* have backbones, are cold-blooded, and live on land and in water at different times. Three types of amphibians are frogs and toads, salamanders, and caecilians. Caecilians are primitive amphibians that resemble earthworms. They are found in the tropics.

*Birds* have backbones and feathers and lay eggs; most can fly (although penguins cannot).

*Fish* have backbones, breathe through gills, and live in water; most are cold-blooded and lay eggs (although sharks give birth to live young).

*By definition, an animal is a living thing that can move, obtain food, rid itself of waste, and reproduce.*

*Mammals* have backbones and four-chambered hearts, are warm-blooded, and are nourished by their mothers' milk; most are born live (however, the platypus lays eggs).

Some lesser-known animal groups are:

*Arthropods,* such as crabs, lobsters, shrimp

*Coelenterates,* such as jellyfish, corals, sea anemone

*Echinoderms,* such as starfish, sea urchins

*Insects,* such as beetles, ants, bugs, butterflies

*Mollusks,* such as clams, oysters

*Sponges,* such as spongia, mollissima

*Worms,* such as flatworms (flukes), roundworms (hookworms), segmented worms (earthworms), and rotifers (philodina)

*Warm-blooded animals regulate their own body temperatures; their bodies use energy to maintain a constant temperature.*

*Cold-blooded animals depend on their surroundings to establish their body temperatures.*

# WHERE IN THE WORLD DO ANIMALS LIVE?

Animals live only where they can survive. Koala bears, for example, eat only the leaves of certain

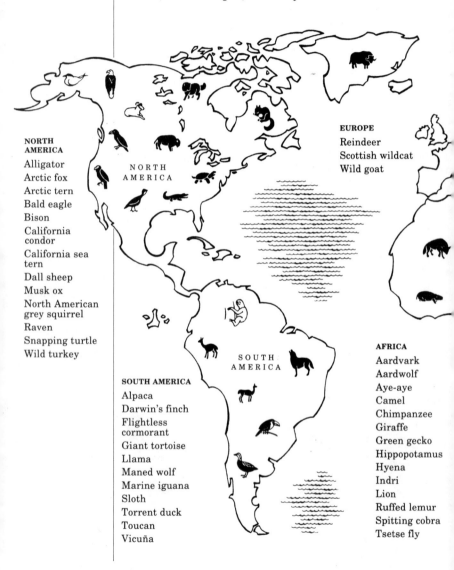

**NORTH AMERICA**

Alligator
Arctic fox
Arctic tern
Bald eagle
Bison
California condor
California sea tern
Dall sheep
Musk ox
North American grey squirrel
Raven
Snapping turtle
Wild turkey

NORTH AMERICA

**SOUTH AMERICA**

Alpaca
Darwin's finch
Flightless cormorant
Giant tortoise
Llama
Maned wolf
Marine iguana
Sloth
Torrent duck
Toucan
Vicuña

SOUTH AMERICA

**EUROPE**

Reindeer
Scottish wildcat
Wild goat

**AFRICA**

Aardvark
Aardwolf
Aye-aye
Camel
Chimpanzee
Giraffe
Green gecko
Hippopotamus
Hyena
Indri
Lion
Ruffed lemur
Spitting cobra
Tsetse fly

eucalyptus trees, so they must live in Australia, where these trees grow. All of these animals can survive in only one place on earth—and many of them are endangered.

**ASIA**

Asiatic lion
Giant panda
Komodo dragon
Przewalski's horse
Snow leopard
Zeren

**AUSTRALIA AND NEW ZEALAND**

Archie's frog
Dingo
Duck-billed platypus
Emu
Kakapo
Kiwi
Koala
Quokka
Short-nosed rat kangaroo
Short-tailed wallaby
Tasmanian devil

**ANTARCTICA**

Adélie penguin
Penguin
Ross seal
Weddell seal

EUROPE

ASIA

AFRICA

AUSTRALIA

11

## WHAT DO YOU CALL THEM?

Although these words sound scientific, they are commonly used to describe animal families or behavior.

Marsupials *are families of mammals, such as kangaroos and opossums, whose females carry their young in an external pouch.*

*Arachnids* are arthropods, such as spiders, scorpions, mites, and ticks.

*Carnivores* are flesh-eating animals, like lions.

*Cetaceans* are ocean mammals, including whales and dolphins.

*Diurnal* animals, such as squirrels, are awake during the day.

*Herbivores* are animals, such as deer, who eat plants.

*Invertebrates* are animals without backbones, such as worms.

*Nocturnal* animals, such as owls, are awake at night.

*Omnivorous* animals, such as bears, eat meat and plants.

*Pinnipeds* are aquatic mammals with flippers, like seals and walruses.

*Predators* are animals, such as tigers, who stalk and kill other animals for food.

*Primates* are mammals, including chimps, gorillas, and monkeys.

*Quadrupeds* are animals with four feet, such as cows.

*Rodents* have large front teeth for gnawing and cheek teeth for chewing, like squirrels and gerbils.

*Vertebrates* are animals with backbones, such as horses.

## ANIMALS ON THE MOVE

Have you ever wondered if you could outrun an elephant or outswim a dolphin? Here is a list of top speeds over short distance . . . see how you would do!

*Black mamba snake, 20 mph*

*Cheetah, 70 mph*

*Dolphin, 30 mph*

*Domestic cat, 30 mph*

*Dragonfly, 36 mph*

*Elephant, 25 mph*

*Garden snail, 0.03 mph*

*Giraffe, 30 mph*

*Greyhound dog, 39 mph*

*Grizzly bear, 30 mph*

*Human being, 27.89 mph*

*Leatherback turtle, 22 mph*

*Lion, 50 mph*

*Peregrine falcon, 217 mph*

*Sailfish, 68 mph*

*Spider, 1.17 mph*

*Three-toed sloth, 0.15 mph*

*Tortoise, 0.17 mph*

*Wild turkey (flying), 55 mph*

## SORRY, WRONG ANIMAL

The *American buffalo* is not a buffalo; it is a bison.

The *bald eagle* is not bald; it has a cap of white feathers on top of its head.

The *koala* is not a bear; it is a marsupial, which is a mammal with a pouch.

The *Komodo dragon* is not a dragon; it is a lizard.

The *prairie dog* is not a dog; it is a rodent similar to a squirrel.

The *scorpion* is not a spider; it is a relative of the spider. (The scorpion has a stinger in its tail. A spider has an appendage on its head which it uses to catch and paralyze prey.)

The *titmouse* is not a mouse; it is a bird.

The *water hog* is not a pig; it is a rodent, also called Capybara.

*The seahorse is not a horse; it is a fish.*

## FANTASTIC ANIMAL FACTS

- A chameleon (small lizard) can move its eyes in two directions at the same time.

- The embryos of tiger sharks fight each other while in their mother's womb. The survivor is the baby shark that is born.

- Dolphins sleep at night just below the surface of the water. They frequently rise to the surface for air.

- A cockroach can live up to 10 days without a head.

- An albatross can sleep while it flies. It apparently dozes while cruising at 25 mph.

- Amazon ants (red ants found in the western U.S.) steal the larvae of other ants to keep as slaves. The slave ants build homes for and feed the Amazon ants, who cannot do anything but fight. They depend completely on their slaves for survival.

- The hummingbird is the only bird that can fly straight up, backward, and upside down!

- A leech is a worm that feeds on blood. It will pierce its victim, fill itself with three to four times its own body weight in blood, and will not feed again for months.

- Lovebirds are small parakeets who live in pairs. Male and female lovebirds look alike, but most other male birds have brighter colors than the females.

- Only female mosquitoes bite. Females need the protein from blood to produce their eggs.

## ANIMAL SCAVENGERS

Scavengers are animals that feed on dead or injured animals caught by predators. Scavengers are not usually held in high esteem, but they have a job to do: they clean the earth of organic garbage.

### Five Birds That Scavenge

*California condors* eat the remains of dead animals.

*Crows* can be seen eating small mammals, like squirrels, that have been killed on the roads.

*Marabou storks* of the Eastern Hemisphere eat dead fish and reptiles.

*Seagulls* will eat anything!

*Vultures* (buzzards) are full-time scavengers.

### Three Fish That Scavenge

*Marine eels* will eat dead fish and crustaceans.

*Remoras* swim near large fish and eat their leftovers.

*Sharks* keep the ocean clean by eating dead or wounded fish.

### Seven Mammals That Scavenge

*Bears* often follow ravens in order to find dead fish to eat. Alaskan brown bears feed on dead seals, walruses, and whales that have floated ashore.

*Hyenas* hunt and scavenge in packs. African villagers often leave their garbage out for hyenas to eat.

*Jackals* (African wild dogs) often scavenge in packs beside hyenas.

*Leopards,* like lions, will scavenge when their hunting is unsuccessful.

*Lions* are great predators but will often scavenge or steal prey caught by other animals.

*Raccoons* eat garbage from dumps and cans, especially if it smells of chicken or fish.

*Rats* will eat anything.

## An International Guide to Animal Talk

Didn't you always suspect that animals spoke different languages? They do as far as their country's written word is concerned. So if your dog says "guf-guf" instead of "bow-wow" or "rrruf-ruf," maybe he or she is Russian! Here is a brief guide to international animal talk.

| ANIMAL | ENGLISH | RUSSIAN | JAPANESE | FRENCH | GERMAN |
|---|---|---|---|---|---|
| BIRD | *Tweet-tweet* | *Squick* | *Qui-qui* | *Choon-choon* | *Piep-piep* |
| CAT | *Meow* | *Meau* | *Nyeow* | *Meow* | *Meow-meow* |
| COW | *Moo* | *Mu* | *Mo-Mo* | *Meu-meu* | *Muh-muh* |
| DOG | *Rrruf-ruf* | *Guf-guf* | *Won-won* | *Whou-whou* | *Vow-vow* |
| DUCK | *Quack-quack* | *Quack* | *Qua-qua* | *Coin-coin* | *Quack* |
| GOAT | *Meh-meh* | *Beee* | *Mee-mee* | *Ma-ma* | *Eeh-eeh* |
| HORSE | *Neigh-neigh* | *Eohoho* | *He-heeh* | *Hee-hee-hee* | *Iiiih* |
| OWL | *Whoo* | *Ooooo* | *Hoo-hoo* | *Oo-oo* | *Wooo-wooo* |
| PIG | *Oink-oink* | *Qrr-qrrr* | *Boo* | *Groan-groan* | *Crr-cvl* |
| ROOSTER | *Cocka-doodle-do* | *Kukuriki* | *KoKeKock-ko* | *Cocorico* | *Goockle* |

## CALLING ALL ANIMAL SCIENTISTS

A person who specializes in the study of animals is called a zoologist. Zoologists who study certain species of animals have their own names.

*Apiculturists* specialize in bees.

*Anthropologists* study human beings.

*Entomologists* study insects.

*Herpetologists* study reptiles and amphibians.

*Ichthyologists* specialize in fish.

*Mammalogists* specialize in mammals.

*Ornithologists* study birds.

## ANIMALS FROM START TO FINISH

It takes an average of 270 days for human beings to grow before they are born. This chart shows how long it takes some other animals to gestate or incubate.

*Animals that grow in their mothers gestate. Animals that grow in eggs outside their mothers incubate.*

| ANIMAL | AVERAGE TIME |
|---|---|
| AFRICAN ELEPHANT | 1¾ YEARS |
| BLACK BEAR | 210 DAYS |
| COW | 283 DAYS |
| DOG | 63 DAYS |
| DOMESTIC CAT | 63 DAYS |
| GIRAFFE | 1¼ YEARS |
| HORSE | 337 DAYS |
| OTTER | 280 DAYS |
| PARAKEET | 19 DAYS |
| REINDEER | 7½ MONTHS |
| RHINOCEROS | 650 DAYS |
| SWAN | 42 DAYS |
| WHALE | 420 DAYS |

## Naming Animal Babies

You know that a newborn human is called an infant or a baby. But do you know the names of these other animal newborns? If you know six or more, congratulations!

| ANIMAL | NEWBORN NAME |
| --- | --- |
| COCKROACH | NYMPH |
| DEER | FAWN |
| ELEPHANT | CALF |
| FISH | FRY |
| GIRAFFE | CALF |
| KANGAROO | JOEY |
| NIGHTINGALE | NESTLING |
| SEAL | WHELP |
| SWAN | CYGNET |
| TURKEY | POULT |
| WHALE | CALF |
| ZEBRA | COLT |

## Animal Dads

Most animals never even see their parents! Many are insects, fish, or amphibians that hatched from fertilized eggs to face life completely alone. When animals are raised by parents, it's most often the mother who does the rearing. But we found some unusual animal dads.

*Catfish:* A father sea catfish keeps his eggs in his mouth until they are ready to hatch. He will not eat until his young are born, which may take several weeks.

*Cockroach:* Father cockroach eats bird droppings

to obtain precious nitrogen, which he carries back to feed his young.

*Duck:* Most male ducks live as bachelors, but the ruddy duck of North America helps care for his young.

*Frog:* Father Darwin frog hatches his eggs in a pouch in his mouth. He can eat and continue about his business until his tadpoles lose their tails, become tiny frogs, and jump out of his mouth!

*Monkey:* Marmosets are tiny South American monkeys. The fathers take care of their babies from birth. When the marmoset is born, the father cleans it, then carries it to the mother only when it needs to be nursed. When the baby can eat solid food, the father will feed it.

*Penguin:* Father Emperor penguin withstands the Antarctic cold for 60 days or more to protect his eggs, which he keeps on his feet, covered with a feathered flap. During this entire time he doesn't

eat a thing. Most father penguins lose about 25 pounds while they wait for their babies to hatch. Afterward, they feed the chicks a special liquid from their throats. When the mother penguins return to care for the young, the fathers go to sea to eat and rest.

*Rhea:* Rheas are large South American birds similar to ostriches. Father rhea takes sole care of his young. From eggs to chicks, he feeds, defends, and protects them until they are old enough to survive on their own.

*Sand grouse:* Father Namaqua sand grouse of Africa's Kalahari Desert flies as far as 50 miles a day in order to soak himself in water and return to his nest, where his chicks can drink from his feathers!

*Seahorse:* Father seahorse has a pouch in which the mother lays her eggs. The father then looks after the eggs for about 2 months, until they hatch and leave the pouch. He continues to protect the young until they are able to live on their own.

*Siamese fighting fish:* When the mother lays her eggs, the father catches them in his mouth, then drops them into a nest he has prepared. He guards the nest and protects the baby fish when they hatch.

*Wolf:* When the mother wolf gives birth to pups, the father stands guard outside their den and brings food to the mother and pups. As they grow, he not only plays with them but also teaches them how to survive. Wolves continue to live together much as human families do.

*Since earthworms have both male and female sex organs, every earthworm can be both a mother and a father!*

## BIRDS AS SYMBOLS AND OMENS

From ancient times to the present, certain birds have been considered both symbols and forecasters of events. These eight birds, from every part of the world, have been especially important.

*Cranes* are revered in Asia as symbols of a long life.

*Cuckoos* are welcomed as a sign of spring in Europe and are considered omens of a happy marriage.

*Doves* symbolize love and peace. To dream of doves means happiness is at hand.

*Eagles* are considered sacred by Native Americans, for the claws and bones of the birds are believed to drive illness away. As the symbol of the U.S., the bald eagle stands for endurance, independence, and courage.

*Owls* are considered prophets of doom. In ancient Rome as well as modern European and American folklore, a hooting owl warns of death.

The *phoenix* is a mythical bird that dies by fire, then rises from its own ashes after 500 years! Thus it symbolizes renewed life.

*Ravens* are said to predict death and pestilence. Folklore has it that the raven's sense of smell is so acute that it can smell death before it comes. No one wanted to see a raven fly over a house!

*Storks* are symbols of good luck. In folklore, storks deliver babies.

# WHAT'S THAT ANIMAL NUMBER?

- Mayflies have a life span of about 2 hours.
- A slug has 4 noses.
- Despite its long neck, the giraffe has only 7 neck bones — the same number as a person.
- The mouse deer of Asia, a real deer, is only 9 inches high.
- A lobster has 10 legs.
- The eye of the giant squid, the largest of any animal, is 15 inches across.
- The largest animal brain belongs to the sperm whale. It can weigh 20 pounds.
- Most starfish have 5 arms, but the basket starfish may have 50 arms or more!
- A jellyfish is 95% water.
- A male peacock has 200 long feathers that stand up from his back.
- A millipede (which means "thousand-footed") may have as few as 8 legs or as many as several hundred.

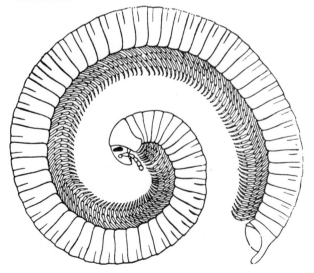

- An elephant eats 250 pounds of plants and drinks 50 gallons of water a day.
- A seahorse can lay 400 eggs at a time.
- The leatherback turtle weighs up to 1,900 pounds.
- A hummingbird may visit 2,000 flowers a day for nectar.
- A tapeworm may grow up to 40 feet long with up to 3,000 segments.
- There are more than 12,000 species of ants in the world.
- There is a tiny insect, called a midge, that beats its wings 62,000 times a minute.
- One beehive can contain up to 80,000 bees at a time.
- There are 200 million insects for each person on earth.

## ANIMAL COMMUNICATION

Most animals (including people) use "body language" as well as sound in order to communicate with one another. Here are some of the movements and gestures animals make to express themselves.

*Bees* dance when they have found nectar. The scout bee will dance in the air, and the dance directs other bees to the location of the nectar.

*Chimpanzees* greet each other by touching hands.

Male *fiddler crabs* wave their giant claw to attract female fiddler crabs.

*White-tailed deer* show alarm by flicking up their tails.

*Dogs* stretch their front legs out in front of them and lower their bodies when they want to play.

*Elephants* show affection by entwining their trunks.

*Giraffes* press their necks together when they are attracted to each other.

*Gorillas* stick their tongues out to show anger.

*Horses* rub noses as a sign of affection.

*Kangaroos* thump their hind legs to warn others of danger.

*Prairie dogs* bare their teeth and press their mouths together to discover if they are friends or foes.

*Whales* breach (leap out of the water) repeatedly to send messages to other whales.

Swans *entwine their long necks both to fight and to court.*

## ANIMAL ARSENAL

Animals are equipped to protect themselves and to attack and kill in order to get food. Here are some of the body parts and methods animals use for defense and attack.

*Antlers:* The deer family, including elk, moose, and caribou, use their antlers to charge and duel with their enemies.

*Camouflage:* Coloring that matches or blends with an animal's surroundings help the animal to hide. The Arctic fox, green tree frog, penguin, and polar bear are a few of the animals who use this method in defense.

*Claws:* Bears, owls, and tigers are some of the animals who use their sharp claws to fight as well as to catch prey.

*Ejection:* Both cuttlefish and squid eject black inky fluids in which to hide from predators. The sea cucumber squirts its insides out to defend itself! (It then grows a new stomach.)

*Explosions:* Self-sacrificing ants explode in the face of the enemy to save their colony. A South American lizard squirts blood from its eyes to repel enemies.

*Feet:* A large bird like the ostrich has a powerful kick. Elephants, cottontail rabbits, and kangaroos also use their feet to fight.

*Horns:* Goats, sheep, and water buffalo use their horns to fight in the same way that deer use their antlers.

*Odor:* Skunks aren't the only animals to use scent glands for defense. Some others are bedbugs, cockroaches, earwigs, foxes, mink, snakes, weasels, and wolverines.

*Poison:* Many animals have poison glands, such as toads, moths, snakes, and spiders. Coral snakes and cottonmouth snakes are poisonous. The platypus has poison in its spurs. The spines of some fish like the stone fish and scorpion fish are poisonous.

*Shocks:* The electric catfish, electric eel, and electric ray all use shock to paralyze or damage their victims.

*Spitting:* The archer fish spits water from a "blowgun" in the roof of its mouth to capture the bugs it eats. The jawfish spits pebbles from its mouth to defend itself. The spitting cobra spits its venom (poison) into the eyes of its enemy.

*Stings:* A sting pierces, hurts, and sometimes poisons the victim. A few of the many stinging animals are the bee, jellyfish, Portuguese man-of-war, sea urchin, and wasp.

*Tails:* Lizards use their tails to hit their enemies or knock them over.

*Teeth:* Baboons, mice, squirrels, rats, wolves, and woodchucks use their teeth as both defensive and offensive weapons.

*Tongues:* Anteaters, chameleons, frogs, and lizards use their tongues to catch prey.

*Tusks:* The African wart hog and the walrus use their tusks to fight enemies.

## ASK ANY ANIMAL

*Do animals cry?*
Most animals don't (with the exception of human beings), but there is a large, gentle marine mammal called a dugong who lives in the Indian Ocean and sheds tears when in trouble or pain.

*Do woodpeckers get headaches from all their hammering?*
No. Woodpeckers' heads are filled with pockets of air that cushion their head bones as they drill for food or bore the tunnels that lead to their nests.

*What's the difference between teeth and tusks?*
Nothing! Tusks are simply large teeth that protrude outside an animal's mouth.

*How do chicks break out of their shells?*
Baby birds have an egg tooth, which they use to

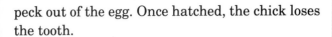

peck out of the egg. Once hatched, the chick loses the tooth.

*Does each bird have one song?*
No, birds have many songs. Birds "sing" to communicate about feeding, nesting, flying, defending, and many other aspects of their lives.

*Are the stripes of any two zebras alike?*
No, each zebra has its own stripe pattern, just as each person has his or her own fingerprint.

*What's the difference between an antler and a horn?*
An *antler* is made up of solid bone; it is shaped like a branch and is shed yearly. Moose, caribou, and deer are some animals with antlers. A *horn* is hollow, made up of a hard skin tissue similar to a fingernail. A horn has no branches and is permanent. Some horned animals are antelope, buffalo, and goats.

*Why do birds fly in a V formation?*
It's efficient! A V formation helps the birds conserve energy because the V-shaped air streams created by the birds in front reduce the wind resistance for the other birds. When the lead bird gets tired, another bird takes over.

*What's the difference between extinct and endangered?*
*Extinct* is forever. It means the entire species of animals has died and can never return. Passenger pigeons are extinct. *Endangered* animals are in immediate danger of becoming extinct. The few remaining ones are dying off. The California condor is an endangered animal.

## PRESIDENTIAL PETS

U.S. presidents and their families have typically liked animals. Barbara Bush, the wife of President George Bush, even wrote a book about her dog Millie. Here are some of the more unusual presidential pets.

| PRESIDENT | PET | NAME |
|---|---|---|
| George Washington | Parrot | Polly |
| John Q. Adams | Alligator | |
| Abraham Lincoln | Turkey | Jack |
| Benjamin Harrison | Goat | His Whiskers |
| Theodore Roosevelt | Garter snake | Emily Spinach |
| Calvin Coolidge | Bobcat | Smokey |
| | Donkey | Ebenezer |
| | Raccoons | Horace & Rebecca |

## ROYAL PETS

From earliest times, royalty has collected strange animals. Power, wealth, and privilege gave them the ability to acquire animals of great beauty, ferocity, or rareness.

*Henry's elephant was the first ever in England. Josephine's orangutan sat at her dinner table wearing a coat!*

| RULER | PET |
|---|---|
| Julius Caesar, emperor of Rome | Giraffe |
| Ramses II, pharaoh of Egypt | Lion (Anta-M-Nekht) |
| Nero, emperor of Rome | Tigress (Phoebe) |
| Charlemagne, emperor of France | Elephant (Abul Abba) |
| Charles V, king of Spain | Seals (7) |
| Louis IX, king of France | Elephant & Porcupine |
| Henry III, king of England | White bear & Elephant |
| Josephine, wife of Napoleon | Orangutan |

## THE WORLD'S FAVORITE PETS

Household pets are common in America, Europe, and Asia.

- In China and Hong Kong, cats are thought to bring good luck and are kept in shops as well as homes.
- The Japanese keep birds and crickets as pets.
- In Arab countries, dogs are considered unclean. Contact with a dog must be followed by a ritual washing.
- The Italians also have little use for dogs but find cats charming and companionable. Thousands of stray cats live in the Forum, the Colosseum, and other historic landmarks in Rome.
- The Inuit Eskimo of northern Canada adopt bear cubs, foxes, birds, and baby seals.
- Animals are rarely kept as pets in Africa.
- The British are especially fond of pets. Half of all the households in England have a pet, usually a cat or bird.

*Australian aborigines capture dingo (wild dog) puppies and raise them for a time before letting them go.*

# ANIMALS THAT REGENERATE

Many animals can regenerate—that is, grow new parts of their bodies to replace those that have been damaged. Here are a few of these amazing creatures.

*Lizards* who lose their tails in battle can grow new ones.

*Planariums* are flat worms. If cut into pieces, each piece can grow into a new worm.

*Sea cucumbers* have bodies that are 6 feet long. If cut into pieces, each one will become a new sea cucumber.

*Sharks* continually replace lost teeth. A shark may grow 24,000 teeth in a lifetime.

*Spiders* can regrow missing legs or parts of legs.

*Sponges* can be divided. In that case, the cells of the sponge will regrow and combine exactly as before.

*Starfish* that lose arms can grow new ones; sometimes an entire arm can grow from a lost one.

## DO ANIMALS HAVE PERSONALITIES?

We don't know whether animals insult their enemies by calling them human beings, but we call on quite a few animals to describe other people in uncomplimentary ways. Here are some animals that seem to embody less desirable human characteristics.

*Bats:* To call someone "batty" or say a person has "bats in the belfry" is to call the person crazy. When a ringing church bell disturbs bats who live in a belfry (the tower where a church bell is rung), they fly around in a frenzied way. The belfry is seen as a person's head; the disordered movements of the bats are his or her thoughts.

*Birdbrain:* A stupid person is often called a birdbrain since a bird's brain is normally small — about the size of the bird's eye.

*Jellyfish:* A person who has a weak character is called a jellyfish, because jellyfish have no spines (they can't stand up straight) and are composed of water and a jellylike substance (soft, wobbly, and insubstantial).

*Leech:* A person who attaches him- or herself to another and takes without giving anything in return is often called a leech, since a leech is a blood-sucking worm.

*Lone wolf:* Someone who is described as a lone wolf is an outsider, one who keeps to him- or herself. Since, like people, wolves live in families and travel in packs, a single wolf is unusual and has either strayed from the pack or been driven away.

*Pig:* A sloppy or messy person is often called a pig, for pigs often wallow in the mud or dust in order to keep cool.

## Disease-Carrying Animals

Animals can carry diseases that are harmful to people. Here is a list of animals and the diseases they may carry.

| DISEASE | SYMPTOMS | CARRIER |
| --- | --- | --- |
| Bubonic plague | Painful swelling, high fever, body aches | Rat, flea |
| Elephantiasis | Rough, thickened skin, body swelling | Worms |
| Lyme disease | Rash, fatigue, muscle and joint pain | Deer tick |
| Malaria | Chills, weakness, fever, excessive perspiration | Mosquito |
| Plague typhus | Fever, skin rashes | Flea, lice, chipmunk, prairie dog, squirrel |
| Rabies | Headaches, muscle spasms, convulsions | Woodchuck, bat, raccoons |
| Rocky Mt. spotted fever | Chills, fever, rash, leg pain | Wood tick |
| Sleeping sickness | Attacks nervous system; results in prolonged sleep | Tsetse fly |
| Trichinosis | Vomiting, fever, pain, face swelling | Worms in pigs |

# Body and Food

*An Owner's Manual*

OUR BODIES ARE INCREDIBLE machines. This "owner's manual" will give you tips 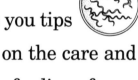 on the care and feeding of your body, insights into the marvels of the "body machine," and delectable tidbits about food.

## BODY SUIT: A PEEK INSIDE

Everyone is unique. We have different skin colors, hair colors, body shapes and sizes — but we all look alike inside. If you could peek inside your own body, what would you see? Hundreds of bones, miles of blood vessels, and trillions of cells, all of which are constantly working together, doing all kinds of different things.

### Skin

*Main job:* To protect your internal (inside) organs from drying up and harmful bacteria from getting inside.

*Anatomists are people who study the human body.*

*How much:* The average person has a total of 6 pounds of skin.

*Main layers:*
Epidermis: Outer layer of skin cells, hair, nails, and sweat glands.
Dermis: Inner layer of living tissue, containing nerves and blood vessels.

*Skin facts:* Your skin . . .
. . . is so flexible that you can bend and stretch.
. . . feels heat, cold, pain, pressure, moisture, irritation, and tickles because it has nerves.
. . . heals itself when wounded.
. . . keeps heat in on cold days and releases it as perspiration on hot days.
. . . is a watertight container for your body.

## Bones

*Main job:* To give shape to your body.

*How many:* At birth you had 300 bones in your body. As an adult you'll have 206, because some fuse together.

*Kinds of Bones*
- *Long* bones are thin; they are found in your legs, arms, and fingers.
- *Short* bones are wide and chunky; they are found in your feet and wrists.
- *Flat* bones are flat and smooth, like your rib and shoulder blades.
- *Irregular* bones, like the three bones in your inner ear and the vertebrae in your spine, come in many different shapes.

## Joints

*Main job:* To allow bones to move in different directions.

*Kinds of Joints*
- The *ball and socket* joint is found in your hip, where the thigh bone sits neatly inside the cup of the hip bone. It is also found in your shoulder.
- The *hinge* joint works like a door hinge and allows movement in only one direction. It is found in your elbows and knees.
- *Plain* joints link the bones in your foot between the toes and the ankle and look like one disk on top of another. They allow your foot to adapt to the weight of your body, whether running or resting.
- A *pivot* joint looks like two flat, diamond-shaped

*The largest bone in the body is the femur, or thigh bone; it is 20 inches long in a 6-foot-tall person.*

*The smallest bone is the stirrup bone, in the ear; it is .1 inch long.*

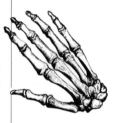

*Bones don't bend. It is the joint that allows two bones next to each other to move.*

disks with a stick through them. It is found in your neck and allows your head to move in all directions.

- The *saddle* joint looks like two bicycle seats facing each other and can be moved in any direction. It is found at the base of your thumbs.

## Ligaments

*Main job:* These bands of tough tissue hold joints together. They are strong and flexible.

## Muscles

*Main job:* To make involuntary or voluntary body movement possible.

*How many:* Your body has more than 650 muscles. Each muscle does only two things: *expand* when being used and *contract* when resting.

*Kinds of Muscles*

- *Skeletal* muscles move your bones. They are called voluntary muscles because you decide when to move them. You have more than 400 voluntary muscles.

- The job of the *cardiac* muscle, or heart, is to pump blood through your body. The cardiac muscle is involuntary; it never stops working during your lifetime.

- *Smooth* muscles control your internal movements, such as moving food around in your intestines. These muscles are also found in the blood vessels, where they assist the flow of blood. Smooth muscles are involuntary.

*Every day, the average person's muscles work as hard as if they were placing 2,400 pounds on a 4-foot-high shelf.*

## Tendons

*Main job:* To hold your muscles to your bones.

*Tendon fact:* Tendons look like rubber bands.

## Viscera

This term refers to the organs that fill your body's chest and abdominal cavity. They belong to many different systems: respiratory, digestive, and urinary.

*Main job:* To provide your body with food and oxygen and to remove waste.

*How many:* The viscera has ten organs: the trachea or windpipe, lungs, liver, gallbladder, spleen, stomach, large intestine, small intestine, and bladder.

*Your fingers are mostly powered by muscles in your palm and wrist.*

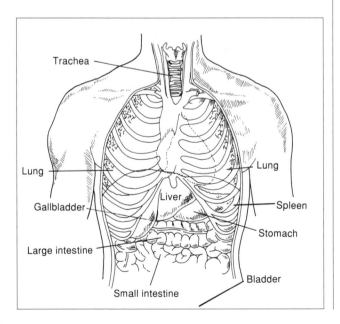

Trachea

Lung

Gallbladder

Large intestine

Small intestine

Liver

Lung

Spleen

Stomach

Bladder

## Glands

*Main job:* To manufacture substances that help your body to function in various ways.

*Kinds of Glands*
- *Endocrine* glands make hormones, which tell the different parts of your body when to work.
- *Oil* glands keep your skin from drying out.
- *Salivary* glands make saliva, which helps to digest carbohydrates in your mouth and aids in swallowing.
- *Sweat* glands make perspiration, which regulates your body temperature.

## Cells

*Main job:* To perform the many jobs necessary to stay alive, such as moving oxygen around your body, taking care of the fuel supply, communications, and waste removal.

*Some Different Cells*
- The *egg* is the largest human cell. Once it is fertilized, all other cells begin forming.
- *Bone* cells help build your skeleton by secreting the fibers and minerals from which bone is made.
- *Fat* cells store fat. They can shrink or grow. Once you have them you can't get rid of them.
- *Muscle* cells are organized into muscles, which move body parts.
- *Nerve* cells pass nerve messages around your body.
- *Red blood* cells carry oxygen around your body.
- *White blood* cells fight disease.

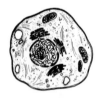

*There are 26 billion cells in a newborn baby and 50 trillion cells in an adult.*

## BODY COUNT

The thickness of your skin varies from ½ to 6 millimeters, depending on the area of your body.

The 4 taste zones on your tongue are bitter (back), sour (back sides), salty (front sides), and sweet (front).

The 5 senses are sight, hearing, smell, touch, and taste.

Your body contains 8 pints of blood.

You use 14 muscles to smile.

The small intestines are 20 feet long.

The large intestines are 5 feet long and are 3 times wider than the small intestines.

Most people shed 40 pounds of skin in a lifetime.

Your body is 70% water.

Normal body temperature is 98.6° Fahrenheit.

When you sneeze, air rushes through your nose at a rate of 100 mph.

An eyelash lives about 150 days before it falls out.

Your brain sends messages at the rate of 240 mph.

About 400 gallons of blood flow through your kidneys in one day.

You blink your eyes about 20,000 times a day.

Your heart beats about 100,000 times a day.

You have about 120,000 hairs on your head.

There are 10 million nerve cells in your brain.

Each of your eyes has 100 million rods, which help you see in black and white.

Each eye has 7 million cones, which help you see in color.

*Placed end to end, all your body's blood vessels would measure about 60,000 miles.*

## FOLK FOOD CURES FOR NATURAL HEALTH

*Cucumber slices* placed on closed eyelids soothe tired eyes. The inner peel cleans and freshens your face.

*Lemonade* is supposed to cure hiccups.

*Licorice* is an old remedy for coughs and colds.

*Parsley* is a natural breath freshener.

*Strawberries* are said to whiten teeth.

## (BE) WELL, WELL, WELL, OR WHY YOU SHOULD DO AS YOU'RE TOLD

*Wash your hands before eating.*
Germs are spread more easily from your hands than, say, your lips. When you have a cold, keep your hands clean and don't worry about kissing someone.

*Wear gloves and cover your head to keep warm.*
As much as 70% of your body's heat can escape through exposed hands, feet, and head.

*Get out of those wet clothes.*
Wet clothes actually conduct heat away from the body.

*Don't chew gum.*
Chewing gum for more than 20 minutes a day stresses your jawbone, gums, and the biting surface of your teeth. *However*, chewing a stick of sugarless gum for a few minutes stimulates your saliva secretion and helps to clean your teeth.

*Brush your hair.*
Brushing distributes protective and moisturizing natural oils along the whole length of the hair

*When the Chinese invented the toothbrush in 1490, the bristles were made of animal hairs. Nylon toothbrushes were first sold in the U.S. in 1938.*

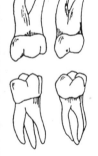

shaft. It also stimulates your scalp and removes loose scales.

*Stand up straight.*
Poor posture can cause rounded shoulders, backaches, and swayback. It also may keep your internal organs from working properly.

## WHERE DID YOU GET THOSE PEEPERS?

| BODY PART | SLANG |
|---|---|
| ABDOMEN | BELLY, BREADBASKET, TUMMY |
| EYES | PEEPERS, HEADLIGHTS |
| FACE | MUG |
| FEET | DOGS |
| HAIR | MANE |
| HANDS | PAWS, MITTS |
| HEART | TICKER |
| LARYNX | ADAM'S APPLE |
| LEGS | WHEELS |
| MOUTH | KISSER |
| NOSE | BEAK |
| TEETH | CHOPPERS, IVORY, FANGS |

## BRAIN FOOD

You don't feel with your heart. Feelings and emotions are stored in your brain.

You don't think with your head. You think with your brain, which is inside your head.

You see with your eyes and hear with your ears, but your eyes must send a message to your brain in order for you to see. Your ears must send a message to your brain in order for you to hear.

*Your brain weighs 2% of your body weight. It uses 20% of your body's energy.*

## SICK KIDS

Most healthy kids get sick once in a while. No matter how well you take care of yourself, you can't always avoid germs that others are carrying. Here are some common illnesses and conditions caused by germs.

*Acne*

Pimples and blackheads usually on the face are known as acne. Acne is caused by bacteria and oil in the skin clogging the pores, which then become inflamed. There is no way to prevent acne; most young people get some form of it.

*Athlete's Foot*

You don't have to be an athlete to get athlete's foot. Sneakers worn without socks make the ideal environment for fungus growth. The fungus

### What's the difference?

Bacteria *are tiny, one-celled living organisms that can only be seen with a microscope. They live and breed in warm, moist environments in the body, growing quickly and causing infection. Bacterial infections can usually be treated with an antibiotic.*

Viruses *are smaller than bacteria and cannot be seen with a microscope. They grow inside the body and produce toxins (poisons) that can cause rashes, aches, and fevers. Viruses cannot be killed with antibiotics.*

causes the skin to itch and peel, especially between the toes.

### Bronchitis

The trachea, a big tube that carries air from the throat to the chest, forks and becomes two main bronchi, one going to each lung. When bacteria or viruses invade the cell lining of the trachea or bronchial tubes, the infection is called bronchitis.

### Chicken Pox

Everyone gets chicken pox (except chickens). Some 98% of children in the U.S. get chicken pox between the ages of 1 and 10. It's caused by a virus that spreads easily when an infected person coughs or sneezes. The chicken pox rash is made up of clear blisters, called vesicles, on the skin. They are very itchy and form scabs when they dry.

### Cold

People get colds more than any other illness, often two or more a year. Colds are caused by viruses in the respiratory tract, *not* because you played in the cool air too long!

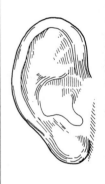

### Croup

When a virus attacks the larynx (voice box), the voice becomes hoarse and squeaky. The accompanying cough may sound like a seal's bark, and it may hurt to cough.

### Ear Infection (acute otitis media)

Fluid normally escapes from the ear through the Eustachian tube, which leads to the back of the nose and throat. Ear infections occur when the

Eustachian tube becomes swollen and does not let the fluid out. This fluid presses on the eardrum and causes pain.

### Head Lice

Head lice are tiny insects that breed in people's hair and spread easily from one person to another. They look like dandruff flakes, but they are stuck firmly to the strands of hair. Head lice won't make you sick but do cause a terrible itch, an allergic reaction to the insects.

### Influenza (flu)

The flu is caused by a virus that infects the entire respiratory tract. Your head, muscles, and throat hurt, and you may have a high fever.

### Strep Throat

This is an infection of the back of the throat caused by the streptococcus bacteria, which affect the cells in the lining of the throat. The damaged cells and other nearby cells send out fluid, which causes the throat to swell and become very red and sore. The redness is caused by additional blood coming into the area.

### Tonsillitis

A painful sore throat can mean tonsillitis, when the tonsils become enlarged and swollen. Pus sacs develop, and it hurts to swallow.

### Warts

Warts are caused by a virus in the skin cells which causes rapid growth of the skin's outer layer. A hard bump forms on the surface of the skin.

*Plantar's warts got their name because the wart "plants" itself within the foot and the roots grow inward. Plantar's warts are very painful because of the pressure placed on them from walking.*

## ARTIFICIAL BODY PARTS

Doctors and bioengineers, scientists who know both the human body and how to build machines, have together created some sixty artificial body parts. In the future, they hope to make artificial organs, called organoids, to replace diseased lungs, livers, and other organs. Here are some of the body parts that can currently be replaced.

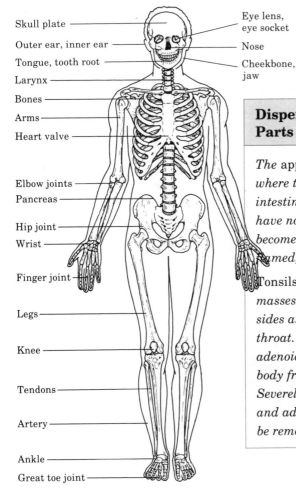

Skull plate

Outer ear, inner ear

Tongue, tooth root

Larynx

Bones

Arms

Heart valve

Elbow joints

Pancreas

Hip joint

Wrist

Finger joint

Legs

Knee

Tendons

Artery

Ankle

Great toe joint

Eye lens, eye socket

Nose

Cheekbone, jaw

### Dispensable Body Parts

*The* appendix *is located where the small and large intestine meet. It seems to have no use. When it becomes infected or in-flamed, it can be removed.*

*Tonsils and* adenoids *are masses of tissue on the sides and upper part of the throat. Healthy tonsils and adenoids help protect the body from infection. Severely infected tonsils and adenoids may have to be removed.*

# FOOD

What's *bouillabaisse*? It's French for a fish stew that combines many kinds of fish and shellfish. Here is a stew of another kind—a variety of food facts.

## Meal Within a Meal

For special occasions, the Bedouin tribes of Africa stuff a fish with eggs and put it inside a chicken. The chicken is put inside a sheep, and the sheep is put inside a camel and roasted. Now that's stuffed!

## Prehistoric Food

Have you ever wondered what people ate before recorded time? They dug wild onions and radishes and searched for wild squash, cabbage, mushrooms, and waterlily seed to eat. They also ate some insects, raw. Certain tasty insects became extinct from being overhunted (or overeaten?).

## Bird's Nest Soup

Yes, this Asian delicacy is made from real bird's nests. In China, a prized food is the soup made from the Asian swift's nest.

*Buffalo wings have nothing to do with bison. They are spicy chicken wings that originated in Buffalo, New York.*

*Breakfast in Egypt*
In Egypt, breakfast is often bought and eaten at a street stall. Usually it is bread wrapped around assorted fried vegetables: eggplant, beans, tomatoes, and peppers.

*Aborigine Food*
The aborigines of Australia call their native food "bush-tucks." It is game meat such as kangaroo, turkey, and goanna, a kind of lizard.

*Pretzels and Prayers*
According to folklore, pretzels were given to children who knew their prayers. The pretzel shape was supposed to signify arms folded across the chest in prayer.

*Gorp*
The energy food of bikers and hikers is called Gorp: *G*ood *O*ld *R*aisins and *P*eanuts.

*Peanut Butter*
A favorite spread for sandwiches, peanut butter was created by a doctor as a health food. In Africa, where they were first grown, peanuts are known as groundnuts.

*The ancient Greeks believed horseradish was worth its weight in gold.*

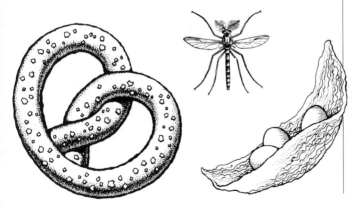

## SMART FOOD, JUNK FOOD

Food for health and well-being is not a new idea. The Egyptians, Greeks, and Romans believed that certain foods were natural cure-alls. Poppy juice was used to kill pain, strawberry roots to treat mad-dog bites. Crocodile blood was recommended for failing eyesight. Here are some foods that are currently thought to be good for you.

*Fiber, found in fruits and vegetables and whole-grain cereal, is not digestible. It helps to rid your body of waste and also makes you feel full.*

| SMART FOOD | WHY |
| --- | --- |
| Banana | Contains potassium and helps to prevent ulcers. |
| Barley | Lowers cholesterol because it is high in the good fat (HDLs, high-density lipoproteins). |
| Cheese | Fights cavities because it contains calcium. |
| Chili peppers | Good for bronchitis, colds, and sinusitis. |
| Cucumber | Breaks up cholesterol deposits. |
| Figs | Helps to stabilize blood sugar, which keeps energy levels high. |
| Horseradish | It's sharp and strong, but fights colds because the root contains an antibiotic and vitamin C. |
| Kale | Contains calcium for building bones plus the same beta carotene found in carrots that helps fight germs. |
| Milk (low fat) | Contains calcium, which helps to build strong teeth and bones. |
| Prunes | An excellent natural laxative because of its fiber content. |
| Yogurt | The live culture in yogurt acidophilus helps the body to fight intestine and yeast infections. |
| Water | The best liquid to drink because it purifies your bloodstream and cleans your cells and tissues. |

You may want these junk foods, but try to stay away!

| JUNK FOOD | WHY |
|-----------|-----|
| Cakes and cookies | Contain too much sugar and not enough vitamins and minerals. |
| Colas | Have lots of sugar and few nutrients; may contain caffeine, an addictive drug. |
| Ice cream | Has many nutrients but is full of sugar and fats. |
| Imitation fruit drinks | Mostly sugar and water, with artificial flavors and colors added. Contain very little pure fruit juice. |
| Potato chips | Although made from potatoes, they are deep fried and contain lots of salt, fat, and cholesterol. |
| Sugar-coated cereal | Half cereal and half sugar. |

## Fast Food: Quick Tips If You Must

Until recently, fast-food restaurants were a nutritional nightmare. Today you can eat well if you are careful to order the right dishes.

| RESTAURANT | SELECTION | FAT | CALORIES |
|------------|-----------|-----|----------|
| Burger King | BK broiler (chicken sandwich) | 8g | 267 |
| Hardees | Real lean deluxe burger | 13g | 340 |
| Kentucky Fried Chicken | Skinfree crispy | 12g | 220 |
| McDonald's | McLean deluxe burger | 10g | 320 |
| Wendy's | Grilled chicken sandwich | 9g | 320 |

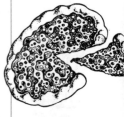

*Pizza may have many toppings. The first pizza, served to Queen Margharita of Italy, was garnished with the colors of the Italian flag: white cheese, green basil, and red tomatoes.*

## Food for Thought

Are french fries from France? Is chop suey Chinese? Here are some commonly mistaken beliefs about food and eating.

- French fries are not from France. They were first made in Belgium in 1876. The term "french" refers to the way of cutting the potatoes before cooking.

- Chop suey was created in America by a Chinese cook who worked in a California mining camp in the 1800s. He stir-fried a variety of vegetables, called it *tsa sui*, Mandarin Chinese for "various things," so people called it chop suey.

- Almost everyone associates potatoes with Ireland. Although they are its main crop, the potato is a native food of Peru, which was brought to Europe by explorers.

- The next time someone says you "eat like a pig," take it as a compliment! Pigs don't overeat, and their diet is the closest to the human diet of any other animal.

- Cool off with ice cream? Wrong. Ice cream feels cool, but it is loaded with calories (units of heat) and actually makes your body warmer.

- "Eating like a bird" means not eating much. In fact, birds eat a lot, and they eat frequently because of their high metabolism (the body's way of making food into energy).

- If sandwiches were named after John Montagu, the fourth earl of Sandwich, why aren't they called Montagus?

- If melba toast and peach melba were named after Dame Nellie Melba, whose real name was Helen Porter Mitchell, why isn't it called Mitchell toast or Peach Mitchell?

*In Morocco, schoolboys are given roasted hedgehog liver to help them remember their studies.*

## FEAST AND FAST

### The New Year

In Madrid, Spain, people count down the last minutes of the old year by popping grapes into their mouths.

In the southern part of the U.S., black-eyed peas are eaten on New Year's Day for good luck.

In Japan, New Year's food is red snapper, which brings good luck because of its color, which the Japanese consider lucky.

In southern India, boiled rice is a New Year's food.

In Hungary, a roast pig, with a four-leaf clover in its mouth, is prepared for New Year's.

In Greece, a cake called *peta* is baked with a coin inside it. The person who gets the slice with the coin will have special luck in the coming year.

The Jewish New Year is celebrated with apples dipped in honey.

The Buddhist New Year is celebrated in Tibet with a dish called *guthok*, which is made of nine special ingredients, including a piece of charcoal. The person who gets the charcoal is said to have an evil heart.

### Presidents' Birthdays

Abraham Lincoln, who was born on February 12, 1809, had a fondness for homemade pies. During his presidency, women from his home state of Illinois frequently mailed him their apple pies.

George Washington was born on February 22, 1732. His favorite dessert was hazelnuts, and his favorite vegetable was onions.

### April Fools' Day

In France, a person who is fooled on this day is called *poisson d'Avril*, an "April fish." Chocolate fish are the treats for the day. In the U.S. at one time, people poured chocolate over pieces of cotton on April 1, to fool others with "cotton candy."

### Halloween

In the U.S., kids dunk for apples in tubs of water, drink apple cider, and eat cakes and cookies decorated with orange and black icing. In Ireland, where Halloween customs began, traditional foods are *barm brach* (a raisin bread), colcannon (baked kale and potatoes), and oatmeal porridge.

### Thanksgiving Day

The first Thanksgiving meal celebrated by the Pil-

ABRAHAM LINCOLN

*The day before Lent is called Fat Tuesday, Shrove Tuesday, or Mardi Gras. Traditionally, people made pancakes to use up their butter and eggs, which were not allowed during Lent.*

grims and the Native Americans included turkey, venison (deer meat), lobster, fish, sweet potatoes, cranberries, and popcorn.

## Hanukkah

This 8-day Jewish Festival of Lights is celebrated with potato pancakes (*latkes*), which are fried in oil. This is a reminder of the oil that burned in the temple for 8 days.

## Christmas

Some traditional Christmas Eve meals are meatless. Italians eat fish soup called *zuppa di pesce*. The Irish eat oyster stew.

Christmas dinner in Denmark is traditionally roast goose. In Greece, it's roast leg of lamb, and in Hungary it's chicken *paprikash* (paprika-flavored).

In the island nation of New Zealand, the Christmas meal is a picnic eaten on one of the beaches.

Kwanza is an African American feast celebrated from December 26 to January 1. A banana custard with raisins and sweet potatoes are traditional fare.

Kwanza *means "first" in Swahili, an African language. This name was picked for the American feast because many African tribes celebrate the* first *harvest of crops.*

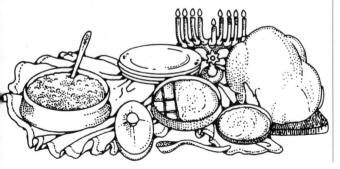

## Fasting

To fast is *not* to eat at all or *not* to eat certain foods for a period of time. Usually people fast for religious reasons. Some people have fasted for political or health reasons, too.

Muslims fast from dawn to sunset during the holy month of Ramadan so that their sins will be forgiven. Before dawn they eat a meal called *suhur*. After sunset they eat a meal called *iflar*.

Jews fast on the holy day of Yom Kippur to atone for their wrongdoings. From sunset to sunset they do not eat or drink anything, not even water.

Christians fast during Lent, 40 days that commemorate the 40 days Jesus fasted in the desert. At one time bread and water were the only foods allowed during Lent. Later, meat was the only forbidden food. Today, people fast in many ways, mainly by giving up favorite foods.

Mahatma Gandhi fasted seventeen times while he was the leader of the people of India. He fasted to be close to the people who were starving and to protest violence.

Cesar Chavez, a leader of the American farmworkers, fasted to stop violence in the struggle for equal rights and fair pay for the workers. His fast lasted 26 days.

Mark Twain, the American writer, thought fasting was a cure for illness. He would cure his colds and fevers by not eating for one or two days.

*People can live without food for a few weeks, but they cannot live without water for more than a few days.*

# FOOD AND SUPERSTITIONS

The ancient Egyptians thought *onions* kept evil spirits away. When they took an oath (made a promise), they placed one hand on an onion.

The custom of throwing *rice* at weddings goes back to the time when people thought rice, a symbol of health and prosperity, would appease evil spirits so they would not bother the wedding couple.

In Hungary, *salt* is thrown on the threshold of a new house because it is thought that salt will protect the inhabitants from evil. Europeans who believed in vampires sprinkled mustard seed on the roof of their homes to keep them away.

| Who grows the most? | |
| --- | --- |
| CORN | U.S. |
| GRAPES | FRANCE |
| POTATOES | FORMER USSR |
| RICE | CHINA |
| SUGAR | BRAZIL |
| TEA | INDIA |

In Japan, during the festival of Setsuben, *beans* are scattered in dark corners and entrances of the home to drive out evil spirits.

For many years, Europeans have used *garlic* as a charm against the evil eye. Some wore bulbs of garlic around their necks. Others placed wreaths of garlic over their doors for protection.

## WHAT'S NEW IN FOOD?

*Ostrich Meat*
This is the low-fat red meat of the 1990s. Ostriches are fed a low-fat diet consisting of alfalfa and corn pellets. The world's largest bird produces about 150 pounds of meat that tastes nothing like poultry but very much like beef.

### Broccoflower

This new vegetable is a combination of broccoli and cauliflower. It looks like a green cauliflower and has the taste of both vegetables.

### Hot Soup

You don't need a stove to cook Super Boil, a new soup developed by Nissan Foods of California. The can comes with a key on top. When you turn the key, a chemical is released which causes the soup to boil. It's ready to eat in 5 minutes.

### Erupting Cookie

Baked in the microwave, this cookie acts like a miniature volcano. When it is heated, the liquid center oozes out of the top. Nabisco is still testing the cookie at this writing.

### Miniature Vegetables

No, they're not baby vegetables, just vegetables in a new size. There's no need to slice them—they cook faster and some even say they taste better. So far there are miniature carrots and eggplants.

# Book Baedeker

*From Cover to Cover*

FROM *PAT THE BUNNY* TO THE  Bible, books contain whole worlds for you to explore. Knowledge, adventure, mystery, laughter, conversation, comfort, and more are possible when you open a book. Books are a special way to "travel"—and wonderful to share with friends. What's in your collection?

A Baedeker is a guidebook for travelers.

## A WORD ABOUT BOOKS

What do books mean to you? People often have a lot to say about books. They talk about what they like and don't like as well as how books have influenced their lives. Do you agree with any of the following quotations?

*"If you would not be forgotten as soon as you are dead and rotten, either write things worth reading, or do things worth the writing."*
Benjamin Franklin, American statesman

*"A good book is the best of friends, the same today and forever."* Martin Tupper, British author

*"Some books leave us free and some books make us free."*
Ralph Waldo Emerson, American author

*"Wherever they burn books they will also, in the end, burn human beings."*
Heinrich Heine, German poet

*"Books, the children of the brain."*
Jonathan Swift, British author

*"I have always come to life after coming to books."*
Jorge Luis Borges, Argentine writer

*"A garden carried in a pocket."*
Chinese proverb

*"People die, but books never die."*
*Publishers' Weekly*, May 9, 1942

*"The oldest books are only just out to those who have not read them."*
Samuel Butler, English author

*"The man who does not read good books has no advantage over the man who can't read them."*

Mark Twain, American author

# HOW TO READ A BOOK INSIDE AND OUT

## Inside

*Leaves:* Each sheet of paper is a leaf.

*Pages:* Each side of a leaf is a page.

*Bookplate:* A label pasted in a book that names the owner or donor.

*Endpapers:* The pages between the cover and body of a book; they may be plain, colored, or printed, such as with a map.

*Front matter:* The pages before the text (title page, etc.)

*Back matter:* The pages following the text (index, etc.)

*Text:* The basic information, or core, of a book.

| | |
|---|---|
| *Verso:*<br>The left-hand page | *Recto:*<br>The right-hand page |

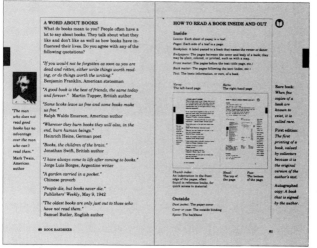

| | | |
|---|---|---|
| *Thumb index:*<br>An indentation in the front edge of the pages, often found in reference books, for quick access to material | *Head:*<br>The top of the page | *Foot:*<br>The bottom of the page |

## Outside

*Dust jacket:* The paper cover

*Cover or case:* The outside binding

*Spine:* The backbone

Rare book:
*When few copies of a book are known to exist, it is called rare.*

First edition:
*The first printing of a book, valued by collectors because it is the original version of the author's text.*

Autographed copy: *A book that is signed by the author.*

# CHILDREN'S BOOK AWARDS

Every year, books written for children receive prizes for being the best in their field. Here are the names of some of the most prestigious awards and their categories of excellence.

*The Caldecott Medal*
For the best illustrated book; given by the American Library Association.

*The Golden Kite Award*
The best fiction book and the best nonfiction book; given by the Society for Children's Book Writers.

*The Newbery Medal*
For the most distinguished literature for children published in the U.S.; given by the American Library Association.

*The Horn Book Award*
For the most outstanding juvenile books in the U.S.: one award for outstanding fiction, one for outstanding nonfiction, one for outstanding illustration; given by the *Boston Globe*.

*The Coretta Scott King Award*
For authors and illustrators whose books promote the contributions of all people to the American dream; given by the American Library Association.

*Randolph Caldecott was a 19th-century British illustrator.*

*John Newbery was an 18th-century British publisher.*

*Coretta Scott King is an African American noted for her tireless work for world brotherhood.*

Since 1980, the following books have received the Caldecott and Newbery medals.

## The Caldecott Medal

1980  Ox-Cart Man, by Donald Hall

1981  *Fables,* by Arnold Lobel

1982  *Jumanji,* by Chris Van Allsburg

1983  *Shadow,* by Blaise Cendrars

1984  *The Glorious Flight,* by Alice and Martin Provensen

1985  *St. George and the Dragon,* retold by Margaret Hodges

1986  *The Polar Express,* by Chris Van Allsburg

1987  *Hey, Al,* by Arthur Yorinks

1988  *Owl Moon,* by Jane Yolen

1989  *Song and Dance Man,* by Karen Ackerman

1990  *Lon Po Po,* translated by Ed Young

1991  *Black and White,* by David Macaulay

1992  *Tuesday,* by David Wiesner

## The Newbery Medal

1980  *A Gathering of Days: A New England Girl's Journal, 1830–32,* by Joan W. Blos

1981  *Jacob Have I Loved,* by Katherine Paterson

1982  *A Visit to William Blake's Inn,* by Nancy Willard

1983  *Dicey's Song,* by Cynthia Voigt

1984  *Dear Mr. Henshaw,* by Beverly Cleary

1985  *The Hero and the Crown,* by Robin McKinley

1986  *Sarah, Plain and Tall,* by Patricia MacLachlan

1987  *The Whipping Boy,* by Sid Fleischman

1988  *Lincoln: A Photobiography,* by Russell Freedman

1989  *Joyful Noise: Poems for Two Voices,* by Paul Fleischman

1990  *Number the Stars,* by Lois Lowry

1991  *Maniac Magic,* by Jerry Spinelli

1992  *Shiloh,* by Phyllis Naylor

# A GUIDE TO LIBRARY BOOKS:
## THE DEWEY DECIMAL SYSTEM

Imagine walking into a house where room after room is filled with shelves, all packed with books in no specific order. Imagine trying to find the one book you want! That's what happened every day to Melvil Dewey, an American librarian who lived from 1851 to 1931. He became so unhappy trying to help people find books that he invented the Dewey Decimal System of Classification, which is still used in libraries today. The system numbers books by their subject matter in the following way.

| | |
|---|---|
| *000–099* | GENERAL WORKS (ENCYCLOPEDIAS, MAGAZINES, ALMANACS, BIBLIOGRAPHIES) |
| *100–199* | PHILOSOPHY, PSYCHOLOGY, ETHICS |
| *200–299* | RELIGION AND MYTHS |
| *300–399* | SOCIOLOGY (CIVICS, ECONOMICS, EDUCATION) |
| *400–499* | PHILOLOGY (LANGUAGE, DICTIONARIES, GRAMMAR) |
| *500–599* | SCIENCE (MATH, CHEMISTRY, BIOLOGY, BOTANY) |
| *600–699* | USEFUL ARTS (MEDICINE, AGRICULTURE, TV) |
| *700–799* | FINE ARTS (PAINTING, MUSIC, PHOTOGRAPHY) |
| *800–899* | LITERATURE (NOVELS, POETRY, PLAYS) |
| *900–999* | HISTORY, GEOGRAPHY, BIOGRAPHY |

# STORYTELLERS

Long ago, in primitive times, stories were passed on by word of mouth. Since the invention of printing, stories have been part of the world's literature. The fairy tales, legends, and fables we know today have often come from far in the past. Lewis Carroll, the author of *Alice's Adventures in Wonderland,* called stories "love gifts." Here are six famous storytellers' "love gifts" to us.

## Aesop's Fables

Aesop was a storyteller who lived in ancient Greece. Animals are the main characters in his fables, which show how a problem is solved and a moral or lesson is learned. Aesop's stories include "The Boy Who Cried Wolf" and "The Tortoise and the Hare." They were first written down in about 300 B.C.

## Andersen's Fairy Tales

Hans Christian Andersen lived in Denmark in the 19th century. He was considered an ugly child and had no friends, so he lived in a dream world, reading about the lives of famous men who had risen from poverty to fame. At the age of 14, when his father died, he moved to Copenhagen and tried to become an actor. When he was still unsuccessful at 30, he decided to try writing down the tales he had been telling children as he traveled around the countryside. Some of his stories are "The Emperor's New Clothes," "The Ugly Duckling," and "The Princess and the Pea."

## Arabian Nights

According to legend, a queen named Scheherazade told these stories to Sultan Schahriah to save her life. Each night she told him tales, stopping at the most exciting part so that he would have to wait until the next night to learn what happened. After 1,001 nights, the sultan granted Scheherazade her life. She became his wife, and her stories were recorded for all the world to read. They include "Ali Baba and the Forty Thieves," "Sinbad the Sailor," and "Aladdin and the Magic Lamp."

### Grimm's Fairy Tales

Jacob and Wilhelm Grimm were brothers who lived in Germany. After their parents died, the brothers traveled about the country and gathered stories. When they published these tales in the early 19th century, they became famous. Their collection includes "Hansel and Gretel" and "Snow White and the Seven Dwarfs."

### The Legend of King Arthur

The story of King Arthur and his Knights of the Round Table was published by Sir Thomas Malory in 1469, while he was in a London jail. These tales had delighted European audiences for centuries before Malory brought them together in one book.

### Perrault's Fairy Tales

Charles Perrault lived in France in the 17th century. When he retired from government service, he began to take popular folk tales and change them into children's fairy tales with morals. He was very successful because he was one of the first French authors to write especially for children. His most famous fairy tales are "Sleeping Beauty," "Tom Thumb," and "Puss in Boots."

# 20 CHARACTERS YOU SHOULD KNOW

Do you know Charlotte, Hans, and Alice? They are friends of your grandparents and parents. When you read about them, they'll become your friends, too.

## Alice

Alice, an impressionable Victorian girl of 7½, falls down a rabbit hole into Wonderland, where she has many strange and curious adventures.

*Alice's Adventures in Wonderland,* by Lewis Carroll

## Amelia Bedelia

Amelia Bedelia is a maid who interprets her duties literally. When she is asked to dust the furniture, she douses it with talcum powder! To change the towels she cuts holes in them! Her confusion makes us see how many ways there are to interpret ordinary statements.

*Amelia Bedelia* series, by Peggy Parish

### Charlie

Charlie Bucket is a poor boy who loves chocolate. He and four other children win the privilege of being shown around the mysterious Willy Wonka's Chocolate Factory.

*Charlie and the Chocolate Factory,* by Roald Dahl

### Charlotte

Charlotte is a spider who lives in a barn above the pen of Wilbur, a young pig. By writing messages in her web, Charlotte saves Wilbur's life. Meanwhile, Charlotte, Wilbur, the other farm animals, and Fern, a young girl, all learn something about the meaning of life and friendship.

*Charlotte's Web,* by E. B. White

### Claudia

When Claudia Kincaid is sick of being told what to do at home, she runs away to live in the Metropolitan Museum of Art in New York City. Her brother, Jamie, joins her on an adventure that leads them to the home of Mrs. Basil E. Frankweiler. Claudia, full of spunk and vitality, proves resourceful, curious, and strong as she unravels a mystery.

*From the Mixed-Up Files of Mrs. Basil E. Frankweiler,* by E. L. Konigsburg

### Dorothy

Dorothy Gale and her dog, Toto, are blown by a cyclone from Dorothy's aunt and uncle's farm in Kansas to the country of the Munchkins in the imaginary Land of Oz. Dorothy, after many adventures accompanied by a Scarecrow, a Tin Man, and a Cowardly Lion, finally finds the Wizard,

who they hope will solve all their problems.
*The Wonderful Wizard of Oz,* by L. Frank Baum

### Eloise
Eloise is 6 years old and lives in the luxurious Plaza Hotel in New York City. She has everything from a nanny to room service, from a day maid to a tutor. Everyone dotes on Eloise.
*Eloise,* by Kay Thompson

### Encyclopedia Brown
Leroy Brown, nicknamed Encyclopedia, is a 10-year-old boy who can solve any mystery. He and his father, the chief of police of Idaville, try to crack hard cases together. With his sharp ear for detecting flaws in a culprit's story, Encyclopedia Brown never loses a case or misses a clue.
*Encyclopedia Brown* series, by Donald J. Sobol

### Fudge
Farley Drexel Hatcher, also called Fudge, first appeared in *Tales of a Fourth-Grade Nothing.* His brother Peter would say that Fudge is the biggest pain ever invented. He is also troublesome and messy, uses a lot of big words, and is very funny.
*Superfudge,* by Judy Blume

### Hans Brinker
Hans Brinker's father is desperately ill from an accident that leaves the family poor. Hans and his sister, Gretel, enter a skating competition to earn money. This story of loyalty and gumption takes place among the canals and windmills of Holland.
*Hans Brinker, or, The Silver Skates,*
by Mary Mapes Dodge

## Harriet

Harriet M. Welch, age 11, wants to see and know everything in her quest to become a famous writer. Notebook in hand, she spies on her friends, trying to trap them in wrongdoings. When her notes accidentally fall into her friends' hands, Harriet learns an important lesson.

*Harriet, the Spy,* by Louise Fitzhugh

## Homer Price

Homer Price lives in Centerburg, a small midwestern town. Inquisitive and friendly, he has a knack for getting himself into humorous and zany situations.

*Homer Price* series, by Robert McCloskey

## Laura

The central character is really the author, who started to write about her childhood in 1932, when she was 63 years old. These memoirs tell the story of 5-year-old Laura, who moves with her family from a log cabin in Wisconsin across the prairie states. The books recall her life from her young tomboy days to her adulthood.

*Little House on the Prairie* series,
by Laura Ingalls Wilder

## Madeline

Madeline is a 6-year-old girl who attends boarding school in Paris. An individualist, she is the envy of her eleven classmates, for she is both the bravest and the naughtiest.

*Madeline* series, by Ludwig Bemelmans

## Mafatu

Mafatu became afraid of the sea as a 3-year-old child when he saw his mother drown. He learns to overcome this fear when he battles danger and faces hardship on an island inhabited by cannibals. With only his dog and pet albatross for companionship, Mafatu emerges, at 15, a true hero when he returns to his Polynesian fishing village.

*Call It Courage,* by Armstrong Sperry

## Nancy Drew

Nancy Drew is a detective who has appeared in dozens of books. She tries to help her father, a district attorney, solve his cases. Her curiosity and clear thinking always prove successful.

*Nancy Drew* series, by Carolyn Keene

## Pippi

Pippilolta Provisionia Gaberdina Dandeliona Ephraimsdaughter Longstocking is a 9-year-old who lives in the villa Villekula with her purple spotted horse and other animal friends as a result of her father's being lost at sea. Carrot-haired Pippi's spunky and optimistic outlook on life leads her and her two neighbors into fantastic adventures.

*Pippi Longstocking,* by Astrid Lindgren

## Mr. Popper

Mr. Popper, a disheveled house painter, dreams of exploring the South Pole and having a penguin as a pet. To his astonishment Admiral Drake, an explorer, sends him a penguin. Eventually he has a family of penguins.

*Mr. Popper's Penguins,* by Richard Atwater

## Ramona

Ramona Geraldine Quimby lives in an American town with her older sister, Beezus. Ramona is a lively, naughty girl whose parents think she is adorable and forgive all her inventive, crazy ideas (which usually misfire).

*Ramona* series, by Beverly Cleary

## Tom Sawyer

Tom is a young boy who lives with his aunt Polly and brother Sid in a small town on the Mississippi River. Clever and adventurous, Tom and his friend, Huckleberry Finn, get into one scrape after another in the days of the Old South.

*The Adventures of Tom Sawyer,* by Mark Twain

# BOOKS IN TROUBLE

The banning of books and other forms of censorship are not new. Since at least the 4th century B.C., some groups and individuals have encouraged the banning or outright destruction of reading material in the name of morality or for political or religious reasons. Here is a list of the most frequently attacked children's books in recent years and the objections to them.

| | |
|---|---|
| **Book** | *Anne Frank: The Diary of a Young Girl* |
| **Reason** | Too depressing. |
| **Book** | *Blubber,* by Judy Blume |
| **Reason** | The characters curse, and the leader of the taunting is never punished for her cruelty. |
| **Book** | *Bony-Legs,* by Joanna Cole |
| **Reason** | Deals with subjects such as magic and witchcraft. |
| **Book** | *The Chocolate War,* by Robert Cormier |
| **Reason** | Offensive language. |
| **Book** | *Confessions of an Only Child,* by Norma Klein |
| **Reason** | Use of profanity by the lead character's father. |
| **Book** | *Harriet, the Spy,* by Louise Fitzhugh |
| **Reason** | Teaches children to lie, spy, talk back, and curse. |
| **Book** | *A Hero Ain't Nothin' but a Sandwich,* by Alice Childress |
| **Reason** | Anti-American and immoral. |
| **Book** | *The House Without a Christmas Tree,* by Gail Rock |
| **Reason** | Uses the word *damn.* |
| **Book** | *In a Dark, Dark Room, and Other Scary Stories,* by Alvin Schwartz |
| **Reason** | Too morbid for children. |
| **Book** | *In the Night Kitchen,* by Maurice Sendak |
| **Reason** | Nudity; Mickey loses his pajamas during his fall in the kitchen. |
| **Book** | *A Light in the Attic,* by Shel Silverstein |
| **Reason** | Suggestive illustrations that might encourage kids to break dishes so they won't have to dry them. |
| **Book** | *Sylvester and the Magic Pebble,* by William Steig |
| **Reason** | The characters are all shown as animals; the police are presented as pigs. |

A Light in the Attic

*poems and drawings by*
Shel Silverstein

## REFERENCE BOOKS:
## WHEN YOU WANT TO LOOK IT UP

### Atlas

A book of maps with or without text. The word *atlas* was first used as the title of a book by Gerardus Mercator in 1585.

Examples: *Atlas of the World, Rand McNally Atlas of the Earth's Resources*

### Biographical Index

A book of information about people who are well known in a particular field.

Examples: *Who's Who, Current Biography*

### Dictionary

Definitions, spellings, and pronunciations of words, arranged in alphabetical order.

Examples: *The American Heritage Dictionary, The Misspellers' Dictionary, Young People's Science Dictionary*

### Directory

The names and addresses as well as other facts about specific groups, persons, or organizations.

Examples: *Guide to Summer Camps, Children's Media Marketplace*

### Encyclopedia

Information on just about every subject arranged in alphabetical order.

Examples: *World Book Encyclopedia, Encyclopaedia Britannica*

### Gazetteer

A geographical dictionary or index with the names of places and their locations in alphabetical order.

Example: *Chambers World Gazetteer: An A–Z of Geographical Information*

**Guidebook**
Information and directions, often for travelers.
Examples: *Fodor's Travel Guides, Guide to the Ski Touring Centers of New England, Barron's Guide to the Most Prestigious Colleges*

**Manual/Handbook**
Instructions on how to do or make something.
Examples: *A Manual for Writing Term Papers,* by Kate L. Turabian; *The Manual of Martial Arts,* by Ron van Clief

**Thesaurus**
Synonyms, or near synonyms, for words as well as related terms.
Example: *Roget's Thesaurus*

**Yearbook/Almanac**
Current information on a wide range of topics.
Examples: *Information Please Almanac, Guinness Book of World Records*

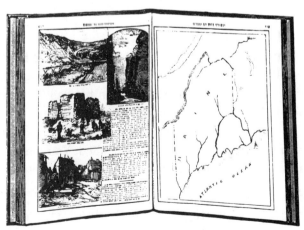

## The Best-Selling Children's Books of All Time

These books were selected from a list of 64 best-selling children's books. All have sold more than a million copies.

*Charlie and the Chocolate Factory,* by Roald Dahl, 1964, 1 million

*Charlotte's Web,* by E. B. White, 1952, 2 million

*The Children's Bible* (Golden Books), 1965, 3.5 million

*The Clear and Simple Thesaurus Dictionary,* by Harriet Wittels and Joan Greisman, 1976, 1 million

*E.T. the Extra-Terrestrial Storybook,* by William Kotzwinkle, 1983, 1 million

*Hardy Boys #1: The Tower Treasure,* by Franklin Dixon, 1927, 1 million

*The Macmillan Dictionary for Children,* 1975, 1.5 million

*Nancy Drew #1: The Secret of the Old Clock,* by Carolyn Keene, 1930, 1 million

*The Real Mother Goose,* illustrated by Blanche F. Wright, 1916, 3.5 million

*The Secret Garden,* by Frances Hodgson Burnett, 1921, 2 million

*The Velveteen Rabbit,* by Margery Williams, 1926, 1 million

*Where the Sidewalk Ends,* by Shel Silverstein, 1974, 3 million

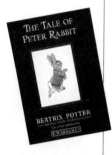

*The best-selling book of all time is* The Tale of Peter Rabbit, *by Beatrix Potter (1902). More than 9 million copies have been sold.*

## CHILDREN AS AUTHORS

Many children have written books that have been published. One of the first we know about is Francis Hawkins. In 1641, when he was 8 years old, he wrote a book of manners for children called *Youth Behavior.* Listed below are other children who have had their writing published. You may be able to find their books in a library or bookstore.

Katherine Hull, 14, and Pamela Whitlock, 15, went to school together in England. One day, while taking shelter from a rainstorm, they decided to collaborate on a book by children, about children, and for children. Their novel, *The Far Distance Oxus,* was published one year later, in 1937, and was said to be a classic by critics in both Europe and the U.S.

Anne Frank's diary was published in English in 1952 as *The Diary of a Young Girl.* Written when Anne was a teenager, it describes her family's life in hiding because they were Jewish during World War II. After two years of confinement in the attic of a warehouse in Amsterdam, Holland, the family was found, taken to a concentration camp, and killed by the Nazis. Only her father survived. When the diary was found, he saw that it was published in 1947. It has been translated into more than fifty languages.

ANNE FRANK

Dorothy Straight of Washington, D.C., was only 4 years old when she wrote *How the World Began.* Her book was published in 1964, two years later.

Susan Eloise Hinton started her writing career in high school, beginning the first draft of *The Outsiders* at the age of 15; it took her a year and a half to complete it. A book about youth gangs and their confrontations, it was published in 1967, when she was 17. It has sold more than a million copies.

The West Indian girl Manghanita Kempadoo wrote *Letters of Thanks,* which was published in 1969, when she was 12 years old. The book is a series of thank-you notes that parody the gifts in the carol "The Twelve Days of Christmas."

Alexandra (Ally) Elizabeth Sheedy published *She Was Nice to Mice* in 1975, when she was 12 years old. It is the story of Esther Esther, an extraordinary mouse who is taken back in time through her family history to the days of Queen Elizabeth I and William Shakespeare.

A group of young Native American children in Arizona told their stories to their teacher, Byrd Baylor, who had them published in 1976 as *And It Is Still That Way*.

Jamie DeWitt was 12 years old when he entered his true adventure story "Jamie's Turn" in the 1984 Raintree Publish-a-Book Contest. His story describes an accident on his family's farm in Wisconsin. What is truly remarkable is that Jamie has a learning disability that makes it difficult for him to write down what he is thinking.

When Jason Gaes was stricken with Burkitt's lymphoma, a rare form of cancer, at the age of 7, he decided to write *My Book for Kids with Cansur*. His twin brother, Tim, and 10-year-old brother, Adam, illustrated the book, which was published in 1987. It provides comfort and inspiration to people of all ages.

When he was 9, David Klein wrote "Irwin the Sock" for a school assignment. The story of Irwin and Irina, matching argyle socks, was submitted to the Raintree Publish-a-Book Contest and won. It was published in 1988.

Gordon Korman wrote his first book, *This Can't Be Happening* at MacDonald Hall, as a 7th-grade

English project. By the time he graduated from high school, he had written and published five more books, including *Go Jump in the Pool* and *Beware the Fish.* All are available in paperback editions.

## WHERE TO GET PUBLISHED

If you are interested in having your writing published, you can send your work to some of the publications listed below. Always enclose a stamped, self-addressed return envelope when sending material to any publication. Good luck!

## Publications

*Alive for Young Teens,* Christian Board of Publication, Box 179, St. Louis, Mo. 63166. Publishes fiction, nonfiction, poetry, puzzles, riddles, tongue-twisters, and crazy definitions written by 12-to-15-year-olds.

*Bitterroot Poetry Magazine,* P.O. Box 489, Spring Glen, N.Y. 12483. Publishes poetry. You may submit up to 4 poems at a time.

*Boy's Life Magazine,* 1325 Walnut Hill La., Irving, Tex. 75038

*Children's Digest,* 1100 Waterway Blvd., P.O. Box 567, Indianapolis, Ind. 46206. Publishes original fiction and nonfiction, poetry, and readers' favorite jokes and riddles.

*Children's Express,* 20 Charles St., New York, N.Y. 10014. This news service is reported by kids age 13 and under. The twice-weekly column is distributed by UPI to 2,500 newspapers around the world. Write for information.

*Children's Magic Window,* 6125 Olson Memorial, Minneapolis, Minn. 55422. Publishes letters, poems, drawings, and stories on special Kidstuff pages.

*Cobblestone,* 20 Grove St., Peterborough, N.H. 03458. Publishes a variety of material; however, you are asked to write first and ask for guidelines and upcoming themes.

*Creative Kids, GCT,* Mobile, Ala. 36660. Gives children an opportunity to publish their work.

*Jack and Jill,* P.O. Box 567, Indianapolis, Ind. 46206. Publishes stories, poems, riddles, and jokes written by students in grades 2 through 6.

*Just About Me (JAM),* Ensio Industries, 247 Marlee Ave., Suite 206, Toronto, Ont., Canada M6B 4B8. Publishes both fiction and poetry written by girls from age 12 to 19.

*Probe,* Baptist Brotherhood Commission, 1548 Poplar Ave., Memphis, Tenn. 38104. Publishes stories about personal experiences by boys from age 12 to 17.

*Seventeen,* 850 Third Ave., New York, N.Y. 10022. Features fiction, nonfiction, and poetry written by teenage girls. Teens can also write for the Free for All column, which includes essays, book reviews, and puzzles.

*Stone Soup, The Magazine by Children,* Box 83, Santa Cruz, Calif. 95063. Publishes stories, plays, poems, and book reviews by children under 14.

*Writing, General Learning Corp.,* 60 Revere Dr., Northbrook, Ill. 60062. Seeks feature stories by junior high school students.

## Writing Contests

### Publish-a-Book Contest
Winners of this contest will have their books published by Raintree Publishers. Writers in the 4th, 5th, and 6th grades can submit their stories to Raintree Publishers, 310 W. Wisconsin Ave., Milwaukee, Wis. 53203.

### Seventeen
This contest is open to all U.S. teenagers (ages 13–20) who submit a short story on any subject by September 1, yearly. Write to *Seventeen* Magazine, 850 Third Ave., New York, N.Y. 10022.

# Business and Technology

*Money Matters*

CALL IT COMMERCE, TRADE, vocation, employment, profession, or maybe just busy-ness, work has been  around for a long time — and  shows no sign of going away soon. Its partner, technology, accounts for many of the changes that societies have undergone since the beginning of mankind.

## BUSINESS CARDS: BUTCHER, BAKER, CANDLESTICK MAKER

Tracing the origin of your family name, you may be able to find out not only who your ancestors were but also what they were. In 12th-century England, when family names began to be used, people were identified by what they did as much as by what they were called. If a baker were named John, he became John Baker. The name Archer meant a professional with a bow and arrow. Barber was the name given to a man who cut hair. Does *your* family name come from the work one of your relatives did long ago?

*Last Name:* Barker
*Occupation:* Shepherd
*Origin:* Barker comes from the Norman word *barches*, meaning "shepherd," the person who watches over a flock of sheep.

*Last Name:* Black
*Occupation:* Dyer
*Origin:* Men named Black were cloth dyers who specialized in black dyes. In those days, all cloth was originally white, so it had to be dyed different colors.

*Last Name:* Carter
*Occupation:* Delivery person
*Origin:* A person who drove a cart pulled by oxen, carrying goods from town to town, was named Carter.

*Last Name:* Chamberlain
*Occupation:* Personal servant
*Origin:* Noblemen required servants to cook,

clean, and generally care for their large estates. Chamberlains cleaned the chambers, or rooms, of a nobleman's home.

*Last Name:* Chandler
*Occupation:* Candlemaker
*Origin:* The French word *chandelier* refers to a man who makes candles.

*Last Name:* Cooke
*Occupation:* Cook
*Origin:* The name Cook was given to people who made their living cooking for others. The *e* in Cooke was added to disguise the name's meaning.

*Last Name:* Cooper
*Occupation:* Barrelmaker
*Origin:* Cooper was the name for someone who made wooden barrels.

*Last Name:* Fisher
*Occupation:* Fisherman
*Origin:* People named Fisher were professional fishermen.

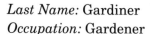

*Last Name:* Gardiner
*Occupation:* Gardener
*Origin:* This is a variation of the Norman word *gardinier,* which means a gardener, a person who cares for plants and lawns.

*Last Name:* Hansard
*Occupation:* Swordmaker
*Origin: Hansard* in French means "a long pointed sword." Swordmakers were given this name to identify their craft.

*Last Name:* Kellogg
*Occupation:* Slaughterer
*Origin:* Kellogg was a nickname for a pork butcher. Its literal meaning is "kill hog."

*Last Name:* Kemp (Kempe)
*Occupation:* Wrestler
*Origin:* These were unusually strong fellows who wrestled for a living. The name comes from the Old English word *cempa,* meaning "warrior."

*Last Name:* Leach
*Occupation:* Doctor
*Origin:* Leach comes from the word *laece*, meaning "doctor." Medieval doctors also used blood-sucking worms called leeches on their patients. They believed these worms would purify the patient's blood and rid him of disease.

*Last Name:* Parker
*Occupation:* Park keeper
*Origin:* Noblemen often kept beautiful parks on their estates. Watchmen, or "parkers," guarded the parks from outsiders.

*Last Name:* Smith
*Occupation:* Metalworker
*Origin:* Anyone who worked with metal was called a smith. This name was originally a friendly nickname referring to the person or his business. Eventually it became one of the most popular English names.

*Last Name:* Stone
*Occupation:* Stoneworker
*Origin:* Stone is the nickname for someone who worked with stone, a mason or stonecutter.

*Last Name:* Wall
*Occupation:* Mason
*Origin:* Wall was the name given to a special kind of mason, one who had great speed and skill in building straight wall structures.

*Blacksmith:*
*A person who worked in iron.*

*Goldsmith:*
*A person who worked in gold.*

*Whitesmith:*
*A person who worked in tin.*

## BUSINESS THEN AND NOW

Since biblical times, people have worked for food, clothing, and shelter. They still do, but the jobs themselves have changed a great deal, and many professions are now obsolete, no longer useful. For instance, old-fashioned lamplighters have been replaced by electrical switches. Other professions have been modernized. The pony express driver is now a mailperson driving a truck. Yet some jobs haven't changed at all. Farmers in the Holy Land grew olives, figs, and grapes. Today, farmers in this region do the same. But no matter how tools change with time and jobs disappear or change, it seems that people will always have to work to get what they need.

THEN / NOW

### Apothecarist / Pharmacist

In biblical times, the main job of apothecarists was to grind minerals, vegetable oils, and animal fats to make medicines as well as cosmetics and perfumes for women. Today, pharmacists buy perfumes and cosmetics to sell. Their main role is to prepare and fill prescriptions ordered by doctors for their patients.

### Carter / Garbage Collector

Animals used to be the principal means of transportation for both people and things. Although useful, they were also messy, and one of the carter's jobs was to remove animal waste from the streets. Today's garbage collector, unfortunately, has to transport much more than dung.

*Coachman / Limousine Driver*
Coachmen transported wealthy people in a comfortable, closed, four-wheeled carriage pulled by one or more horses. Today, wealthy people are driven in limousines, very large, luxurious cars often equipped with telephones and television.

*Cotter / Groundskeeper*
Cotters were hired by wealthy landowners to work on farms at harvest time, dig ditches, plant crops, and thatch roofs. Groundskeepers today are responsible for the upkeep and management of the lawns and gardens of estates for wealthy people, corporations, or nonprofit organizations such as museums.

*Doorkeeper / Doorman, Security Guard*
For a long time, the people guarding the entrances to temples and private homes have been called doorkeepers. In the past, they were also responsible for guarding the sheep at night. Our

modern city doormen in uniform announce visitors, call for taxis, and also guard the building entrance. There's one big difference between then and now—no sheep.

## Fuller / Cleaner

This job in Hebrew is called *mikabes*, one employed as a person who either cleans dirty clothes or removes natural oils from freshly woven cloth. Detergents were placed in hot water to wash the cloth, which was then stamped on, banged with a metal instrument, and scraped repeatedly. It was a time-consuming and difficult job. Dry cleaners today have machines that use chemicals to remove stains from clothes and then press, shape, and iron them.

## Juggler, Wandering Minstrel / Street Entertainer

In the 13th century, jugglers and wandering minstrels entertained people on the street. They tossed balls in the air and sang songs, hoping people would give them money. Some things never change. They are still found in many large cities and sometimes at country fairs.

## Peddler / Salesperson

Peddlers rode their horses laden with pots, pans, needles, and cutlery throughout villages and towns, trading their goods for other products people wanted. Sometimes they would trade for food or clothing for themselves. Today our world is full of different kinds of salespersons, from travelers to telemarketers to shop workers. They no longer trade goods for other goods but earn a salary so that they can buy their own necessities.

### Scribe / Secretary

The job of scribe dates from at least 3000 B.C., when few people knew how to write. Those who did held positions of importance in the temple or palace. Scribes first recorded information on clay tablets. Later they used parchment, quills, and ink. Today, secretaries use typewriters and word processors, copiers, fax machines, and many other tools in order to communicate and keep records.

### Tinker / Handyman

The tinker rode a horse and carried his tools in his saddlebag. He plugged holes in leaky basins, made new handles for iron dippers, and remade spoons and bowls. Handymen today still carry their tools with them as they travel about, making small repairs.

### Town Crier / TV News Announcer

Every village had a town crier who announced the important news of the day. The job required a loud, clear voice so that all the villagers could hear the information. Television now carries news broadcasts to millions of people throughout the world. Today we are just as likely to see events as they happen rather than hear about them later.

### Vizier / Judge

The medieval vizier is the judge of today. Viziers listened to problems and impartially decided who was right and who was wrong. Today the judge is the highest court official, but in most cases, a jury of twelve people determines the guilt or innocence of the accused person. The judge decides the sentence, or punishment, if necessary.

*They were once called chiffoniers, then ragpickers, then junk dealers; now they are secondhand clothes dealers.*

*They were once called baggage smashers or baggagers, now they are porters or redcaps.*

## PRESIDENTS' OCCUPATIONS

Presidents of the U.S. weren't always presidents. Most of them were lawyers, but almost a third followed other professions.

| | |
|---|---|
| GEORGE WASHINGTON | SURVEYOR, PLANTER |
| JOHN ADAMS | TEACHER, LAWYER |
| THOMAS JEFFERSON | WRITER, INVENTOR, LAWYER, ARCHITECT |
| ANDREW JACKSON | SOLDIER |
| ZACHARY TAYLOR | SOLDIER |
| ANDREW JOHNSON | TAILOR |
| JAMES A. GARFIELD | TEACHER |
| THEODORE ROOSEVELT | RANCHER |
| WOODROW WILSON | TEACHER |
| WARREN HARDING | NEWSPAPER EDITOR |
| HERBERT C. HOOVER | ENGINEER |
| HARRY S. TRUMAN | HABERDASHER |
| DWIGHT D. EISENHOWER | ARMY GENERAL |
| JOHN F. KENNEDY | NEWSPAPERMAN |
| LYNDON B. JOHNSON | TEACHER |
| JIMMY CARTER | PEANUT FARMER |
| RONALD W. REAGAN | ACTOR |
| GEORGE H. W. BUSH | OILMAN |

ANDREW
JACKSON

## KIDS AT WORK

When you help with household chores after school, you may dust or wash dishes. If you grew up a hundred years ago, you may not have gone to school at all. You may have worked full time as a powder monkey or a loblolly. Take a look at these and other historical jobs for kids.

*Chimney sweeps:* Small children, 6 to 8 years old, crawled up chimneys and loosened the soot with a broom. They often worked 12-hour days.

*Gillie boys:* These boys helped fishermen, baited hooks, pulled nets, and prepared food.

*Loblollies:* These boys were surgeon's assistants and worked on military ships.

*Office boys:* Young boys worked in offices sharpening pencils, stuffing envelopes, sweeping floors, and running errands.

*Powder monkeys:* These boys worked on warships and at forts, carrying gunpowder to the cannons during battle.

*Vendors:* Children often sold things on city

*Instead of sending children up a chimney, a goose would be tied to a rope and sent up to clean the soot with its feathers.*

streets. There were newspaper boys, muffin boys, and hot corn girls.

*Waterboys:* Farm and construction crews had waterboys, who brought water to them while they worked.

## FADS: BELIEVE IT OR NOT, THEY'RE BUSINESS

Once in a while, someone has a great idea that becomes a fad, a product that is immensely popular for a short time. Some of the following have gone from fad to classic; others have just gone. There are some interesting things about fads. Anyone can have an idea that becomes a fad, and fads usually make their originators rich.

### *Silly Putty (1944)*

Chemists at General Electric working with silicone stumbled across this material that can be kneaded, bounced, and stretched. In 1949, Peter Hodgson thought it would make a great toy. After an investment of $150, Hodgson sold 1-ounce bags of putty in plastic eggs. It was an instant success. Millions of eggs of Silly Putty have been sold and continue to sell to this day.

### *Slinky (1945)*

When he was 26, Richard James of Philadelphia invented the Slinky. It consists of 87 feet of flat wire coiled into 3-inch-diameter circles and stands less than 2 inches high when stacked. The Slinky's ability to "walk" down stairs and open and close like an accordion made it a favorite toy during the 1950s, and it is still popular today.

## Hula Hoop (1958)

Arthur Melin and Richard Knerr, founders of the Wham-O Toy Company, took an idea from Australia, where gym students exercised using bamboo hoops, and turned it into the biggest fad of all time. The Hula Hoop is a round plastic tube that can be rotated around the waist by swinging the hips; it can also be jumped through, used as a jump rope, or spun around the neck. More than 25 million had been sold only 4 months after it was introduced.

## Mood Rings (1975)

Mood rings were made of heat-sensitive liquid crystals encased in quartz. When the body temperature of the wearer changed, the crystals changed color, supposedly indicating how the wearer felt at the moment. Blue meant happy; reddish brown meant insecure; green meant active; black meant the wearer was tense and upset. Joshua Reynolds, a 33-year-old New Yorker, created and marketed the original mood ring.

## Pet Rocks (1975)

More than a million people bought Pet Rocks as Christmas gifts in 1975. Gary Dahl, of Los Gatos, California, had the idea while joking with friends about his easy-to-care-for pet, a rock. This pet ate nothing and didn't bark or chew the furniture. Pet Rocks were sold with a funny manual that included tips on how to handle an excited rock and how to teach it tricks. By 1976, Gary Dahl was a millionaire and Pet Rocks were the nation's favorite pet.

# TIMELINES

## 20th-Century Toys and Games

| 1900 | Baseball cards |
|------|----------------|
| 1901 | Ping-Pong |
| 1902 | Teddy Bear |
| 1909 | Jigsaw puzzle |
| 1918 | Raggedy Ann doll |
| 1926 | Miniature golf |
| 1929 | Yo-yo |
| 1933 | Monopoly |
| 1943 | Scrabble |
| 1945 | Silly Putty |
| 1957 | Frisbee |
| 1958 | Barbie doll |
| 1960 | Toy Trolls |
| 1975 | Skateboarding |
| 1983 | Cabbage Patch Kids doll |
| 1989 | Teenage Mutant Ninja Turtles |
| 1990 | Rollerblading |

# Entertainment

| | |
|---|---|
| 1877 | Phonograph invented |
| 1892 | First phonograph records sold |
| 1895 | Movies and movie theaters |
| 1897 | Radio first sent over long distance |
| 1919 | Shortwave radio |
| 1920 | Technicolor invented for movies |
| 1929 | FM radio introduced in U.S. |
| 1930 | Jukebox marketed in U.S. |
| 1931 | Pinball machine marketed in U.S. |
| 1931 | Electronic TV demonstrated in Britain |
| 1941 | TV broadcast begins in U.S. |
| 1948 | LP (long-playing) records sold in U.S. |
| 1949 | 45 rpm (revolutions per minute) records sold in U.S. |
| 1952 | Transistor radio invented |
| 1954 | Color TV broadcast in U.S. |
| 1957 | Stereo phonograph introduced |
| 1962 | Telstar satellite broadcasts TV worldwide |
| 1962 | Video games created |
| 1970 | VCR (videocassette recorder) marketed |
| 1970 | CDs (compact discs) marketed |
| 1979 | Sony Walkman sold |
| 1980s | Cable TV networks aired in U.S. |
| 1981 | MTV (music television video) broadcast in U.S. |
| 1982 | Wristwatch TV introduced in Japan. |

*In the future, holography (three-dimensional photography) will enable viewers to walk around TV and movie images as if they were real scenes.*

## Copycats

| 1875 | Typewriter |
|------|------------|
| 1900 | Photocopying (camera takes a photo of an original) |
| 1906 | Photostats (copies made on light-sensitive paper instead of film) |
| 1938 | Xerography (a dry process, with no liquid developer) |
| 1938 | Tape recorder |
| 1963 | Home video recorder |
| 1988 | Facsimile (fax) machine |

## What Counts

| 3000 B.C. | Abacus (board with beads for mathematical functions) |
|------|------------|
| A.D. 1623 | Mechanical calculator |
| 1642 | Adding machine |
| 1946 | Electronic computer |
| 1963 | Disk storage for computer |
| 1970 | Floppy disk |
| 1971 | Pocket calculator |
| 1975 | Desk top computer |
| 1981 | Personal computer |
| 1984 | Laser disk storage |
| 1991 | About 30,000 computer bulletin boards in U.S. |

*Computers of the Future: Scientists predict that biological computers will be grown instead of manufactured. A molecular storage system could contain all human knowledge in the space of a paperback book.*

# Bits and Pieces

1832 Matches

1845 Rubber bands

1879 Mechanical pencil

1888 Ball-point pen

1900 Paper clips

1937 Cellophane tape

1960 Felt-tip pens

*A 13-year-old boy invented golf tees made from recycled paper, which were first sold in 1992.*

# Let There Be Light

1906 Light bulbs (tungsten)

1910 Neon light

1915 Searchlight arc

1936 Fluorescent light

1960 Laser light used in U.S.

*By the 21st century, telephones with computer translators will make it possible to have "phone pals" all over the world.*

# High Tech Talking

1876 Telephone patented

1951 Long-distance dialing in the U.S.

1956 Transatlantic telephone cable

1963 Pushbutton telephone in U.S.

1970 Picturephone in U.S.

1983 Cellular phones in U.S.: *mobile* phones for cars, *transportable* phones carried in a case, and *portable* phones carried in hand

# An "Overall" Look at Clothing

|  |  |
|---|---|
| 3000 B.C. | Cotton is woven in the Indus Valley, Asia. |
| 1600 | Shoes (like moccasins) are made by the Babylonians. |
| 1500 | Silk is woven by the Chinese. |
| 1200 | Linen is made from flax by the Egyptians. |
| 1100 | Assyrian soldiers fashion the first boots. |
| 200 A.D. | Romans make different shoes for left and right feet. |
| 1200 | Buttons are used in Europe. |
| 1580 | Pockets are sewn in men's trousers in Europe. |
| 1823 | Waterproof cloth is invented by Mackintosh, a Scotsman. |
| 1849 | The safety pin is invented by Walter Hunt, an American. |
| 1851 | The home sewing machine is patented by Isaac Singer, an American. |
| 1873 | Jeans are made by Levi Straus, an American. |
| 1893 | The zipper, first used to fasten shoes, is patented by the American Whitcomb Jackson. |
| 1910 | Asian pajamas replace nightshirts in Europe. |
| 1917 | Keds produces the tennis shoe. |
| 1927 | Synthetic fibers are made by combining coal and petroleum. |
| 1930 | American women wear trousers for golf and horseback riding. |
| 1935 | Polyurethane is developed and used for stretch cloth. |
| 1940 | Nylon stockings are sold in America. |
| 1942 | Polyester fabric is marketed in America. |
| 1957 | Velcro is patented by George de Mestral of Switzerland. |
| 1975 | Calvin Klein begins the "designer" jeans era. |

*Who makes the most?*

*Wool:
Australia,
USSR,
New Zealand,
China,
Argentina*

*Cotton:
China, USSR,
U.S., India,
Pakistan*

# Making Life Easier: Household Heroes

1836 ● Gas stoves are used in homes.

1901 ● Electric washing machine is invented.

1907 ● Electric vacuum cleaner is introduced.

1909 ● Electric toaster is made.

1911 ● Air conditioning is invented.

1940 ● Automatic dishwasher is manufactured.

1967 ● Compact microwave ovens are sold.

# Transportation: On Land

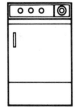

6500 ● The wheel is invented by the Sumerians.
B.C.

3500 ● Animals pull wheeled vehicles in Mesopotamia.

44 ● The wheelbarrow is invented by the Chinese.

A.D.
1769 ● The first steam-powered vehicle, with 3 wheels, is invented in France.

1791 ● The bicycle is invented in Scotland.

1792 ● The ambulance is created for Napoleon's army.

1803 ● The steam locomotive is invented for railroads.

1869 ● The modern motorcycle is invented.

1874 ● The cable streetcar is invented.

1885 ● The automobile is invented.

1892 ● The tractor is invented.

1924 ● The diesel truck is invented.

*Who makes the most cars? Japan, U.S., West Germany, France, USSR (in order)*

## Transportation: On Water

| 4500 B.C. | Sailing ships are made in Mesopotamia. |
| 3500 | Oar-powered ships sail the seas. |
| A.D. 1620 | The submarine, human powered, is invented. |
| 1787 | The steamboat is invented in America. |
| 1886 | The electric-powered submarine is invented. |
| 1909 | The hydrofoil is invented. |
| 1954 | Nuclear-powered submarines are used. |
| 1988 | The world's largest passenger ship, the 73,000-ton *Sovereign of the Seas,* sails from Norway. |

## Transportation: In Air

| 1783 | Hot-air balloon |
| 1783 | Parachute |
| 1852 | Dirigible |
| 1853 | Zeppelin |
| 1903 | First airplane flight |
| 1911 | Hydroplane |
| 1926 | Liquid-propelled rocket is invented. |
| 1939 | First successful helicopter flight. |
| 1955 | Hovercraft |
| 1968 | Supersonic transport (SST) |
| 1970 | Jumbo jet |
| 1971 | First space station orbited |
| 1981 | Solar-powered airplane |

*The first man in space was Yuri Gagarin of the USSR in 1961.*

*The first man to walk on the moon was Neil Armstrong, an American, in 1969.*

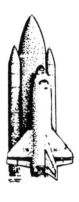

## MOST PEOPLE THINK SO, BUT . . .
*Most people think . . .*

*. . . Christopher Columbus discovered America.*

In fact, the Vikings, led by Leif Ericson, landed on North America near Newfoundland in the year 1000. Christopher Columbus landed on the island of San Salvador in 1492, thinking he had reached the East Indies.

*. . . Ferdinand Magellan was the first to sail around the world.*

In fact, he was dead before the voyage was over. Magellan set sail from Spain in 1519 with 5 ships and 270 men and was killed in a fight with the natives of Macatan Island in the Pacific Ocean in 1521. In 1522, one of his ships, with 18 original crewmen, completed the journey.

*. . . Robert Fulton invented the steamboat.*

In fact, John Fitch, an American, built and operated a steamboat on the Delaware River in 1787, but his passenger business failed. Fulton's steamboat, the *North River*, later known as the *Clermont* after its port town, was financially successful in 1807 and became famous.

*. . . Phineas Fogg traveled around the world in 180 days.*

In fact, he was an imaginary character in a Jules Verne novel, *Around the World in Eighty Days*. Nellie Bly, an American journalist, accepted a challenge to go around the world in fewer than 80 days. In 1889, she made the journey in 72 days.

*. . . Charles Lindbergh was the first to fly across the Atlantic Ocean.*
In fact, he was the first to fly solo (alone) across the Atlantic in 1927. The first nonstop flight across the Atlantic was made by Alcock and Brown, two British aviators, in 1919.

*. . . Henry Ford invented the automobile.*
In fact, the modern automobile was invented in Germany by Otto Benz in 1885. The first American cars were made by the Duryea Brothers in 1895. In 1896, Ford produced an inexpensive assembly line car, the Model T.

## KLEENEX IS REALLY A BRAND NAME
Yes, Kleenex is a brand name for facial tissues. Some product names, or trademarks, have become so common that often they are used to name the product. Here are a few examples.

| BRAND NAME | GENERIC NAME |
| --- | --- |
| ACE BANDAGE | ELASTIC BANDAGE |
| BAND-AIDS | PLASTIC BANDAGES |
| CHAPSTICK | LIP BALM |
| JELL-O | GELATIN DESSERT |
| KLEENEX | FACIAL TISSUES |
| Q-TIPS | COTTON SWABS |
| SCOTCH TAPE | CELLOPHANE TAPE |
| STYROFOAM | PLASTIC FOAM |
| TEFLON | NONSTICK COATING |
| VASELINE | PETROLEUM JELLY |
| VELCRO | HOOK AND LOOP FASTENER |
| WALKMAN | PORTABLE CASSETTE PLAYER WITH HEADPHONES |
| XEROX | PHOTOCOPIER |

# Creature Catalogue

*Angels, Fairies, Giants, and Monsters*

OUR IMAGINATIONS ARE FILLED with creatures of every description. From horrible to beautiful, tiny to tremendous, evil to angelic, they all exist in the minds of people throughout the world. Creatures are all around us—in movies, songs, stories, and art. Are they real or not? Only you know the answer.

## ANGELS

The angel is a heavenly being, superior to humans, who serves as an attendant and messenger of God, or a guardian for someone on Earth. Angels typically have wings, are delicately beautiful and either glow or are surrounded by halos. *Angelology* is the study of angels. In 1978, over half the people in the U.S. who were asked, said they believed in angels. Angels are drawn on greeting cards, painted on ceilings and mentioned in one of every top ten songs. Angelfood cake, the California Angels baseball team, and the city of Los Angeles (Spanish for "city of angels") all show our fondness for and fascination with angels. Whether you are an "angelologist" or not, you'll want to know all about angels.

### Angel Profile

| | |
|---|---|
| *Appearance:* | Bright, glowing, ethereal, winged |
| *Characteristics:* | Intellect and powers superior to humans |
| *Habitat:* | Heaven |
| *Specialties:* | Messengers, guardians |

### Who's Who of Angels

*Archangel Gabriel,* the only female angel, is described as having 140 pairs of wings!

*Archangel Michael* is considered the "greatest" of angels, a hero who defeated Satan. Michael takes souls to the "other world."

*Archangel Raphael* is the angel of healing who is the friendliest and merriest of all the angels.

*Archangel Uriel* is the angel of repentance and the angel who warned Noah of the flood. Uriel is also the angel of the month of September.

*Lucifer* is Satan, once the mightiest Seraphim, now the fallen angel, the Devil.

# Angels in Order

There are nine orders, or groups, of angels that surround God. These nine are further divided into groups of three, or triads. The angels in the first triad communicate directly with God, then pass their knowledge on to the second triad, who pass it on to the third triad, who pass it on to human beings. Here is the order of angels, from highest to lowest.

FIRST TRIAD

**Seraphim**
Angels closest to God who appear to humans with 6 wings and 4 heads. They are angels of love.

**Cherubim**
God's charioteers who have 4 wings and 4 heads. They are angels of knowledge.

**Thrones**
Huge, they are known as "many-eyed ones." They make up God's chariot.

SECOND TRIAD

**Dominions**
Angels who oversee other angels to make sure they do their duties.

**Virtues**
Known as "the shining ones," they are miracle makers.

**Powers**
The "border guards" between the first and second level of heaven. They are also the guardians of human souls.

*According to Christian belief, everyone has two guardian angels.*

THIRD TRIAD

**Principalities**
Angels in charge of Earth's nations and cities.

**Archangels**
The go-betweens or messengers from God to humans who also fight the Devil.

**Angels**
The "watchers" who never sleep. Among these are the guardian angels who are assigned to every human at birth.

*According to the Jewish faith, each child has 11,000 guardian angels at birth.*

## Angel Lore

*Hell's angels* are fallen angels, now the devils and demons of the underworld. One named Zephon planned to set fire to heaven but was cast out before succeeding.

*Angel wings,* as painted by the great artists, were modeled after large and beautiful birds such as eagles and swans.

*Angel music* is thought to be the vibration of the universe, the song of creation and life. Angels make music with their voices and by beating their wings.

*Angel dress* is almost always a long, flowing robe of blue or white with gold belts and gold jewelry.

*Angels speak* all languages, and always know which ones humans will understand.

*Angel fever* peaked in the 13th century, when angels were thought to move the stars and govern the planets, seasons, months, days, and hours.

*Some believe fairies to be fallen angels who weren't bad enough for Hell.*

# BEASTS

Imaginary beasts lurk in the legends of most countries of the world. Usually they are monsters, described as mutants, or creatures with strange and horrible bodies. Although these beasts can touch our deepest fears, they are very popular. It seems that people like to be scared.

Teratology *means the study of monsters.*

## Who's Who of Beasts

| WHO | WHERE | WHAT |
| --- | --- | --- |
| Aigaumcha | Africa | A tiny monster with eyes on its feet; its diet consists of human flesh. |
| Al(s) | Armenia | These have iron teeth, brass claws and eat babies. |
| Bunyip | Australia | A water devil who hides in isolated wetlands and lakes and drowns swimmers. |
| Galactic ghoul | Solar system | A force in space some 35 million miles from Earth on the way to Mars. It supposedly causes electrical or mechanical problems with spacecraft in the area. |
| Kappa | Japan | An ugly green monster with a monkey's head and a turtle's shell, it drags people into its watery home to eat them. |
| Logaroo | Caribbean Islands | Like vultures by day, they shed their skin at night, hide in fog, and suck blood from their victims. |
| Manticora | West Indies | A lion with human features, eyes that burn blue fire, and deadly quills it can shoot from its tail. |
| New Jersey devil | U.S. | Part ram, part kangaroo with bat wings, a horse's feet, and a pointed tail, this bellowing monster kills barnyard animals. |
| Ping feng | China | A huge, piglike beast, with a head at each end, that attacks people and other animals. |
| Rakshasa | India | A beast who appears in any ugly shape, it comes from nowhere to kill its victims with a single scratch from its poisonous tail. |
| Vodyany | Eastern Europe | A green-haired monster with horns, paws, and blood-red eyes. Its victims are swimmers. |

## DRAGONS

Dragons deserve a category all their own because they are beasts found all over the world. But there are two distinct types of dragon: the dragon of the Western world and the dragon of the Eastern world.

*Western Dragons*
These enormous, fire-breathing serpents have scaly green bodies and huge red wings. Greedy creatures, they hoard gold treasure in dens under the earth. Fierce and always hungry, a Western dragon will eat anything but especially likes weak, young, human flesh. Dragons live in caves, mountains, or lakes. They were particularly active in the Middle Ages, when brave knights challenged them to battle.

*Eastern Dragons*
Compared to Western dragons, these beasts are quite small. Their bodies are long, and they have

*Native Americans believed in snake dragons, supernatural wisdom.*

two horns for ears. They have no wings, and their soft breath is said to form clouds. They do not roar; instead they make the sounds of beating gongs and jingling bells. Chinese dragons dine on sparrows. They live wherever there is water. They are kind and wise friends of human beings.

## WATER SERPENTS

In the Old Testament of the Bible, *Leviathan* is a large sea monster who represents the forces of evil. In Arabian folklore, *Behemoth* is an enormous fish swimming in a bottomless sea carrying all of creation on its back.

| Cousins of the Loch Ness Monster? | |
| --- | --- |
| **WHO** | **WHERE** |
| Champ | Lake Champlain, U.S. |
| Chessie | Chesapeake Bay, U.S. |
| Ogopogo | Okanagan Lake, British Columbia |

In present times, the *Loch Ness Monster* remains one of the world's most famous mysteries. "Nessie" is thought to be a giant creature with a huge rounded body, maybe 100 feet long, and a long neck. Some think it is a prehistoric seagoing dinosaur, pleiosaur. It lives in the inky black waters of the immense, 700-foot-deep Loch (Lake) Ness in Scotland. "Nessie" has been sighted many times. An expedition in 1934 at the height of "monster fever" claimed 21 sightings and took 5 pictures. No one has yet caught this elusive creature or scientifically proved its existence. Tales of the Loch Ness Monster may be the basis for stories of similar freshwater serpents in other places.

## FAIRIES

Perhaps you think of Pinocchio's Blue Fairy, the Good Witch of the West from *The Wizard of Oz,* or

Peter Pan's Tinkerbell when you imagine a fairy. But in fact, fairies don't like to be seen by people at all. These tiny creatures can appear and disappear in the blink of an eye. You may never know if you've seen one or not! But you can be sure of one thing: there is a wealth of fascinating lore about these little people who can vanish at will.

**Who's Who of Fairies**

*The Banshee:* This Irish fairy is more often heard than seen. Her mournful wail, called keening, is heard outside the home of a dying person.

*The Bogeyman:* Also called bogies or bugbears, these fairies are nasty to children and frighten them in the dark. Only children can see their furry bodies and fiery red eyes.

*Fairy food is milk, cream, and butter.*

*Brownies:* Brownies are helpful little men with brownish skin and brown clothing. They have been said to visit farms in Scotland and do house-

hold chores while the family sleeps. All they ask in return for their work is a bowl of cream.

*Changelings:* A changeling is a fairy child who takes the place of a human baby who the fairies think is being fussed over too much. The baby is then used to "strengthen" the fairy race.

*Dwarfs:* These aged creatures of the mountains are miners with magical powers. They won't appear aboveground in daylight because they'll turn to stone. They wear long clothes to cover their feet, which are deformed or point backward.

*Elves:* Elves are merry creatures who live in colonies under the earth. They love parties, music, and dancing, but they kidnap people who are caught listening to their music.

*Flower fairies:* In the gardens of China, flower fairies dress like young girls and spread the scent of flowers as they dance.

*Many small cottages in Ireland built in a "fairy path" have front and back doors directly opposite each other which are left ajar to allow fairies free passage.*

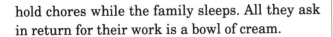

111

*Gnomes:* Gnomes are bearded men with broad, leathery features who never age and who always wear hoods. They guard hidden treasure in the woods and hills where they live.

*Goblins:* Goblins, the thieves of the fairy world, have a bad reputation. They have deformed bodies with huge, bulging eyes and live in underground caves.

*Huldre:* These Icelandic fairies look like beautiful girls from the front, but in back they may have cow tails or they may be one-sided. They demonstrate that beauty is only one part of something.

*Jinni (genie):* In Arabian folklore, these spirits have supernatural powers and can appear in many shapes and sizes. They may be good or evil, depending on their Master. They live in unusual places like empty bottles.

*Leprechauns:* These clever, independent little men wear three-cornered hats. They are shoemakers who make only one shoe, not a pair. Every leprechaun has a hidden pot of gold.

*Menehunes:* These hard-working Hawaiian fairies work at night building bridges and roads. They are small, dark-eyed creatures with shaggy eyebrows and deep, gruff voices.

*Monaciello:* This Italian fairy is dressed in a hooded robe. It comes out at night to lead poor and needy people to hidden treasure.

*Pixies:* These green dancing fairies have a king, a queen, and a full royal court. Pixies live in England, where they pull pranks on people.

*Fairies love to dance and are fond of the music of fiddles, harps, tambourines, and cymbals.*

*Sandman:* He travels the world over, sprinkling sleep dust in children's eyes to help them fall asleep.

*Tooth fairy:* No one has seen a tooth fairy, so their appearance has not been described. When a child's tooth falls out, the tooth fairy takes it away and leaves a reward in its place.

*Trolls:* Trolls, usually men, may be huge or tiny, but they are all stingy and nasty. They hate the light and loud noises.

*Vilas:* These fairy sisters live in the Alps, where they heal the sick and foretell the future.

*Wanagemeswah:* Thin as a knife, this fairy lived among the Penobscot Indians of Maine in the U.S.

*Will-o'-wisps:* Will-o'-wisps are mischievous fairies who light up on dark nights. They snatch the lights of travelers and try to lead them astray.

*"Elf locks" are tangles of hair made by pesty fairy elves.*

*A sock under the bed helps to keep troublesome fairies away.*

## GIANTS

Giants have enormous size and strength packed in a human form. They can roar like thunder, make the earth shake, and snack on grown people. Their characteristics depend on their nationalities. Irish giants are pleasant, English giants are openly evil, and Welsh giants are clever and cunning. All giants have a keen sense of smell, and they are always smelling out little boys (fee fi fo fum). But their brains never match their bodies. The smallest person can always outsmart the most terrible giant. Giants are proof that intelligence is more important than size.

*Albanian giants are as tall as pine trees, with black beards that reach to their knees. They catch men to eat and women to fan the flies away.*

## Who's Who of Giants

*Super Giant*
*Atlas* was one of the Titans in Greek mythology. After the Titans lost a battle with the god Zeus, Atlas's punishment was to carry the earth on his shoulders for eternity.

*Gentle Giant*
*Paul Bunyan*, an American folk hero, was a giant of the north woods. He was taller than the trees, and when his footprints filled with water, they created the ten thousand lakes of Minnesota.

*Biblical Giant*
*Goliath*, a warrior giant, terrorized whole armies with his size and strength. Only a young boy named David would challenge him. With a slingshot and a stone, David beat Goliath.

*One-Eyed Giant*
The *Cyclops* was a man-eating giant who had one eye in the middle of his forehead. In Greek mythology, the Cyclops captured the hero Odysseus, who escaped after he put out the Cyclops' eye.

*Mountain Giants*
*Yeti*, the Abominable Snowman of Tibet, *Yerin*, the Wildman of China, and *Sasquatch*, the Big Foot of America, are all mysterious giants who live in the mountains. There are many stories of sightings or attacks by these mysterious creatures.

*Man-Eating Giant*
An *ogre* is a man-eating giant. Rakshas was an ogre who lived in a palace in India. His gold and

*Scientists have found gigantic skulls and enormous jaws that may have belonged to a race of giants half a million years ago.*

jewels made him rich, but he was dirty and dumb. Like all ogres, he enjoyed eating people.

### Giantess
Most giant wives are depicted as stay-at-homes who spend their time making bread out of ground-up human bones. *Befri*, a French giantess, carried off young girls who did not want to spin thread into cloth. But *Grendel's Mother*, in the story of *Beowulf*, was an ogress who could sneak up on sleeping warriors and eat 15 of them at a time. She was killed by the hero Beowulf, who used a magic sword of the giants to slay her.

### Cold Giant
*Jack Frost* is an enormous, hoary giant whose cold breath freezes the earth, covering it with frost. His fierce roar can shatter icebergs.

Gruagachs *are Scottish giants and giantesses.*

# Disaster Digest

---

*The Worst of Times*

---

DISASTERS ARE EXTREME, SUD-
den events that damage people
and property. Earthquakes, wind-
storms, floods, and disease all
strike anywhere on earth, often

 without warn-
ing. As exam-
ples, we've cho-
sen disasters
that have occurred around the
world throughout history.

## AVALANCHES

An *avalanche* is any swift movement of snow, ice, mud, or rock down a mountainside or slope.

*Where:* Italian Alps
*When:* 218 B.C.
When Hannibal, the Carthaginian general, crossed the Alps to conquer Rome, 18,000 soldiers, 2,000 horses, and many elephants died. Most of the deaths were caused by Alpine avalanches.

*Where:* United States
*When:* 1910
The worst snowslide in U.S. history occurred in the Cascade Mountains in Wellington, Washington, when 118 people were trapped when their train became snowbound. An avalanche then swept them to their deaths in a gorge 150 feet below the tracks.

*Where:* Peru
*When:* 1962
When tons of ice and snow slid down Huascaran Peak in the Andes Mountains, nearly 4,000 people were killed. Some 30 years later, it is still considered the world's worst avalanche.

### Devastating Accidents

| WHEN | WHAT | WHERE | NUMBER DEAD |
|------|------|-------|-------------|
| 1865 | Ship explosion | Mississippi River | 1,653 |
| 1912 | *Titanic* sank | North Atlantic | 1,500 |
| 1977 | Airplane collision | Canary Islands | 583 |
| 1985 | Airplane crash | Japan | 520 |
| 1987 | Ship collision | Philippines | 1,840 |

## BLIZZARDS AND HAILSTORMS

A *blizzard* is a severe snowstorm. A *hailstorm* is precipitation in the form of balls or lumps of clear ice and compact snow.

*Where:* India
*When:* 1888
A hailstorm hit the city of Moradabad, killing 246 people. It was the worst hailstorm ever recorded.

*Where:* United States
*When:* 1978
The blizzard of 1978 was the most powerful and damaging snowstorm to hit the East Coast. It crippled New York and New England for days, dumping 20–30 inches of snow carried by winds of 40 mph on land, 90 mph at sea. An estimated 400 people died and 200 boats sank.

*Where:* USSR
*When:* 1923
In Rostov, 23 people and even more cattle were killed by hailstones weighing up to 2 pounds each.

*Where:* India
*When:* 1939
A hailstorm over a 30-square-mile area in the southern part of the country killed cattle and sheep and damaged crops. Some of the hailstones were said to weigh 7½ pounds.

## DROUGHTS AND FAMINES

*Droughts* are unusual periods of dryness that damage food crops. *Famines* are extreme shortages of food that cause people to die of starvation.

*Where:* Egypt
*When:* 1200–02
The Egyptian people relied on the annual flooding of the Nile River to leave soil for growing crops. After a shortage of rain, however, the Nile didn't rise. People were unable to grow food and began to starve to death. The final death toll was 110,000, due to starvation, cannibalism, and disease.

*Where:* Ireland
*When:* 1845–49

Potatoes were the mainstay of the Irish diet. When the crop was struck by a potato blight (a fungus that killed the crop), farmers and their families began to starve. The grain and livestock raised in Ireland were owned by the English, and the laws of the time prevented the Irish people from importing grain to eat. This combination of plant disease and politics resulted in the Great Potato Famine, which killed 1.5 million people and caused a million more to move to America.

*Where:* Northern China
*When:* 1959–61
The world's deadliest famine killed an estimated 30 million people in China. Drought was followed by crop failure, which was followed by starvation, disease, and cannibalism. News of the famine was not revealed to the rest of the world until 1981, some 20 years later.

*Where:* Biafra (Africa)
*When:* 1967–69
As a result of civil war, famine conditions killed an estimated 1 million people and left another 3.5 million suffering from extreme malnutrition.

# EARTHQUAKES AND TIDAL WAVES

An *earthquake* is a trembling movement of the earth's crust. A *tidal wave* is an unusually high sea wave which follows an earthquake or volcano. *Tsunami* is the Japanese word for tidal waves caused by undersea earthquakes.

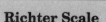

*Where:* Near East & Mediterranean Sea
*When:* 1201
The worst recorded earthquake in history took an estimated 1 million lives.

*Where:* China
*When:* 1556
More than 830,000 people in the Shensi Province were killed by this earthquake. It caused the collapse of caves that people had carved out of cliffs and used for homes.

*Where:* Japan
*When:* 1933
A deadly *tsunami* killed 3,000 people on the island of Honshu. The tidal wave, caused by an earthquake, sank 8,000 ships and destroyed 9,000 homes.

*Where:* Armenia
*When:* 1988
Nearly 4,000 square miles of densely populated land was ravaged by an earthquake. Three cities were leveled, killing more than 25,000 people. Other countries were able to send the Armenians supplies and rescue workers. Miraculously, 15,000 people were recovered from the rubble.

## Richter Scale

Earthquakes are measured on a 1–9 scale devised by two seismologists, Charles Richter and Beno Gutenberg.

1. Felt by scientific instruments
2. Felt by some people and animals
3. Felt by most people
4. Felt by all people
5. Building walls crack
6. Structures tremble

MAJOR QUAKE

7. Destroys buildings and people
8. A disaster
9. So devastating, none has yet been recorded

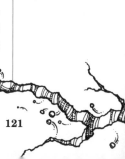

## FLOODS

A *flood* occurs when a body of water rises and overflows onto normally dry land.

*Where:* The Netherlands and England
*When:* 1099
A combination of high tides and storm waves on the North Sea flooded coastal areas of England and the Netherlands, killing 100,000 people.

*Where:* United States
*When:* 1889
The Johnstown Flood, in Pennsylvania, was considered one of the worst disasters in U.S. history. After an unusually heavy rainstorm, a dam 74 miles upriver from Johnstown broke. One out of every 10 people in the path of the flood died, a total of 2,000 people in less than an hour.

*Where:* Italy
*When:* 1966
After a heavy rainfall, the Arno River overflowed, flooding the streets of Florence. Many great works of art in the museums were damaged, as was the architecture of the city. In two days, more than 100 people died and the city was covered with half a million tons of mud, silt, and sewage.

## HURRICANES, TYPHOONS, AND CYCLONES

A *tropical cyclone* is the general term for violent circular winds with torrential rains that originate in the tropics. When they occur in the Atlantic Ocean, they are called *hurricanes.* In the Pacific Ocean, they are called *typhoons.* In the Indian Ocean, they are called *cyclones.*

*Where:* Caribbean Islands
*When:* 1780
The worst hurricane on record killed more than 20,000 people and destroyed the naval fleets of the British, Spanish, and French. The hurricane destroyed everything in its path from the island of Barbados to Puerto Rico.

*Where:* Japan
*When:* 1954
Packing 100-mph winds, this typhoon killed 1,600 people on the island of Hokkaido. Many of the victims were on a harbor ferry that capsized.

## Beaufort Wind Scale

The Beaufort Wind Scale was designed in 1805 by Sir Francis Beaufort, a rear admiral in the British navy, to describe the wind's effect on sailing ships. The scale is a series of numbers from 0 to 17 that indicate wind speed.

| NUMBER | NAME | MILES PER HOUR |
| --- | --- | --- |
| 0 | Calm | less than 1 |
| 1 | Light air | 1–3 |
| 2 | Light breeze | 4–7 |
| 3 | Gentle breeze | 8–12 |
| 4 | Moderate breeze | 13–18 |
| 5 | Fresh breeze | 19–24 |
| 6 | Strong breeze | 25–31 |
| 7 | Moderate gale | 32–38 |
| 8 | Fresh gale | 39–46 |
| 9 | Strong gale | 47–54 |
| 10 | Whole gale | 55–63 |
| 11 | Storm | 64–73 |
| 12–17 | Hurricane | 74 and above |

*Where:* East Pakistan (Bangladesh)
*When:* 1970
The total death count ranged between 300,000 and 500,000 people after this cyclone, the worst natural disaster of this century. Severe winds and high waves destroyed a 3,000-square-mile area.

## PESTILENCE
Pestilence is contagious disease that spreads out of control, killing many people.

### Black Death
*Where:* Western Europe
*When:* 1347–51
This plague, thought to be the Bubonic plague, spread throughout Europe, killing about half its population. It was called the Black Death because of the black blotches that appeared on the victims' bodies. This plague was carried by infected fleas of the black rat.

### Influenza
*Where:* Worldwide
*When:* 1918–19
This flu was a highly contagious virus that killed 20 million people throughout the world. Without antibiotics to treat the illness, most people died of complications from the disease, like pneumonia. This pestilence, along with the Black Death, resulted in the highest number of deaths worldwide in history.

### AIDS
*Where:* Worldwide
*When:* 19??–present
AIDS (acquired immune deficiency syndrome) is a

disease that destroys the body's immune system, its ability to fight sickness. This virus may have developed as long as 50 to 150 years ago, but it was not identified until 1981. The virus may take years to produce symptoms, but it is always fatal. Scientists estimate that 270,000 people will die from AIDS each year.

## TORNADOES

Tornadoes, also called "twisters," are black, spinning, funnel-shaped columns of terrific winds that suck up everything in their paths. Tornado winds may roar up to 300 mph.

*Where:* United States
*When:* 1965
Tornadoes raced through five midwestern states, killing 271 people, injuring 5,000 more, and destroying $200 million worth of property. The state of Indiana, which lies in "Tornado Alley," was the hardest hit.

*Where:* Bangladesh
*When:* 1989
The world's deadliest tornado ripped through Shaturia, Bangladesh, killing more than 1,300 people in April 1989.

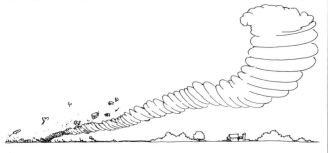

## VOLCANIC ERUPTIONS

A volcanic eruption occurs when molten rock ash and steam pour through a vent in the earth's crust. Some volcanos explode. Some are slow-flowing lava fountains. Lava is hot fluid rock.

*Where:* Italy
*When:* A.D. 79
The eruption of Mount Vesuvius buried the towns of Pompeii and Herculaneum under 20 feet of ash and lava, killing an estimated 20,000 people. The ash that buried the town and the people also preserved them. The work of uncovering the ancient cities began in 1748 and continues to this day.

*Where:* Indonesia
*When:* 1883
The greatest explosion in modern times occurred when Krakatoa erupted. The power of the explosion was thought to be 26  times the power of the greatest H bomb, and the roar was heard over one-thirteenth of the surface of the earth. The eruption wiped out 163 villages, killing 36,380 people.

# Environment
# Examination

*An Earthly View*

YOU KNOW HOW IMPORTANT

 our earth is and that there are many things you can do to help out in the environmental crisis. Being educated and well informed when it comes to the state of the earth is one of them, so here are some interesting and helpful things to know.

# EARTH'S ADDRESS BOOK

Have you visited any *biomes* lately? A biome is a large ecosystem where plants, animals, insects, and people live in a certain type of climate. If you were in Fairbanks, Alaska, you would be in a frosty biome called the Arctic. Taking a plane, you could be in Brazil, in a hot and humid biome called the rain forest, just a few hours later. The world contains many biomes: grasslands, deserts, forests, and mountains, to name a few. The plants and animals living in each are as different as their climates. Which is your favorite?

## Arctic

The Arctic is the territory north of the Arctic Circle. It includes the northern lands of Europe (Lapland and Scandinavia), Asia (Siberia), and North America (Alaska and Canada) as well as most of Greenland.

*Special features:*

This is the earth's coldest biome. It receives less sun than any other area. Since the sun does not rise for nearly six months of the year, the Arctic winters are long and bitterly cold. It is not unusual for the temperature to be below –30˚F in winter. Most of the animal life in this area lives in or around water. The waters teem with fish such as cod, shark, salmon, Alaskan King crab, and coalfish. The rich marine life of the seas provides food for the animals of this area, such as the walrus, seal, and polar bear.

## Coniferous Forest

The coniferous forest biome is south of the tundra

(see Tundra). It stretches from Alaska straight across North America to the Atlantic Ocean and across Eurasia. The taiga is the largest stretch of coniferous forest in the world, circling the earth in the Northern Hemisphere. It supplies the bulk of the world's commercial softwood timber, which is used to make paper.

*Special features:*
These forests consist of cone-bearing trees such as fir and pine, which are well suited to the cold climate. The soil is not very fertile, however, because there are no leaves to decompose and enrich it. Some animals that thrive in this biome are birds such as the crossbill and great horned owl, squirrels, lynx, caribou, and reindeer.

## Deciduous Forest
This biome is in the mild temperate zone of the Northern Hemisphere. Major regions are found in eastern North America, Europe, and Eastern Asia.

*Special features:*

Deciduous trees lose their leaves in fall. The natural decaying of the fallen leaves enriches the soil and supports all kinds of plant and animal life. The deciduous forest is a lively place, where oak, beech, ash, and chestnut trees are typical and wildflowers, berries, and many types of insect and animal life abound. But the fertile soil is also good for people, and in Europe most of the deciduous forest has been destroyed to make room for farms and homes. This biome, or habitat, has been altered more than any other natural habitat in the world. In the U.S., the deciduous forest is a home for deer, the American gray squirrel, wood mouse, rabbit, woodpecker, and finch, to name a few!

## Desert

A desert is an area where little or no life exists because of a lack of water. Scientists estimate that about 5% of the earth's surface is desert. Deserts can be found on every continent except Europe. There are different kinds: hot and dry (the Sahara in Africa, Atacama in South America) and cold and dry (Antarctica, the Gobi in Central Asia).

*Special features:*

The lack of water and intense heat or cold make this biome inhospitable to most life. A few animals—reptiles, like snakes and lizards, and amphibians, like frogs and toads—are well adapted to the hot desert. The most famous desert animal is the camel, who can make water from the fat it stores in its hump. The Emperor and Adélie penguins are well-known animals living at the edge of the Antarctic desert. In the Middle East, unfortunately, the desert biome is rapidly changing as oil is drilled and people move in, causing damage to the environment.

## Grasslands

Grasslands are places where the hot, dry climates are perfect for growing food. They are known throughout the world by different names. In the U.S. they are called prairies and extend from the Midwest to the Rocky Mountains. In South Africa, grasslands are called the veld. Hot, tropical grasslands called savannas are found in South America and Africa. In Eurasia, temperate zone grasslands are called steppes; in South America, pampas.

*Special features:*
This inland biome is made of vast areas of grassy field. It receives so little rain that trees cannot grow. The U.S. prairie is used to graze cattle and to raise cereal crops. There is little variety of animal life but those animals that live there are nu-

merous. Some original prairie animals like the wolf and bison have been eliminated from the habitat by hunters. Today's prairie animals include the prairie dog and the mule deer.

## Mountains

Mountains exist on all continents, covering one-fifth of the surface of the earth. Many of the world's mountains lie in two great belts. One, called the Ring of Fire, runs from the west coast of the Americas through New Zealand and Australia and up through the Philippines to Japan. The other major belt stretches from the Pyrenees in Spain and France through the Alps and on to the Himalayas before ending in Indonesia.

*Special features:*
Mountains may be found in groups called chains or ranges, although some stand alone. A mountain biome is very cold and windy. The higher the mountain, the colder and windier the environment. There is also less oxygen at high elevations. The animals of this biome have adapted to the cold, the lack of oxygen, and the rugged landscape. They include the mountain goat, ibex (wild goat), sheep, mountain lion, puma, and llama. All of them are excellent climbers, which means they can move freely in the steep, rocky landscape.

## Rain Forest

Tropical rain forests are found in Asia, Africa, South and Central America, and on many of the Pacific islands. Almost half of the world's rain forest is in Brazil in South America, and many are along the equator.

*Special features:*
Rain forests receive at least 70 inches of rain each year and have more species of plants and animals than any other biome. Anywhere from 25 to 500 species of tree can grow on a single acre! Thick vegetation absorbs the moisture that then evaporates and falls again as rain. A rain forest grows in three levels. The canopy, or tallest level, has trees between 75 and 150 feet tall. They block most of the sunlight from the levels below. The second level, or understory, contains a mix of

small trees, vines, and palms as well as shrubs and ferns. The third and lowest level is the forest floor, where herbs, mosses, and fungi grow. Rain forests are an endangered biome. People have cut the trees and sold the wood to build homes and firewood. Parts of the rain forest have been burned to make space for grazing and farming. In the time it takes you to read this paragraph, between 50 and 100 acres of rain forest have been destroyed. The combination of heat and moisture makes this biome the perfect environment for more than 15 million plants and animals. Some of the animals are the anteater, jaguar, brocket deer, lemur, orangutan, marmoset, macaw, parrot, sloth, and toucan.

## Tundra

The tundra is a vast, treeless area of low, swampy plains in the far north around the Arctic Ocean. Siberia, northern Alaska, and northern Europe are in this biome.

*Special features:*
The earth of the tundra has a permanently frozen subsoil, called permafrost, which makes it impossible for trees to grow. Prehistoric animal remains have been found preserved in the permafrost. In summer, a thin layer of topsoil thaws and creates many pools, lakes, and marshes, a haven for mosquitoes, midges, and blackflies. Migrant birds by the millions are attracted by the insect food and the safe feeding ground. More than 100 migrant bird species nest on the tundra. It is also famous for the beauty of its flowers during early autumn.

# EARTH REPORT

**2 billion years ago:** Life on earth begins.

**10,000 years ago:** More than 15 billion acres of land are covered with forest.

**1750–1850:** The Industrial Revolution. Fossil fuels used in factories.

**1957:** The International Geophysical Year. Scientists in the Antarctic and Hawaii monitor atmospheric gases and the ozone layer.

**1960s:** Dangers to the ozone layer from jet planes are investigated.

**1970 April 22:** Earth has its first worldwide birthday celebration. The Environmental Protection Agency (EPA) is formed by the U.S. government to enforce laws that protect the environment.

**1972:** The Clean Air Act identifies the six most common dangerous pollutants (lead, sulfur oxide, carbon monoxide, particulates, ozone, nitrogen oxide).

**1973:** The Endangered Species Act is passed to protect wildlife. Every year the names of 35 to 50 insects, plants, and animals are added to the list of species threatened with extinction. There are now 11,000 animals on the list. Ten species have increased enough to be removed from the list.

**1974:** The Safe Drinking Water Act outlaws pollutants (substances in water that make people sick) to ensure that people drink safe water.

**1976:** The Toxic Substance Control Act is passed to prevent farmers from using pesticides to kill insects that damage their crops.

**1982:** A hole is discovered in the ozone layer over the Antarctic by a British scientist, Joe Farman.

**1982:** The EPA creates a superfund, setting large amounts of money aside to clean up harmful waste sites across the U.S.

**1988:** Scientists discover a second hole in the ozone layer, this time over the Arctic.

**1990s:** "The Decade of the Environment." People are increasingly committed to protecting the environment. Mandatory recycling begins in many cities and towns; cars must pass annual emission tests to protect the air quality; people are more careful about how they use energy at home. It is hoped that by the end of the decade, planet Earth will be in better health.

## Happy Birthday, Earth!

*Earth had its first official birthday celebration in the U.S. on April 22, 1970. More than 20 million people marched in parades, sang songs, and attended teach-ins on the environment. Earth Day 2 was celebrated on April 22, 1990. This time 100 million people around the globe celebrated.*

# EARTH RECIPES

## A Natural Biosphere: A Prescription for Life on Earth

*Directions:*

To create the perfect biosphere (all parts of the earth that support plant, animal, and human life), mix these ingredients carefully: one part hydrosphere (the earth's water resource), one part lithosphere (the earth's rock and mineral resources), and one part atmosphere (the earth's air).

## Biosphere 2: Made with Artificial Ingredients

*Ingredients:*

| | |
|---|---|
| Arizona desert | Atmosphere |
| A large glass building | A sampling of biomes: an ocean, a savanna, a desert, a rain forest, and a marsh |
| Hydrosphere | |
| Lithosphere | |

*The atmosphere accounts for the largest section of the biosphere. Gases from the air are found as far away as 600 miles (965 km) from Earth.*

*Directions:*

Biosphere 2 is in a large glass building in the Arizona desert. It has everything that animals, plants, and human beings need to live. On September 26, 1991, Biosphere 2 was completely sealed for two years. The eight scientists who live there are called biospherians. During this time, no air, water, waste, or supplies are supposed to go in or out. Everything will be recycled, including water and air. Food will be grown and raised. The biospherians hope that this project will teach us more about life on Earth as well as the ingredients needed for life on other planets.

## Earth Emergency Stat

*Patient's Name:* Planet Earth

*Condition:* Dying

*Cause:* In the last 25 years, new technology, increasing population, and the wasting of natural resources have threatened the life-sustaining balance between humanity and nature. As a result, our planet is dying. But it can be cured if the prescribed treatment is followed.

*Stat comes from* statim, *which is Latin for "immediately."*

*Treatment:* Everyone needs to become responsible for the environment if the earth is to get better. These ten reminders, some of which you can do every day, are just a few things that will help.

1. Use all writing paper on both sides.

2. Use paper grocery bags for garbage instead of plastic bags.

3. Use paper grocery bags to make book covers rather than buying new ones.

4. Pack your lunch in reusable containers.

5. Use silverware and dishes instead of disposable plastic utensils and plates.

6. Use plastic containers to store food.

7. Return all deposit soda bottles and cans.

8. Separate glass, paper, and other recyclable materials and take them to a recycling center.

9. Carpool with friends.

10. Give your old toys and clothes to people who can use them rather than throwing them away.

## OUR EARTH OUT OF CONTROL

Accidents happen, but when they destroy the delicate balance of nature and cause the whole world to suffer, they become disasters, and we should do all we can to prevent them from happening again.

*Bhopal chemical leak, December 1984, Bhopal, India*

An explosion in the Union Carbide chemical plant in Bhopal, India, released a deadly gas called methyl isocyanate, which is used to make pesticides. The gas formed a cloud that killed 2,500 people; another 50,000–100,000 people became ill. Trees and plants in the area became yellow and brittle. The explosion was caused by a mechanical failure that was not noticed in time to stop it.

Exxon Valdez *oil spill, March 1989, Alaska, U.S.*

On March 24, 1989, 11 million gallons of crude oil spilled into Prince William Sound from the tanker *Exxon Valdez* when its hull hit a reef and tore open. The oil, which is not yet cleaned up after billions of dollars have been spent and the millions of birds, fish, and other wildlife have died, was caused by human error and could have been avoided.

*Chernobyl, April 1986, USSR*

At 1:23 A.M. on Saturday, April 26, 1986, the reactor blew at the nuclear power plant in Chernobyl, ripping open the core, blowing the roof off the building, starting more than 30 fires, and allowing radioactive material to leak into the air. Some 31 people were killed and 200 people were treated for radiation poisoning. Still at risk are 135,000 people from the 179 villages within 20 miles of the plant who were exposed to the radiation before being evacuated. Glaring violations of safety rules were at the bottom of this tragic event.

*Love Canal, 1953, New York, U.S.*
Love Canal, a small town in upstate New York near Niagara Falls, was destroyed by waste from chemical plants. Beginning in 1947, chemical companies could legally dump their waste products into the canal. The area developed a foul smell, trees lost their bark, and leaves fell throughout the year. A health survey found that the drinking water contained excessive levels of 82 industrial chemicals, 7 of which were thought to cause cancer. The people of Love Canal had an unusually high rate of cancer and birth defects. Eventually, many of the houses had to be abandoned. Today, the town has been partly cleaned up and some families have moved back to the area.

*Three Mile Island, 1979, Pennsylvania, U.S.*
On March 28, 1979, the worst accident in U.S. nuclear reactor history occurred at the Three Mile Island power station, near Harrisburg, Pennsylvania. No one was killed, and very little radioactivity was released into the air when coolant (the fluid that keeps a machine cool) escaped from the reactor core due to a combination of mechanical failure and human error. After 10 years and $1 billion in cleanup costs, the lower extremes of the reactor are still so radioactive that workers must use remote-control equipment to remove the remaining fragments of fuel core.

## NATURAL REMEDIES

Every year, Americans throw away 50 billion food and drink cans, 27 billion glass bottles and jars, and 65 million plastic and metal jar and can covers. Where does it all go? Some 85% of our garbage is sent to a dump, or landfill, where it can take from 100 to 400 years for cloth and aluminum to decompose. Glass has been found in perfect condition after 4,000 years in the earth!

We are quickly running out of space. It's time to learn the three R's of the environment: reduce, reuse, recycle. Then practice what you preach: don't buy things you don't really need, that come in wasteful packaging, or that cannot be recycled. Reuse whatever you can, and recycle as much as you can.

### Step I. Preparing Material at Home
1. Wash out cans, bottles, and jars.
2. Remove paper labels from cans.
3. Remove metal seals from bottlenecks.
4. Sort materials: brown or yellow glass, green glass, clear glass, aluminum cans, paper.

### Step II. Reclamation Center
This center pays cities for materials that can be recycled. They are sorted and sent off to recycling plants.

### Step III. Activity at Recycling Plants

*Paper*
1. Paper is sorted by type and sent to a paper mill.
2. Hydrapulper cooks the paper until it is a thick soup of fibers. Detergents and chemicals re-

move inks. The paper is now pulp, which looks like cottage cheese.

3. Impurities are removed by a moving screen, spinners, and a series of washers.
4. Pulp is bleached with chlorine to make it white and washed again.
5. Machine rolls out pulp and dries new paper.
6. Paper is cut to size, wrapped, and shipped.

*Glass*

1. Impactor crushes glass into chunks of cullet ¾ inch in diameter.
2. Cullet is dropped into weighing bin along with ingredients to make new glass.
3. Cullet is put into furnace, which melts it into a thick syrup at 2,800°F.
4. "Syrup" flows out of furnace into an automatic feeder, where it is cut into bottle-size portions.

5. Bottle-size portions flow down a chute into molds, where they are shaped and cooled.
6. A small hole is made in the center by a machine, and air is blown into the bottle to hollow it out. A neck is shaped for a cap or lid.

| Percentage of Old Glass Used to Make a New Glass Around the World | |
| --- | --- |
| THE NETHERLANDS | 57% |
| JAPAN | 55% |
| U.S. | 20% |
| BRITAIN | 17% |

7. Annealing oven, or leer, slowly heats, then cools, the glassware, which makes it strong.

*Aluminum Cans*

1. Cans are smashed and cut into dime-size shreds.
2. Shreds are placed in a gas-powered aluminum furnace, making liquid metal.

3. Liquid flows into molds that form ingots, or bars of metal.
4. Rollers squeeze the ingots into sheets for new cans.
5. Sheets are rolled into coils and sent to a plant, where they are shaped into cans again.

## A TWO-PART USER'S GUIDE TO THE LANGUAGE OF THE ENVIRONMENT

### Part I: User Friendly

*Biodegradable:* Able to decompose or be broken down by the earth's natural elements. These materials will rot and completely disappear into the earth.

*Compost:* Decayed organic refuse. Composting turns garbage into moist soil.

*Energy:* The power that makes things go. It can come from the sun, fossil fuels, or water.

*EPA:* The Environmental Protection Agency is a department of the U.S. government. Its job is to enforce all laws that affect the environment.

*Fossil fuel:* A source of energy such as oil, coal, and natural gas. There are limited amounts of fossil fuels, so we must not waste them.

*Garbologists:* Scientists who study, measure, and weigh the things people throw away. They want to discover better ways to deal with garbage.

| What Americans Throw Away | |
| --- | --- |
| Paper products and cardboard | 36% |
| Yard wastes | 20% |
| Food wastes | 9% |
| Metals | 9% |
| Glass | 8% |
| Plastics | 7% |
| Rubber and leather goods | 3% |
| Other | 8% |

*Greenhouse effect:* Though many people think the greenhouse effect is entirely bad, without this warming of the atmosphere, the earth would be too cold. It is only when the atmosphere's natural balance is disrupted that the greenhouse effect makes the environment too hot.

*Natural resources:* Valuable materials made by nature such as water, land, minerals, and plants. All are necessary for life.

*Ozone layer:* A paper-thin sheet of ozone, an invisible gas, that surrounds the earth 15 miles above its surface. A form of oxygen, ozone protects us from the sun's harmful rays.

*Photodegradable:* A type of plastic that is broken down by the sun's ultraviolet rays.

*Recycle:* To put through a process or use again in another way.

*Renewable energy:* Energy that keeps on reproducing and never runs out, such as solar energy.

*The six main resources that provide energy in the U.S. are oil, gas, coal, nuclear power, hydropower (water), and wood.*

## Part II: User Unfriendly

*Acid rain:* Rain contaminated with pollutants such as sulfur dioxide and nitrogen oxide. These gases come from fuels being burned at high temperatures and from car exhausts. When acid rain falls, it pollutes the environment, damaging trees, plants, fish, and other wildlife.

*Chlorofluorocarbons (CFCs):* Man-made gases that contain chlorine, fluorine, and carbon. They

---

### The pH Scale

The pH scale shows how acidic or alkaline a substance is.

- Vinegar, battery acid, and wine are acids. They have a low pH.
- Substances like milk and bleach are alkalis, the opposite of acids. They have a high pH.
- Pure rain has a pH of about 5.6. Acid rain has been recorded with a pH as low as 2.4. This may not sound bad, but every decrease of 1 pH reflects 10 times more acidity.

143

are found in refrigerator coolants and air conditioners as well as aerosol cans. They destroy the ozone layer, which protects life on earth.

*Deforestation:* Cutting down trees and not replacing them. It hurts the air quality because it reduces the number of trees that produce oxygen for us to breathe. Trees also help delay the greenhouse effect because they use carbon dioxide, which helps maintain air quality. In addition, trees protect the soil and hold it in place.

*Disposable:* An item that is made to be used once and then thrown away. Disposable items create unnecessary garbage.

*Endangered animals:* Animals that may become extinct. Any animal overhunted by people or whose food needs are not met will not survive. Each day three species on earth become extinct, a rate 400 times greater than that 1,000 years ago. Though there are laws to protect endangered animals, it is often too late to save more than a few of the species.

*Hazardous waste:* Anything potentially dangerous that is thrown away, such as paint, oven cleaner, furniture polish, and pesticides.

*Oil spills:* Oil spills occur from tankers (accidents caused by human error), pipelines (bombed by terrorists), and storage tanks (struck by lightning). There is an oil spill almost every week.

*Pollution:* The contamination of air or water by harmful substances.

*Soil erosion:* The wearing away of the soil by water, wind, waves, and glaciers. Water is respon-

*Major hazardous wastes include medicinal wastes, sewage, and pollution from factories.*

sible for two-thirds of the erosion of farmland, usually from rain, oceans, or rivers. Planting the same crop year after year is another major cause of soil erosion. Deforestation adds to this process as well. If erosion continues at the present rate, 7% of the earth's soil will be used up each decade.

*Toxic:* Anything with poisonous ingredients.

*Water pollution:* The contamination of water caused by the dumping of liquid waste and sewage into our streams, rivers, and oceans.

## EARTH CARE ORGANIZATIONS
There are many things you can do to help save the environment. You can begin by reading the books and pamphlets in your school or public library. Then write to the organizations listed below, asking for more information on what you can do.

*Better World Society,* P.O. Box 96051, Washington, D.C. 20077. Funds TV programs about environmental issues and human rights.

*The Children's Rainforest,* P.O. Box 936, Lewiston, Me. 04240. Gives tips on how children can raise money to purchase and protect an acre of rain forest.

**Rainforest Alliance**

*The Cousteau Society,* 870 Greenbriar Circle, Suite 402, Chesapeake, Va. 23320. Educates the public about natural ecosystems.

**The Cousteau Society**

*Environmental Defense Fund,* 257 Park Ave. South, New York, N.Y. 10010. Tells people how they can reduce the use of CFCs.

*Greenpeace, USA,* 1436 U St. NW, Washington, D.C. 20009. Works to preserve the earth and the life it supports. It has almost 2 million supporters.

*National Audubon Society,* 950 Third Ave., New York, N.Y. 10022. Tells people how to use wildlife, land, water, and other natural resources intelligently.

*National Wildlife Federation,* 1400 Sixteenth St. NW, Washington, D.C. 20036. Educates people about the intelligent use of natural resources.

*Project P.E.O.P.L.E.,* P.O. Box 932, Prospect Heights, Ill. 60070

*Rainforest Alliance,* 270 Lafayette St., Suite 512, New York, N.Y. 10012. Works to save tropical rain forests worldwide.

*The Sierra Club,* 730 Polk St., San Francisco, Calif. 94109. Works to preserve national parks and wilderness areas.

*Trees for Life,* 1103 Jefferson, Wichita, Kans. 67203. Helps people in Third World countries to plant and care for food-bearing trees.

# Speaking of Language

## *Talk, Talk, Talk*

DID YOU KNOW THAT THE AVER-age person who speaks English has a vocabulary of  some 3,000 words? William Shakespeare, the great English writer, had an active vocabulary of 24,000 words! The average American 10-year-old probably understands some 7,000 words and uses 700 different words an hour.

## WHO TALKS WHAT?

- There are more than 2,700 languages in the world. In addition, there are more than 7,000 dialects. A dialect is a regional variety of a language that has a different pronunciation, vocabulary, or meaning.

- The most difficult language to learn is Basque, which is spoken in northwestern Spain and southwestern France. It is not related to any other language in the world. It has a extremely complicated word structure and vocabulary.

- All pilots on international flights identify themselves in English.

- Somalia is the only African country in which the entire population speaks the same language, Somali.

- The language in which a government conducts business is the official language of that country.

- More than 1,000 different languages are spoken on the continent of Africa.

*The most widely spoken language in the world is Mandarin Chinese, the language of 885 million people. Hindustani is second, with 461 million, English is third, with 450 million, and Spanish, fourth, with 352 million.*

- The Berbers of North Africa have no written form of their language.

- Many languages in Africa include a "click" sound that is pronounced at the same time as other sounds. You must learn these languages in childhood to do it properly.

## SPEAKING ENGLISH DOWN UNDER

English is so widely spoken, it is unofficially known as the international language. But when Americans go "down under" to Australia or Australians come to the U.S., it's hard to believe we speak the same language! Next time you pack for Australia, take this list along and give it a burl.

| AMERICAN ENGLISH | "DOWN UNDER" ENGLISH |
|---|---|
| AFTERNOON | ARRO (INFORMAL) |
| BILL (RESTAURANT/STORE) | DOCKET |
| BOAST | SHITE |
| CAR ACCIDENT | PRANG CAR |
| HOOD | BONNET |
| COOKIE | BISCUIT |
| ELECTRIC TEAKETTLE | JUG |
| ELEVATOR | LIFT |
| FLASHLIGHT | TORCH |
| FRENCH FRIES | CHIPS |
| FUNNY PERSON | HARDCASE |
| "I'M STUFFED" | "I'M PREGNANT" |
| "IT WILL BE OK" | "SHE'LL BE RIGHT" |
| GO TO THE BATHROOM | SPEND A PENNY |
| TOILET | CLOAKROOM |
| TRUE | FAIR |
| TRY SOMETHING | GIVE IT A BURL |
| UMBRELLA | BROLLY |
| "YOUR TURN TO PAY" | "YOUR SHAIT" |

*English has more words than any other language, about 1 million.*

## THE LANGUAGE OF WHATCHAMACALLITS

Are you often stumped by the name of a little thing? Do you call common objects whatchamacallits? Help is on the way! There *are* names for those little things in life.

*Belt:* tongue, punch holes, keeper

*Broom:* neck (where stick is attached to broom)

*Clothespin:* grinning hole, claw end

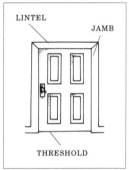

*Comb:* spine, teeth

*Door:* lintel, jamb, threshold

*Eyeglasses:* eye wires (surround glass), budge (bridges the nose), temples (hook over the ears)

*Hair dryer:* barrel, air vents

*Hat:* brim, crown

*Hot dog roll:* hinge

*Hot dog string:* linker twine

*Nail:* shank, head

*Padlock:* shackle (movable arched bar)

*Pail:* ears (where handle attaches to pail)

*Paper clips:* legs (straight), bends (rounded)

*Safety pin:* shaft

*Scissors:* blades, pivot, bow handle (large), ring handle (small)

*Shoe:* aglet (tip of shoelace), welt (between upper and sole), counter (back panel)

*Sock:* toe, gore (back)

*Stairs:* tread, riser, railing, banister, newel post

*Staple:* crown, legs

*Toothbrush:* block handle, block head (where bristles are inserted)

*Window:* lintel, sill, panes, sash

*Zipper:* pull tab, slide, teeth

## SAY WHAT YOU MEAN

### Everyday Expressions

If you say, "The cat's out of the bag" instead of "The secret is given away," you're using an idiom. The meaning of an idiom is different from the actual meaning of the words used. "An apple a day keeps the doctor away" is a proverb. Proverbs are old but familiar sayings that usually give advice. Both idioms and proverbs are part of our daily speech. Many are very old and have interesting histories. See how many of these sayings you know.

*"An apple a day keeps the doctor away."*
This proverb comes from the ancient Romans, who believed the apple had magical powers to cure illness. In fact, apples are filled with vitamin C, protein, pectin, natural sugars, copper, and iron. They *do* promote health.

*To "climb on the bandwagon."*
Long ago, bands on the platforms of traveling wagons played music to announce a parade or political speech. To show their support, people would often jump onto the platform and join the band. Today, this idiom usually refers to someone who hopes to benefit from supporting another person's idea.

*"Saved by the bell."*
In 17th-century England, a guard at Windsor Castle was accused of falling asleep at his post. He claimed he was wrongly accused and could prove it; he had heard the church bell chime thirteen times at midnight. Townspeople supported

*Bakers once gave an extra roll for every dozen sold, so a baker's dozen is thirteen.*

his claim and he was not executed. Today we think of the bell that ends a round in boxing, often saving the boxer from injury, or the bell at the end of a class period, saving you from more work. Regardless, this idiom means rescue from a situation at the last possible moment.

*"Bury the hatchet."*

Native Americans used to bury weapons to show that fighting had ended and enemies were now at peace. Today, the idiom means to make up with a friend after an argument or fight.

To *"have a chip on one's shoulder."*
In 19th-century America, a boy who thought he was pretty tough would put a wood chip on his shoulder and dare anyone to knock it off. Today the idiom refers to anyone who is "touchy" or takes offense easily.

*"A close shave."*
In the past, student barbers learned to shave on customers. If they shaved too close, their clients might be cut or even barely escape serious injury. Today, we use this idiom if a person narrowly escapes disaster.

*"Dot the i's and cross the t's."*
When only handwritten documents were used, it was very important for the clerk to write everything properly, especially letters like *i* and *t*, which could easily be confused. The phrase has since come to mean paying attention to every little detail.

*"He who pays the piper calls the tune."*
In medieval times, people were entertained by strolling musicians. Whoever paid the price could choose the music. This proverb means that whoever pays is in charge.

*"The pen is mightier than the sword."*
In 17th-century England, a free press was banned by the government. This meant that people who disagreed with the government and printed their views were punished. In spite of this, people published their ideas and opinions in illegal pamphlets that were distributed to the public. The proverb means that the written expression of ideas cannot be stopped by physical force.

*"The pot calling the kettle black."*
In the 17th century, both pots and kettles turned black because they were used over open fires. Today, this idiom means criticizing someone else for a fault of one's own.

*"Raining cats and dogs."*
In Norse mythology, the dog is associated with wind and the cat with storms. This expression means it's raining very heavily.

To *"shed crocodile tears."*
Crocodiles have a reflex that causes their eyes to tear when they open their mouths. This makes it look as though they are crying while devouring their prey. In fact, neither crocodiles nor people who shed "crocodile" tears feel sorry for their actions.

## THE RIGHT WORD

When you're sick, do you have a temperature or a fever? Do you put jam or jelly on your toast? It isn't always easy to know which word to use. Although the words in these questions are often used for each other, they mean different things. A temperature is the degree of heat or cold measured by a thermometer. A fever in a person is a body temperature above 98.6°F. Jelly is a combination of fruit juice and sugar; jam is boiled fruit pulp and sugar. Many words in our language are similar but not the same. Think before you use any of the words below.

### Amusement Park/Theme Park

An *amusement park* is a place where people go to have fun. It has games, food, rides, and shows for entertainment.

A *theme park* is an amusement park with a theme, a subject that everything in the park has in common. The rides, games, food, and shows all deal with this subject in some way. At Disney World, a famous theme park, everything has some connection to the Disney characters.

## Cologne/Perfume

*Cologne* is a scented liquid made from alcohol and fragrant oils.

*Perfume* is a quickly evaporating scented oil either obtained from flowers or manmade. It is more concentrated (stronger) and much more expensive than cologne.

## Dinner/Supper

*Dinner* is always the main meal of the day, whether it is eaten at noon or in the evening.

*Supper* is eaten only in the evening, whether it is a large or small meal.

## Dough/Batter

*Dough* is a thick mixture of flour, liquid, and other ingredients that is usually rolled or shaped into bread and other baked goods.

*Batter,* made of flour and liquid, is a thinner mixture than dough. Batter can be poured into pans to make pancakes, biscuits, and cakes.

## Earth/Universe

*Earth,* the planet on which we live, is the third planet from the sun in our solar system.

The *universe* includes everything that exists, including all the planets, the stars, and space.

## Envy/Jealousy

*Envy* is the desire to have something that another person has and the feelings of resentment or unhappiness at the person's having it. For example, you may feel envy when someone you know gets something you've always wanted.

*Jealousy* is like envy but includes suspicion. Jealousy is often associated with competition, especially in love. Sometimes you may be jealous of a brother or sister because you think your parents love him or her more than they love you.

### Information/Knowledge

*Information* is a fact or knowledge about a specific event or subject.

*Knowledge* is having information and understanding it through experience.

### Melody/Tune

A *melody* is a group of notes in a certain order that results in a sweet or agreeable sound.

A *tune* is an easily remembered melody.

### Part/Portion

A piece of something that has been divided is a *part.* When all the pieces are put together, they equal a whole.

A *portion* is a share or part used or given in a specific way.

### Passport/Visa

A *passport* is a document, usually a booklet, that states a person's official identity and citizenship and allows that person to visit another country.

A *visa* is stamped on a passport. It shows that the passport has been examined by the officials of a country and permits entry into that country.

### Soap/Detergent

*Soap* is a cleansing agent that comes from natural fats and oils.

*Detergent* is a cleansing agent that is usually made from synthetic, or manmade, products.

### THE SECRET OF "ONYM"

How many words can you think of that end in *-onym*? *Antonym* and *synonym* are two. Antonyms are words with opposite meanings. Synonyms are words that mean the same thing. The ending, or suffix, comes from the Greek word *onyma,* which means "name." Words that end in *-onym* are names for a type of word. Now that you know the secret, here are some more.

*Acronym*
A word or name formed by combining the first letters or groups of letters from a phrase. For example, SCUBA comes from *s*elf-*c*ontained *u*nderwater *b*reathing *a*pparatus.

*Aptronym*
A name that's especially suited to the profession of its owner. For example, Sally Ride, the astronaut.

*Capitonym*
A word that takes on a new meaning when capitalized. For example, polish (*pol*-ish), Polish (*Po*-lish).

*Charactonym*
The name of a literary character that especially suits his or her personality. For example, Charles Dickens's Scrooge is a miser.

*Eponym*
A real or mythical person from whose name a place, a thing, or an event is taken. The earl of Sandwich, for example, the first person to ask for meat between two slices of bread, is the eponym of the modern sandwich.

*Heteronym*

Two or more words with identical spelling but different meaning and pronunciation. There are so many bows. How about bow and arrow? Bow of a boat?

*Homonym*

Words that sound alike (and are sometimes spelled alike) but name different things. For example, die (to stop living) and dye (color).

*Pseudonym*
From the Greek *pseud* (false) and *onym* (name), a false name or pen name, used by an author. Mark

Twain is a pseudonym for Samuel Langhorne Clemens.

*Toponym*
A place name or word that began as the name of a place, such as hamburger (from Hamburg, Germany) and afghan (a soft blanket from Afghanistan).

## GREETINGS AROUND THE WORLD

Some people shake hands, some kiss and hug. Others just say hello. These exchanges are common in the U.S., but how do people in other countries greet each other? In most of Europe, a handshake will do. Here are a few of the ways to say hello in Asia.

*In Malaysia people* greet *each other by saying "Where are you going?" Because it is not really a question, the polite response is "Just for a walk."*

| COUNTRY | GESTURE |
|---|---|
| China | a nod or bow |
| Hong Kong (older Chinese) | clasp hands together at throat level and nod |
| India | palms together as though praying and bend or nod, called *namaste* |
| Indonesia | say *selamat,* which means peace |
| Japan | bow from the waist, palms on thighs, heels together |
| Korea | a slight bow and handshake (right hand in one or both hands) |
| Malaysia | both hands touch other person's hands, then are brought back to the breast, called *salame* gesture |
| Philippines | a limp handshake |
| Sri Lanka | place palms together under chin and bow slightly |
| Thailand | place palms together, elbows down, and bow head slightly, called *wai* |

## WHEN THE BODY SPEAKS

Did you know that in some parts of the world putting your hands on your hips is impolite? the thumbs-up sign is downright offensive? a wink is unacceptable?

- In Australia, it is rude to wink at women.

- In Brazil, pulling down the lower lid of the right eye means that the listener doubts what you are saying.

- In China, point with an open hand and beckon or signal with the hand facing palm down. To use a finger to point or beckon is rude.

- In Hong Kong, only animals are beckoned with a finger. To signal someone to come to you, reach out, palm down and flutter your fingers.

- In India, grasping your ear means either "honestly" or "I'm sorry."

- In Indonesia, hands on hips while talking means that you're angry and is impolite. Beckon with your palm down and your fingers moving in a swooping motion.

*Thumbing your nose (raising your thumb to your nose and fanning your fingers) is a sign of mockery throughout most of the world.*

- In Japan, it is unacceptable for two adults of the same sex to hold hands while walking together. A smile can mean happiness, anger, embarrassment, or sadness. It is an insult to point at someone with four fingers spread and thumb tucked in. When someone compliments you, respond by waving your hand back and forth in front of your face. Because it is considered impolite to show their teeth, women cover their mouths when they laugh. To make a promise, two people hook their pinky fingers together.

- In Korea, it is rude to blow your nose in front of people. When talking to someone, keep your hands in full view. It is rude to keep your hands behind your back or in your pockets.

- In Pakistan, it is *not* rude to stare at other people. It is impolite to show the soles of your feet or point a foot while sitting on the floor.

- In Spain, snapping the thumb and first finger together a few times is a form of applause. If you think the person you are talking about is stingy, tap your left elbow with your right hand. If you've heard the story before, put your right hand behind your head and pull your left ear.

- In Sri Lanka, moving your head from side to side means *yes* and nodding your head up and down means *no*!

- In Taiwan, say no by extending your palm forward and waving your hand from side to side. It is impolite to use your feet for touching objects or people. Keep your feet off that chair!

- In Thailand, people point to an object with their chins, not their hands.

## SECRET LANGUAGES / MYSTERY MESSAGES

*Moparopyop hopadop a lopitoptoplope lopamopbop.* That means "Mary had a little lamb" in the secret language of Opish. Have you ever thought of using a language all your own? How about Double-Dutch, Na, or Skimono Jive? If you speak a secret language, no one will understand a word you say (until you tell them how it's done). Sound like fun? Try it! We've used "Mary had a little lamb" for each example.

## Double-Dutch
Vowels are pronounced normally, but consonants become syllables.

| | | | | | |
|---|---|---|---|---|---|
| b - bub | k - kuk | s - sus |
| c - cash | l - lul | t - tut |
| d - dud | m - mum | v - vuv |
| f - fuf | n - nun | w - wash |
| g - gug | p - pub | x - xux |
| h - hutch | q - quack | y - yub |
| j - jug | r - rug | z - zub |

Example: *M*uma*r*ug*y*ub *h*utcha*d*ud a *l*uli*t*ut*t*ut*l*ule *l*ula*m*um*b*ub.

## Eggy-Peggy
This secret language is used mostly in England. Add "egg" before each vowel.
Example: Meggary heggad egga leggittle leggamb.

## Gree
Add "gree" to the end of every word.
Example: Marygree hadgree agree littlegree lambgree.

## Na
Add "na" to the end of every word.
Example: Maryna hadna ana littlena lambna.

## Pig Latin
This is the most popular and well-known secret language. Move the first letter to the end of the word and add "ay" to it.
Example: Arymay adhay aay ittlelay amblay.

## Skimono Jive
Add "sk" to the beginning of every word.
Example: Skmary skhad ska sklittle sklamb.

## WISHING WELL

The ancient Greeks threw coins in their wells, hoping to keep the wells from running dry. Today, people throw coins in fountains to make wishes come true. But don't throw all your coins into one fountain; there is more than one way to make a wish.

- "Touch blue and your wish will come true."

- Make a wish each time you eat a green M&M.

- Make a wish when you see three birds on a telephone wire.

- Put a watermelon seed on your forehead and make a wish before it falls off.

- Make a wish before you blow out the candles on your birthday cake.

- Make a wish on the first star you see at night.

- Throw a coin in a fountain; make a wish when the water clears so you can see your reflection.

- Make a wish on a new pair of shoes before you wear them for the first time.

- Make a wish with another person on a wishbone. Each takes an end and pulls until it breaks. The person with the largest piece of bone gets the "lucky break" and the wish.

- Make a wish on the first robin you see in the spring.

- Find a penny, wear it in your left shoe, and your wish will come true.

- Wishes made on Midsummer's Eve (June 23) are most likely to come true.

- Hold your breath and make a wish while crossing a short straight bridge.

## SLANGUAGE

If someone offered you a cannonball, would you accept it? If someone called you cosomo, how would you react? If you were asked for a bee, would you dig it? It all depends on the company you keep. Words mean different things to different groups of people. In the world of sports, the hall of fame is where everyone wants to be, but in the criminal world it's just the reverse—the police mug book. Here's more:

### Service Slang

ARMY BRAT: A small child of army personnel

BIG BOOT: The general

BRAIN FOOD: Noodle soup

CANNONBALL: Grapefruit

COME ON THE GREEN: A challenge to fight

DOODLEBUG: Tank

GI LEMONADE: Water

JACK: Money

Q COMPANY: A recruit

SPUD CALL: Call for kitchen work

### Surfer Speak

BARNEY: A thoughtless jerk

BIG-WAVE MEN: Expert surfers

CRANK: To have a good surf

DROP IN ON: To steal a wave after someone is on it

EPIC: Awesome

GET OUT: Relax

GNARLY: Messy

GUN: A special surfboard used mainly by pros

LINEUP: Where one goes to wait for waves

SET: A group of waves

# Pickpocket Prose

BANG: To steal

BEE: One-dollar bill

BEEFER: A victim who reports a theft to the police

BUTTON: A detective's badge

CUSH: Money

FAT ONE: A wallet containing a lot of money

GLOMMED: Arrested

JUG: A bank

TAIL: To follow

## Police ... in other words

*Cops, coppers, fuzz, the man, the heat, men in blue*

## Jail ... in other words

*Clink, behind bars, slammer, joint, pen, cooler, can, stir, jug, pokey, hoosegow, calaboose, drunk tank, cell block, cross bar hotel*

# Talk of the '60s and '70s

AT: The place to be, where things are happening

DIG IT: To understand

DO A NUMBER: Try to influence

FLOWER POWER: The belief in the power of natural beauty and that the world can be changed through peace and love

GET DOWN: To have a good time

HAIRY: Scary

HANG ME UP: To keep someone waiting

PAD: Home

SCENE: Where the action is

TRASH: Destroy

# '90s Teen Talk

AIRHEAD: Dumb

AWESOME: Fabulous

BARF: Throw up

BARNEY: A misfit

CHILL OUT: Calm down

COSOMO: Popular

FOSSIL: An old person

| | |
|---|---|
| HEMORRHOID: | An annoying person |
| LIKE: | To say |
| POSSE: | A pack of good friends |
| ROLL: | A fat person |
| SPAZZ ATTACK: | To get overly excited |
| TOTALLY: | Completely |

## COLORFUL LANGUAGE

We live in a colorful world. In many countries, colors represent various holidays; they are also used to express feelings and enliven language. Find your favorite color and see what it means around the world.

### Red

For the ancient Romans, a *red* flag was a signal for battle.

The ancient Egyptians considered themselves a *red* race and painted their bodies with *red* dye for emphasis.

In Russia, *red* means beautiful. The Bolsheviks used a *red* flag as their symbol when they overthrew the tsar in 1917. That is how *red* became the color of communism.

In India, *red* is the symbol for a soldier.

In South Africa, *red* is the color of mourning.

It's considered good luck to tie a *red* bow on a new car.

In China, *red* is the color of good luck and is used as a holiday and wedding color. Chinese babies are given their names at a *red*-egg ceremony.

Superstitious people think *red* frightens the devil.

A "*red*-letter day" is one of special importance and good fortune.

In Greece, eggs are dyed *red* for good luck at Easter time.

To "paint the town *red*" is to celebrate.

*Red* is the color most commonly found in national flags.

In the English War of the Roses, *red* was the color of the House of Lancaster, which defeated the House of York, symbolized by the color white.

The "*Red*shirts" were the soldiers of the Italian leader Garibaldi, who unified modern Italy in the 19th century.

To "see *red*" is to be angry.

A "*red* herring" is a distraction, something that takes attention away from the real issue.

A "*red* eye" is an overnight airplane flight.

If a business is "in the *red*," it is losing money.

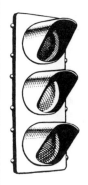

*Because of its visibility, stop signs, stoplights, brake lights, and fire equipment are all painted* red.

### Green

Only one national flag is a solid color: the *green* flag of Libya.

Ancient Egyptians colored the floors of their temples *green*.

In ancient Greece, *green* symbolized victory.

For Muslims, *green* is a sacred color. Muslim prayer rugs are designed with a *green* background.

In the highlands of Scotland, people wore *green* as a mark of honor.

*Green* is the national color of Ireland.

*Green* means "go." When "all systems are *green*," it means everything is in order.

The *green*room of a concert hall or theater is where performers relax before going onstage.

The "*green*-eyed monster" is jealousy.

A *green*horn is a newcomer or unsophisticated person.

*Green* is youthful.

Being "*green* around the gills" is looking pale and sickly.

"*Green* with envy" means full of envy or jealousy.

A person with a "*green* thumb" is good at making plants grow.

A *green,* or common, is a town park.

*Green* is a healing color, the color of nature.

## Blue

In ancient Rome, public servants wore *blue*. Today, police and other public servants wear *blue*.

In China, *blue* is for little girls.

In Iran, *blue* is the color of mourning.

*Blue* was used as protection against witches, who supposedly dislike the color.

If you are "true *blue*," you are loyal and faithful.

*Blue* stands for love, which is why a bride carries or wears something *blue* on her wedding day.

A room painted *blue* is said to be relaxing.

"Feeling *blue*" is feeling sad. "*Blue* devils" are feelings of depression.

Something "out of the *blue*" is from an unknown source at an unexpected time.

A *blue*book is a list of socially prominent people.

A *blue* blood is a person of noble descent. This is probably from the *blue* veins of the fair-complexioned aristocrats who first used this term.

"Into the *blue*" means into the unknown.

A "*blue*nose" is a strict, puritanical person.

A "*blue*stocking" used to be a scholarly or highly knowledgeable woman.

The pharaohs of ancient Egypt wore *blue* for protection against evil.

*The first prize gets a blue ribbon.*

The *"blues"* is a style of American jazz.

*"Blue* laws" are used to enforce moral standards.

A *blue* ribbon panel is a group of especially qualified people.

*Purple is a royal color.*

## Purple, Violet

The Egyptian queen Cleopatra loved *purple*. To obtain one ounce of Tyrian *purple* dye, she had her servants soak 20,000 *Purpura* snails for 10 days.

In Thailand, *purple* is worn by a widow mourning her husband's death.

A *"purple* heart" is a U.S. military decoration for soldiers wounded or killed in battle.

*Purple* robes are an emblem of authority and rank.

*"Purple* speech" is profane talk.

*"Purple* prose" is writing that is full of exaggerated literary effects and ornamentation.

Leonardo da Vinci believed that the power of meditation increases ten times when done in a *purple* light, as in the *purple* light of stained glass.

*Purple* in a child's room is said to help develop the imagination according to color theory.

Richard Wagner composed his operas in a room with shades of *violet*, his color of inspiration.

## Yellow

In Egypt and Burma, *yellow* signifies mourning.

In Spain, executioners once wore *yellow*.

In India, *yellow* is the symbol for a merchant or farmer.

In 10th-century France, the doors of traitors and criminals were painted *yellow*.

Hindus in India wear *yellow* to celebrate the festival of spring.

If someone is said to have a *"yellow* streak," that person is considered a coward.

A *yellow* ribbon is a sign of support for soldiers at the front.

*Yellow* is a symbol of jealousy and deceit.

In the Middle Ages, actors portraying the dead in a play wore *yellow*.

To holistic healers, *yellow* is the color of peace.

*Yellow* has good visibility and is often used as a color of warning. It is also a symbol for quarantine, an area marked off because of danger.

*"Yellow* journalism" refers to irresponsible and alarmist reporting.

*In Japan during the War of Dynasty in 1357, each warrior wore a* yellow *chrysanthemum as a pledge of courage.*

## White

A *white* flag is the universal symbol for truce.

*White* means mourning in China and Japan.

Angels are usually depicted wearing *white* robes.

The ancient Greeks wore *white* to bed to ensure pleasant dreams.

The Egyptian pharaohs wore *white* crowns.

The ancient Persians believed all gods wore *white*.

A *"white* elephant" is a rare, pale elephant considered sacred to the people of India, Thailand, Burma, and Sri Lanka; in this country, it is either a possession that costs more than it is worth to keep or an item that the owner doesn't want but can't get rid of.

*A "white knight" is a rescuer.*

It's considered good luck to be married in a *white* garment.

*White* heat is a state of intense enthusiasm, anger, devotion, or passion.

To *white*wash is to gloss over defects or make something seem presentable that isn't.

A *white* list contains favored items (as opposed to a blacklist).

A *"white*out" occurs when there is zero visibility during a blizzard.

A *"white* sale" is a sale of sheets, towels, and other bed and bath items.

A *"white*d sepulcher" is a person who is evil inside but appears good on the outside, a hypocrite.

*"White* lightning" is slang for moonshine, a home-brewed alcohol.

A *white* room is a clean room as well as a temperature-controlled, dust-free room for precision instruments.

*White* water is the foamy, frothy water in rapids and waterfalls.

## Black

The ancient Egyptians and Romans used *black* for mourning, as do most Europeans and Americans today.

The *"Black*shirts" were the security troops in Hitler's German army, also known as the S.S.

*Black* often stands for secrecy.

*Black* humor is morbid or unhealthy and gloomy humor.

In China, *black* is for little boys.

A *"black*hearted" person is evil.

If a business is "in the *black*," it is making money.

A *"black*list" is a list of persons or organizations to be boycotted or punished.

*Black* is associated with sophistication and elegance. A *"black* tie" event is formal.

A *black* belt in karate identifies an expert.

A *black* flag in a car race is the signal for a driver to go to the pits.

A *black*guard is a scoundrel.

*Black* lung is a coal miner's disease caused by the frequent inhaling of coal dust.

*Black*mail is getting things by threat.

*Black* market is illegal trade in goods or money.

A *black* sheep is an outcast.

*"Black*wash" (as opposed to "whitewash") is to uncover or bring out in the light.

A *black*out is a period of darkness from the loss of electricity, for protection against nighttime air raids, or, in the theater, to separate scenes in a play.

When you *"black* out," you temporarily lose consciousness.

*The ancient Egyptians believed that* black *cats had divine powers.*

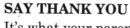

## SAY THANK YOU
It's what your parents always remind you to say. Now you can dazzle your friends and relatives by saying it in thirteen different languages.

| LANGUAGE | THANK YOU | PRONUNCIATION |
|---|---|---|
| Australian English | ta (informal) | |
| Chinese, Cantonese | xie xie | syeh-syeh |
| Chinese, Mandarin | do jeh | daw-dyeh |
| French | merci | mare-*see* |
| German | danke | *dahn*-kah |
| Hindi, Hindustani | sukria | shoo-kree-a |
| Indonesian | termi kasih | t'ree-ma kas-seh |
| Italian | grazie | *gra*-see |
| Japanese | arigato | ahree-gah-tow |
| Korean | kamsa hamnida | kahm-sah=ham-nee-da |
| Spanish | gracias | *gra*-see-us |
| Sri Lanka (Sinhak) | istutiy | isst-too-tee |
| Thai | kawp-kun krap/ka' | kowpkoom-krahp/khak |

## LATIN PER SE
What's the language of scholars, doctors, lawyers, scientists, and priests? It's Latin, and it's not a dead language, as you can see. Here are some fun phrases and words in Latin. Learn them cum laude (koom *lou*-da).

*Per se:*
*In or of itself.*

*Cum laude:*
*With distinc-*
*tion.*

| ENGLISH | LATIN | PRONUNCIATION |
|---|---|---|
| Silly me | me ineptum | may in-*ep*-toom |
| Really | vero | we rr oh |
| No way | nolo modo | noh-loh moh-doh |
| What's happening? | quid fit? | kwid feet |
| Bubble gum | manducabulla | mahn-doo-kah-boo-lah |
| Really rad dude | radicus comes | rah di coos koh mees |
| Read my lips | labra lege | lah-brah lay-gay |
| I'm out of here | a beo | ah *bay*-oh |

# Laws and Rights

HAVE YOU EVER HEARD SOME- one say "an eye for an eye, a tooth  for a tooth"? This phrase expresses a belief held thou- sands of years ago that people should be punished appropriately for their crimes. The punishment for the crime of murder was death; for theft, hands were cut off.

## ORDER IN THE COURT

Courts of law are the umpires of the American legal system. Two types of cases are taken to court, civil and criminal. Civil cases usually deal with disagreements about people's rights and duties to-

## Setting the Scene

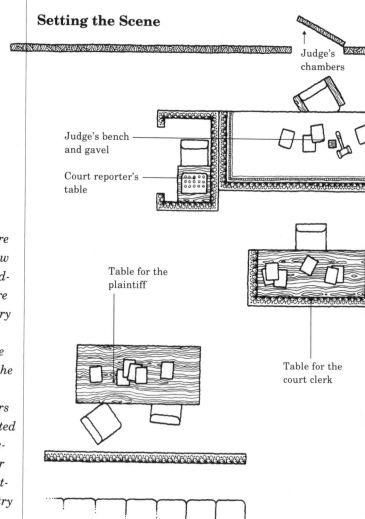

Judge's chambers

Judge's bench and gavel

Court reporter's table

Table for the plaintiff

Table for the court clerk

*Bar examinations are given to law school graduates before they may try a case in court. Once they pass the exam, the new lawyers are permitted to stand before the bar in the courtroom and try a case.*

ward one another. Criminal cases are brought by the government (either state or federal) against people accused of committing crimes. All courts have the same set and cast of characters. Take your seat for the courtroom drama.

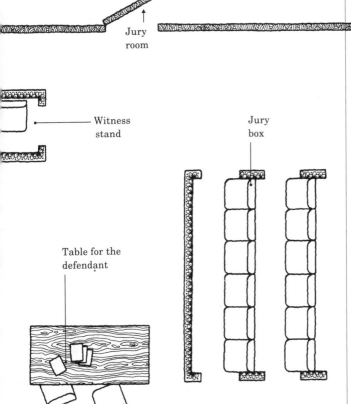

Jury room

Witness stand

Jury box

Table for the defendant

*Judge's chambers:* A small room off the courtroom where the judge changes into robes and confers with lawyers

*Jury room:* A room outside the courtroom where the jury deliberates

*Bar:* Separates spectators from the court

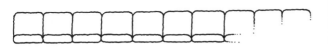

# Cast of Characters

*Court reporter:*
A person who types every word said during the trial. The typewritten document is a permanent record of the trial.

*Judge:* The legal officer who presides over the courtroom and directs and controls the trial.

*A verdict of guilty or not guilty is handed down by the jury.*

*Bailiff:*
The police officer who maintains order in the court.

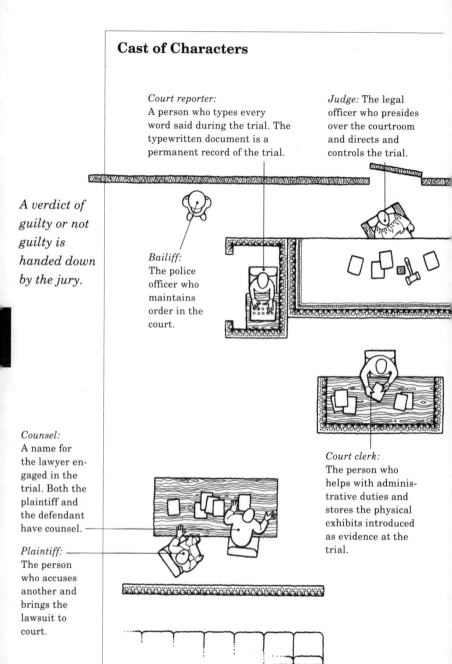

*Court clerk:*
The person who helps with administrative duties and stores the physical exhibits introduced as evidence at the trial.

*Counsel:*
A name for the lawyer engaged in the trial. Both the plaintiff and the defendant have counsel.

*Plaintiff:*
The person who accuses another and brings the lawsuit to court.

## Words from the Script

*Motion:* How the lawyer asks the judge to make a decision.

*Objection:* The opposing side finds fault with the question being asked the witness.

*Sustained:* The judge, following an objection, agrees that the line of questioning should not continue.

*Overruled:* The judge, following an objection, decides the questions may continue.

*Denied:* Not allowed.

*Your Honor:* The way a judge is addressed in a courtroom.

*Mistrial:* A trial that becomes invalid, is essentially canceled, because of a mistake in procedure.

*Appeal:* A request for a higher court to review a decision made by a lower court.

*Cross-examination:* The questioning of a witness by the lawyer for the opposing side.

*Jury:*
The number of jurors varies from state to state. In most states, six or twelve jurors decide a case.

*Foreman:* The foreman of the jury speaks for the entire jury.

*Witness:*
A person who gives the jury information about the case.

*Defense Attorney, Public Defender:*
The lawyer who defends the accused person. A public defender is appointed if the accused is unable to pay for an attorney.

*Defendant:*
The person who is accused of a crime and is being tried.

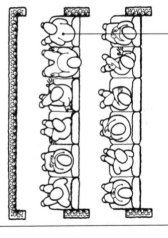

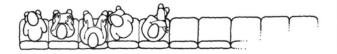

## LAWS TO KNOW

The next time someone says it's the law, you could ask, "What kind?"

*Blue Laws*

These are also known as Sabbath laws. They were passed to restrict or forbid business and recreation on the Sabbath, which is the Christian day of rest. One blue law in some states forbids the sale of alcoholic beverages before noon on Sundays.

*Common Laws*

Rules based on custom or long usage which are usually not recorded as laws. They began in England.

*Law of the Land*

A phrase from the Magna Carta, the basic document of English law. Today the term refers to laws that are fundamental to democracy.

*Martial Law*

Temporary rule by the military which is imposed on citizens during a war, an emergency (like a natural disaster), or a political or economic crisis. Under martial law, military laws are followed instead of civil laws.

*Moral Law*

The law of one's conscience.

*Murphy's Laws*

No one is sure who Murphy was, but these laws are well known. They are:

1. Nothing is as easy as it looks.
2. Everything will take longer than you think.
3. If anything can go wrong, it will.

In times of frustration, people will often remark that things are going according to Murphy's laws.

*Parkinson's Law*
C. Northcote Parkinson, a British writer, formulated this rule: "Work expands to fill the time allotted to it; or, conversely, the amount of work completed is in inverse proportion to the number of people employed." Simply said: If you have an hour to do a 5-minute job, it will take an hour to do it. A large number of people accomplish less work than a smaller number of people.

## WACKY (AND NOT SO WACKY) LAWS IN THE U.S.
It's hard to believe that these laws are actually on the books throughout the U.S. Most of them were passed many years ago, when the times and thinking were very different. Some seem so silly, it's hard to believe the lawmakers weren't joking.

*It's against the law . . .*

- to slurp your soup in a public eating place in New Jersey.
- to holler "snake" within the city limits of Flowery Branch, Ga.
- for frogs to croak after 11:00 P.M. in Memphis, Tenn.
- to read comics while riding in a car in Norman, Okla.
- to remove your shoes if your feet smell while you're in a theater in Winnetka, Ill.
- to buy ice cream after 6:00 P.M. in Newark, N.J., unless you have a written note from a doctor.

*Hammurabi, the king of Babylon in the 18th century B.C., was the first to record the laws and their consequences.*

- for cars to drip on the pavement in Green Bay, Wis. There is a $1 fine for each drip.
- to enter a public theater or a streetcar within 4 hours of eating garlic in Gary, Ind.
- for dogs to get in the way of people walking in Pateros, Wash.
- to ride a bike into a swimming pool in Baldwin Park, Calif.
- to wipe dishes dry in Minneapolis, Minn. Dishes should be left to drip dry.
- for kids to buy lollipops in Spokane, Wash.
- to push dirt under a rug in Pittsburgh, Pa.
- for a barber to shave a customer's chest in Omaha, Nebr.
- for *boys* to throw snowballs at trees in Mount Pulaski, Ill.

## WACKY (AND NOT SO WACKY) LAWS AROUND THE WORLD

Here are some unusual or surprising laws in countries around the world.

In China, families are allowed only one child by law.

In England, it's unlawful to kiss in a movie theater in London.

In Finland, people must be able to read in order to get married.

In Greece, if you are unbathed or poorly dressed while driving on the public roads of Athens, you may have your license taken away.

In Iceland, only seeing-eye dogs are allowed in the country.

In Japan, it's against the law to buy or eat rice grown in another country.

In Micronesia, men are not allowed to wear neckties.

In Sweden, it's illegal for parents to insult or shame their children.

## KNOW YOUR RIGHTS

Throughout history, rulers and dictators have taken away people's rights. In many parts of the world today people can't worship as they please, talk freely, gather with groups of their friends, or travel. If you feel that everyone is always telling you what to do and that you have no rights, you're wrong! Children are protected by the same laws that protect adults, such as the Bill of Rights. Children also have their own rights, which were developed by the United Nations. It's important to know your rights and to stand up for yourself.

### The Bill of Rights

The Bill of Rights was added to the Constitution in the form of amendments. Their chief purpose was to protect the rights of individuals from the government's interference. They guarantee rights

such as religious freedom, freedom of the press, and trial by jury to all American citizens.

*First Amendment:* Freedom of religion, freedom of speech and the press, the right to assemble, the right to petition government.

*Second Amendment:* The right to form a militia and to keep and bear arms.

*Third Amendment:* The right not to have soldiers in one's home.

*Fourth Amendment:* Protection against unreasonable search and seizure.

*Fifth Amendment:* No one can be tried for a serious crime unless indicted (accused) by a grand jury. No one can be forced to testify against herself or himself. No one can be punished without due process of law. People must be paid for property taken for public use.

*Americans had been forced to provide lodging for British troops in colonial times.*

## Other Important Amendments

*Thirteenth Amendment (1865):* Slavery shall not be allowed in the U.S.

*Nineteenth Amendment (1920):* Women have the right to vote.

*Twenty-sixth Amendment (1971):* U.S. citizens who are 18 years of age or older have the right to vote. (Previously, they had to be 21 years old.)

*Sixth Amendment:* People have a right to a speedy trial, to legal counsel, and to confront their accusers.

*Seventh Amendment:* People have the right to a jury trial in civil suits exceeding $20.

*Eighth Amendment:* Excessive bail (money to release a person from jail), stiff fines, and cruel and unusual punishment are forbidden.

*Ninth Amendment:* There are so many basic human rights that all of them could not be listed in the Constitution.

*Tenth Amendment:* Powers not given to the federal government by the Constitution belong to the states or the people.

### Your Rights as a Child
In 1989, the United Nations adopted the Convention on the Rights of the Child because "the child, by reason of his physical and mental immaturity, needs special safeguards and care" and because "in all countries of the world, there are children living in exceptionally difficult conditions." Following are highlights of the 41 articles of rights.

1. Every child has a right to life.

2. Every child has a right to a name at birth and a nationality.

3. Every child has the right to live with his or her parent unless it is against the child's best interests.

4. Special protection shall be given to refugee children.

5. Every child has the right to the highest standard of health and medical care possible.

6. The child has a right to education. The state is to ensure that primary education is free and compulsory.

7. No child shall be subjected to torture, cruel treatment, unlawful arrest, or deprivation of liberty.

8. Children under 15 shall not be recruited into the armed forces.

## YOU HAVE THE RIGHT

Before making an arrest, a police officer must read this list of rights to the suspect. It is called the Miranda warning because of a Supreme Court decision, *Miranda v. Arizona,* in 1966. When Ernesto Miranda was arrested and questioned by the police, the information he gave them was used against him at his trial. This was a direct violation of the Fifth Amendment of the Bill of Rights. Miranda appealed, claiming that his rights were violated. The Supreme Court agreed; since then, everyone is read the Miranda warning upon arrest.

## Miranda Warning

1. You have the right to remain silent and refuse to answer any questions.

2. Anything you say may be used against you in a court of law.

3. As we discuss this matter, you have a right to stop answering my questions at any time you desire.

4. You have a right to a lawyer before speaking to me, to remain silent until you can talk to him/her, and to have him/her present when you are being questioned.

5. If you want a lawyer but cannot afford one, one will be provided to you without cost.

6. Do you understand each of these rights I have explained to you?

7. Now that I have advised you of your rights, are you willing to answer my questions without an attorney present?

# LAW ENFORCEMENT

## Police Gear

*Dress and Equipment*

Hat or helmet

Uniform with a bulletproof vest

Identification badge

Belt with holster and gun (different guns, depending on locale)

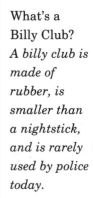

What's a Billy Club? *A billy club is made of rubber, is smaller than a nightstick, and is rarely used by police today.*

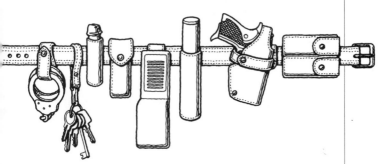

*Attached to the belt or in the pockets are the following:*

Whistle

A flashlight

A reflector (to be used at night)

Handcuffs

Memo book and pencil

Two-way radio

A small knife for cutting rope

A small canister of Mace (impairs vision, burns the skin)

Nightstick (a wooden club with a strap)

*Police dogs attend school daily for 16 weeks before they can work on the police force.*

*Robots:* Small, trucklike vehicles with a camera. They are used primarily to search for bombs.

*Dogs:* Police use specially trained dogs to search for explosives, bodies, and illegal drugs.

*Horses:* Police on horseback usually belong to traffic divisions. They are also used for crowd control.

# Measuring Up

*Count On It*

WHETHER IT'S TIME, MONEY, OR weather, it is certainly  convenient to have a standard system of measurement to rely on. Here are  some old and new ways people have devised to keep track of, compare, and define quantities of things.

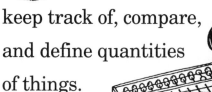

## AS TIME GOES BY

### Measuring Years

- A year is the time it takes for the earth to revolve around the sun once. A calendar year is 365 days.
- A solar or tropical year is 365 days, 5 hours, 48 minutes, and 46 seconds. This year is used for most astronomical calculations.
- A sidereal year is 365 days, 6 hours, and 9 minutes. It is sometimes used by astronomers, because it is the time it takes the earth to return to the same place in its orbit relative to fixed stars.
- Leap year occurs every 4 years, when all the extra hours, minutes, and seconds of the solar year are added up to make an extra day.
- B.C. means "before Christ"; A.D. means *anno Domini,* Latin for "year of our Lord."
- A cosmic year is the amount of time it takes the sun to revolve around the center of the Milky Way, about 225 million years.

| Groups of Years |
| --- |
| Olympiad: 4 years |
| Decade: 10 years |
| Score: 20 years |
| Century: 100 years |
| Millennium: 1,000 years |

| How Often? |
| --- |
| Annual: Yearly |
| Biannual: Twice a year (not equally spaced) |
| Semiannual: Twice a year equally spaced; every 6 months |
| Semicentennial: Every 50 years |
| Centennial: Every 100 years |

### *The Aztec and Mayan Calendars*

The people of these ancient civilizations used two calendars. One was a sacred calendar of 260 days that marked religious feasts. The other was a secular (not religious) calendar of 365 days divided into 18 months of 20 days each. The extra 5 days were added throughout the years, much like the time we add each leap year. Today, many people follow a religious calendar as well as the secular one.

## Religious Calendars
- The Jewish calendar is reckoned from 3761 B.C.
- The Jewish New Year, called Rosh Hashana, occurs on the first and second day of the Hebrew month Tishri, which can come in either September or October.
- The Islamic calendar is based on a lunar (moon) year of 354 days. It is calculated from the Hegira, in A.D. 622, and grouped in 30-year cycles. (The Hegira was the flight from Mecca by Muhammed, the founder of Islam, to escape persecution.)

*The word for the longest measurement of time is* kalpa, *Hindi for 432 billion years.*

## The Chinese Calendar
The Chinese calendar is based on a lunar year of 12 months. Lunar years are measured from the time it takes the moon to go from one new moon to another. This calendar has 29 or 30 days each month.

Years are grouped in cycles of 60. Each year is named after 1 of 12 animals.

| ROOSTER | DOG | PIG | RAT | OX | TIGER |
|---------|-----|-----|-----|-----|-------|
| 1981 | 1982 | 1983 | 1984 | 1985 | 1986 |
| 1993 | 1994 | 1995 | 1996 | 1997 | 1998 |

| CAT | DRAGON | SNAKE | HORSE | SHEEP | MONKEY |
|-----|--------|-------|-------|-------|--------|
| 1987 | 1988 | 1989 | 1990 | 1991 | 1992 |
| 1999 | 2000 | 2001 | 2002 | 2003 | 2004 |

The Chinese New Year occurs on the first new moon after the sun enters Aquarius, sometime between January 21 and February 19.

## Months

- Months are based roughly on the moon. A lunar month is 29½ days, or the time from one new moon to the next.
- 12 lunar months leave 11 days remaining in the solar year.
- To help you remember the days of the month, remember "30 days has September, April, June,

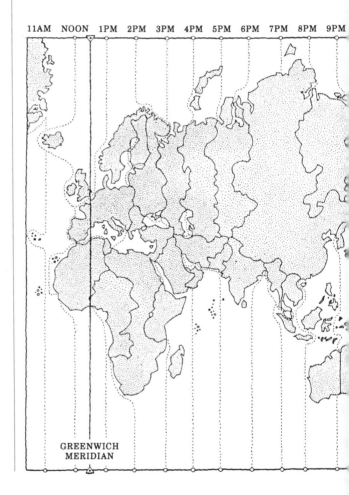

11AM  NOON  1PM  2PM  3PM  4PM  5PM  6PM  7PM  8PM  9PM

GREENWICH
MERIDIAN

and November. All the rest have 31, except February, which has 28."

## Days

- A day is measured by how long it takes the earth to rotate (turn) once: 24 hours.
- The earth is divided into 24 time zones. It takes the sun an hour to cross each zone.

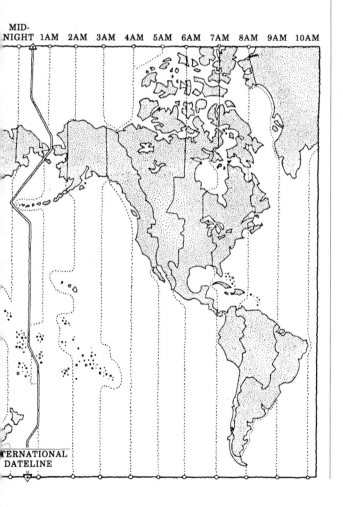

MID-
NIGHT  1AM  2AM  3AM  4AM  5AM  6AM  7AM  8AM  9AM  10AM

INTERNATIONAL
DATELINE

- The time zones are marked by imaginary lines called meridians, which run north and south on the globe.
- The prime meridian is at Greenwich, England. It is 0° longitude. From here, east and west longitude is calculated for the rest of the globe.
- A new day begins at the international date line, which is halfway around the world from the prime meridian.
- East of the international date line it is 1 day earlier than west of it. Remember, "Go ahead west to the new day, go back east to the old."

## Hours

- An hour is 60 minutes.
- The hours between 12 midnight and 12 noon are A.M. (*ante* "before" *meridiem*).
- The hours between 12 noon and 12 midnight are P.M. (*post* "after" *meridiem*)
- Sailor time is used on a ship at sea. The day is divided into 5 "watches" of 4 hours each and 2 of 2 hours each. Bells tell the time. One bell marks the first half-hour of the watch; 8 bells toll the last. On ship, the new day starts at noon.
- Military time is based on a 24-hour clock, making 3:00 P.M. 1500 hours.

## HOW'S THE WEATHER?

### Temperature

Air temperature is measured by a mercury thermometer, which uses the principle of contraction and expansion. When the temperature rises, the

*Here's Pig Latin for military time. Place a zero in front of each hour or minute with single digits. For example: 1 minute after 2 A.M. is said "oh one oh two hours."*

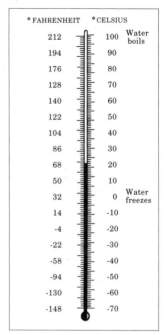

| ° FAHRENHEIT | ° CELSIUS | |
|---|---|---|
| 212 | 100 | Water boils |
| 194 | 90 | |
| 176 | 80 | |
| 128 | 70 | |
| 140 | 60 | |
| 122 | 50 | |
| 104 | 40 | |
| 86 | 30 | |
| 68 | 20 | |
| 50 | 10 | |
| 32 | 0 | Water freezes |
| 14 | -10 | |
| -4 | -20 | |
| -22 | -30 | |
| -58 | -40 | |
| -94 | -50 | |
| -130 | -60 | |
| -148 | -70 | |

mercury expands and rises in the thermometer tube. Cold weather makes the mercury contract and fall.

The *Fahrenheit* scale is used in the U.S. On this scale, 32° is the freezing point of water, 212° the boiling point.

The *Celsius,* or centigrade, scale is used by the World Meteorological Organization and most countries in the world. On this scale, 0° is freezing, 100° is boiling.

*The center of the sun is thought to be 40 million degrees Celsius.*

## Air Pressure and Humidity

• Air pressure is the weight of the atmosphere pressing down on the earth. It is measured by a *barometer* in units called millibars. One thousand millibars equals one bar.

• Warm air is light and reduces pressure, so the barometer reading will be low. Cold air is heavy and increases the pressure, so the barometer reading will be high.

• Warm air holds more moisture than cold air, so low pressure often means stormy weather.

• Relative humidity is the amount of moisture the air can hold before it rains. The most it can hold is 100%. Humidity is measured by a *psychrometer,* which indicates the amount of water in the air at any one temperature.

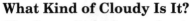

## What Kind of Cloudy Is It?

Clouds are little drops of water or ice hanging in the atmosphere. A *ceilometer* measures the height of clouds.

| CLOUD | DESCRIPTIVE NAME | HEIGHT | DESCRIPTION |
|---|---|---|---|
| Cirrus | Mare's tails | 4 miles + | thin, feathery |
| Cirrocumulus | Mackerel sky | 4 miles + | small patches of white |
| Cirrostratus | Bedsheet clouds | 4 miles + | thin, white sheets |
| Stratus* | High fogs | 0–1 mile | low, gray blanket |
| Cumulus | Cauliflowers | ¼–4 miles | flat-bottomed, white puffy |
| Cumulonimbus* | Thunder-heads | ¼–4 miles | mountains of heavy, dark clouds |

*Indicates rain or snow clouds*

## HOW MUCH DID PETER PIPER PICK?

A *bushel* is the largest dry measure of how much can be held (capacity) for things like fruit, vegetables, and grains. A *pint* is the smallest measure. Dry measures are never used for liquids (there is no such thing as a peck of milk), but liquid measures may be used for dry (a quart of strawberries, for example).

| Dry Measurement | Liquid Measurement |
|---|---|
| 2 pints = 1 quart | 4 gills (16 fluid ounces) = 1 pint |
| 8 quarts = 1 peck | 2 pints = 1 quart |
| 4 pecks = 1 bushel | 4 quarts = 1 gallon |
| 105 quarts = 1 barrel | 31½ gallons = 1 barrel |

## PICK A BALE OF COTTON?

### Measuring Words

A *ream* of paper = 500 sheets

A *bale* of cotton = 500 pounds

A *fortnight* = 2 weeks

A *last* of fish = 20,000 fish

A *drum* of oil = 50–55 gallons

A *hogshead* = 63–140 gallons of drink

A *hand* of bananas = a small bunch
(each banana is called a finger)

A *firkin* of butter = 56 pounds of butter in
England

A *frail* of raisins = 32, 56, or 75 pounds

A *bolt* of cloth = about 40 yards

A *baker's dozen* = 13

A *cran* of herring = 47 gallons

*In China, 2.2
pounds of rice
is called a
kungchin.*

### WHOSE FOOT IS THAT?

In ancient times, the body ruled when it came to
measuring. The length of a foot, the width of a finger, and the distance of a step were all accepted measurements.

| |
|---|
| *Inch = 0.083 feet* |
| *Foot = 12 inches* |
| *Yard = 3 feet or 36 inches* |
| *Mile = 5,280 feet or 1,760 yards* |

*Inch:* At first an inch was the width of a man's thumb. In the 14th century, King Edward II of England ruled that 1

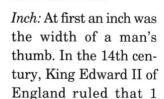

inch equal 3 grains of barley placed end to end lengthwise.

*Hand:* A hand was approximately 5 inches or 5 digits (fingers) across. Today, a hand is 4 inches and is used to measure horses (from the ground to the horse's withers, or shoulder).

| Near and Far |
| --- |
| Around the earth (at the equator): 24,901 miles |
| Across the continental U.S.: 3,000 miles |
| From the earth to the moon: 238,854 miles |
| From the earth to the sun: 93,000,000 miles |

*Span:* A span was the length of the hand stretched out, about 9 inches.

*Foot:* In ancient times, the foot was 11½ inches. Today it is 12 inches, the length of the average man's foot.

*Yard:* A yard was originally the length of a man's belt or girdle, as it was called. In the 12th century, King Henry I of England fixed the yard as the distance from his nose to the thumb of his outstretched arm.

*Cubit:* In ancient Egypt, a cubit was the distance from the elbow to the fingertips. A cubit is 18 inches.

*Lick:* A lick was used by the Greeks to measure the distance from the tip of the thumb to the tip of the index finger.

*Pace:* The ancient Roman soldiers marched in paces, which were the length of a double step, about 5 feet; 1,000 paces was a mile. Today, a pace is the length of one step, 2½ to 3 feet.

# NUMBER PLAY

## How Much Does It Cost?

Would you like to pay for your purchase in camels or cocoa beans? Perhaps you'd like your change in shells. Throughout history, all kinds of things have been used as money. Precious metals have kept their popularity since they're easy to handle (unlike camels) and keep their value. Here is how cold cash is measured around the world.

| COUNTRY | CURRENCY | COUNTRY | CURRENCY |
|---|---|---|---|
| Australia | *dollar* | Malaysia | *ringgit* |
| Brazil | *cruzado* | Mexico | *peso* |
| China | *yuan* | Mongolia | *tugrik* |
| Czechoslovakia | *koruna* | Morocco | *dirham* |
| Denmark | *krone* | The Netherlands | *guilder* |
| Ethiopia | *birr* | Peru | *inti* |
| France | *franc* | Poland | *zloty* |
| Germany | *deutsche mark* | Portugal | *escudo* |
| Ghana | *cedi* | Russia | *ruble* |
| Great Britain | *pound* | Saudi Arabia | *riyal* |
| Greece | *drachma* | South Africa | *rand* |
| Haiti | *gourde* | South Korea | *won* |
| India | *rupee* | Spain | *peseta* |
| Israel | *shekel* | Sweden | *krona* |
| Italy | *lira* | Thailand | *baht* |
| Japan | *yen* | United States | *dollar* |
| Jordan | *dinar* | Venezuela | *bolivar* |
| Laos | *kip* | Zambia | *kwacha* |

## One Million and Still Counting

The *googol* is a number followed by 100 zeros or $10^{100}$. The *googolplex* is the number followed by a googol of zeros.

| |
|---|
| MILLION: 1,000,000 |
| BILLION: 1,000,000,000 |
| TRILLION: 1,000,000,000,000 |
| QUINTILLION: 1,000,000,000,000,000,000 |
| SEXTILLION: 1,000,000,000,000,000,000,000 |
| NONILLION: 1,000,000,000,000,000,000,000,000,000,000 |
| CENTILLION: 1 followed by 303 zeros |

*It would take about 12 days to count to a million, 32 years to count to 1 billion, if each count were about 1 second long.*

## Roman Numerals

The ancient Romans gave us this numbering system. We still use it today for dates on buildings, to number the front matter in books, and for decorative purposes.

| | | | | | |
|---|---|---|---|---|---|
| One | I | Eleven | XI | Thirty | XXX |
| Two | II | Twelve | XII | Forty | XL |
| Three | III | Thirteen | XIII | Fifty | L |
| Four | IV | Fourteen | XIV | Sixty | LX |
| Five | V | Fifteen | XV | Seventy | LXX |
| Six | VI | Sixteen | XVI | Eighty | LXXX |
| Seven | VII | Seventeen | XVII | Ninety | XC |
| Eight | VIII | Eighteen | XVIII | One hundred | C |
| Nine | IX | Nineteen | XIX | Five hundred | D |
| Ten | X | Twenty | XX | One thousand | M |

# WEIGHTY MATTERS

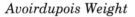

## When It Weighs a Ton

*Avoirdupois,* the French word for "goods of weight," describes the heaviness of objects. The smallest unit is a *grain,* originally a grain of wheat.

*The earth weighs 6 sextillion, 588 quintillion short tons. A class of 27 fifth-graders would weigh about a ton.*

---

### Avoirdupois Weight

| | |
|---|---|
| GRAIN = 0.036 DRAMS | |
| DRAM = 0.0625 OUNCES | |
| OUNCE (OZ.) = 16 DRAMS | |
| POUND (LB.) = 16 OUNCES | |
| HUNDREDWEIGHT = 100 POUNDS | |
| TON (SHORT) = 2,000 POUNDS (USED IN THE U.S.) | |
| TON (LONG) = 2,240 POUNDS | |

---

## Worth Their Weight in Gold

Troy weight is used to measure precious metals. This system may have started in Troyes, France.

*Grain:* The smallest unit in troy weight. Long ago, grains or the seeds of a plant were used as a balance for gold.

*Pennyweight:* The same as the weight of an English penny when troy weight became a legal standard.

*Carat:* Used to express the weight of jewels like diamonds and pearls. The Arabs used a karob

### Troy Weight

| | |
|---|---|
| GRAIN = 0.002083 OUNCES | |
| PENNYWEIGHT = 24 GRAINS | |
| OUNCE = 20 PENNYWEIGHTS | |
| POUND = 12 OUNCES | |

bean, a carat, to weigh against gold, giving us the "K" used in gold weight. A carat was once 4 grains. Today it is 3.086 grains.

## MEASURING POWER

*Horsepower:* A workhorse can lift 550 pounds 1 foot in the air in 1 second; that is 1 horsepower. Engines are measured in horsepower. A 10-horsepower engine can do the work of ten horses.

*Manpower:* An average man lifts 55 pounds 1 foot high in 1 second.

*Candlepower:* The amount of light given off by a candle of a specific size, shape, type of tallow, and type of wick. The brightness of an electric light is measured in candlepower.

*Megaton:* A megaton is the blasting power of a hydrogen bomb. One megaton has the power of 1 million tons of TNT.

## CAN YOU FATHOM THIS?

### Nautical Measurement

A *fathom* is 6 feet, the length of rope a man can extend from open arm to open arm. The rope was lowered into the sea to measure depth.

*1 nautical mile = 1.1515 miles*

A *cable length* is the length of a ship's cable, about 600 feet.

A *nautical mile* is 10 cable lengths, or 6,080 feet.

A *knot* is the measure of speed on water. One knot is 1 nautical mile per hour.

## HOW EARLY MEASURERS MADE THEIR MARK

Dividing things into units is an ancient task. Here are four basic units and the people who first used them. You'll recognize how they are still used today.

*Binary:* This Hindu unit divides things into halves, quarters, and eighths.

*Decimal:* The Chinese and the Egyptians were the first to use decimals, which are tenths. The metric system is based on decimal units.

*Duodecimal:* The Romans used units of 12. Today we have 12 inches in a foot, 12 months in a year, 12 in a dozen.

*Sexagesimal:* The Babylonians used units of 60. Time is measured in 60s: 60 seconds in a minute, 60 minutes in an hour.

## A SPOONFUL OF SUGAR

### A Cook's Measurements

| | |
|---|---|
| 4 CUPS = 1 QUART | |
| 4 CUPS OF FLOUR = 1 POUND | |
| 2 CUPS OF BUTTER = 1 POUND | |
| 1 STICK OF BUTTER = ½ CUP | |
| 3 TEASPOONS = 1 TABLESPOON | |

*Pinch* means just a little of a dry ingredient held between the fingers. A *dash* means just a little of a liquid ingredient. A *clove* of garlic is one small part of the bulb.

*Fannie Farmer was the first to use exact measurements in a cookbook.*

## UMPTEEN MILES OF HIGHWAYS

Knowing your numbers helps you know which direction you are going on U.S. highways. Here's how the highway systems are numbered.

### Interstate Highways

- The interstate system totals 42,500 miles. All interstate highways are marked by blue signs with red tops.
- The north-south highways have odd numbers with 1 or 2 digits, usually including a 5. The

lowest numbers are on the West Coast and increase as they move east. For example, I-5 is on the West Coast, I-95 on the East Coast.

- The east-west highways have even numbers with 1 or 2 digits. The lowest numbers are in the South and increase as they go north. For example, I-4 runs through Florida; I-96 is the northernmost route.

- An interstate highway with 3 digits is a connector or offshoot of a main route.

*Three highways run from coast to coast: I-10, I-80, and I-90. Seven highways run from border to border: I-5, I-15, I-35, I-55, I-65, I-75, and I-95.*

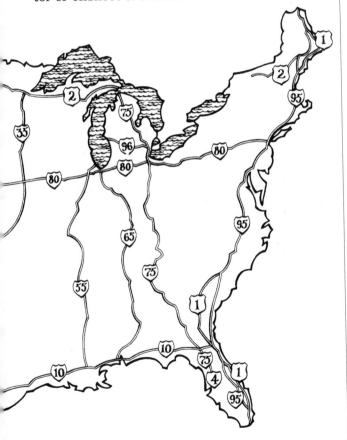

## U.S. Routes

- U.S. routes are posted in black letters on white signs.
- The north-south routes have odd numbers, with 1 to 3 digits. These numbers increase from east to west (just the opposite of the interstate system). For example, U.S. 1 runs along the East Coast; U.S. 101 runs along the West Coast.
- The east-west routes have even numbers, with 1 to 3 digits. The lowest numbers are in the North and increase moving south (just the opposite of the interstates). For example, U.S. 2 runs along the Canadian border; U.S. 90 runs through Texas.

## MEASURING METRIC

Most of the world uses the metric system. The only countries not on this system are the U.S., Burma, Liberia, Muscat, and South Yemen.

The metric system is based on 10s. For example, 10 decimeters make a meter (39.37 inches).

Units smaller than a meter have Latin prefixes: *deci-* means 10; *centi-* means 100; *milli-* means 1,000.

*A millimicron is one thousandth of one millionth of one meter.*

Units larger than a meter have Greek prefixes. *Deka-* means 10; a dekameter is 10 meters. *Hecto-* means 100; a hectometer is 100 meters. *Kilo-* means 1,000; a kilometer is 1,000 meters.

### Helpful Hints

Remember: A *meter* is a little more than a *yard*. A *kilometer* is less than a *mile*. A *liter* is a little more than a *quart*.

# THE METRIC SYSTEM

## Length

| UNIT | VALUE |
|---|---|
| KILOMETER (km) | 1,000 METERS |
| HECTOMETER (hm) | 100 METERS |
| DEKAMETER (dam) | 10 METERS |
| METER (m) | 1 METER |
| DECIMETER (dm) | 0.1 METER |
| CENTIMETER (cm) | 0.01 METERS |
| MILLIMETER (mm) | 0.001 METERS |

## Capacity

| UNIT | VALUE |
|---|---|
| KILOLITER (kl) | 1,000 LITERS |
| HECTOLITERS (hl) | 100 LITERS |
| DEKALITERS (dal) | 10 LITERS |
| LITER (l) | 1 LITER * |
| DECILITER (dl) | 0.10 LITERS |
| CENTILITER (cl) | 0.01 LITERS |
| MILLILITER (ml) | 0.001 LITERS |

*1 liter + U.S. 1.057 quarts*

## Mass and Weight

| UNIT | VALUE |
|---|---|
| METRIC TON | 1,000,000 GRAMS |
| QUINTAL (P) | 100,000 GRAMS |
| MYRIAGRAM | 10,000 GRAMS |
| KILOGRAM | 1,000 GRAMS |
| HECTOGRAM | 100 GRAMS |
| DEKAGRAM | 10 GRAMS |
| GRAM | 1 GRAM * |
| DECIGRAM | 0.10 GRAMS |
| CENTIGRAM | 0.01 GRAMS |
| MILLIGRAMS | 0.001 GRAMS |

*1 gram + U.S. 0.035 ounces*

## Metric Conversions
### Here's all you'll need to know about them!

| MULTIPLY | BY | TO FIND |
|---|---|---|
| Centimeters | .0328 | feet |
| Centimeters | .3937 | inches |
| Feet | 30.4801 | centimeters |
| Feet/minutes | .507 | cent./seconds |
| Foot-pounds | .1383 | meter-kilograms |
| Gallons | 3,785.4 | cubic centimeters |
| Gallons | 3.7853 | liters |
| Grams | .0353 | ounces |
| Grams | .0022 | pounds |
| Inches | 2.54 | centimeters |
| Inches | .0833 | feet |
| Kilograms | 2.2046 | pounds |
| Kilometers | 3,280.833 | feet |
| Kilometers | .6214 | miles |
| Kilometers/hour | 54.68 | feet/minute |
| Kilometers/hour | .6214 | miles/hour |
| Knots | 1.8532 | kilometers/hour |
| Liters | 1.0567 | quarts |
| Meters | 3.2808 | feet |
| Meters | 39.37 | inches |
| Meters | 1.0936 | yards |
| Meter-kilograms | 7.2307 | foot-pounds |
| Meters/minute | 1.667 | centimeters/second |
| Meters/minute | .0547 | feet/second |

one meter

one foot

| MULTIPLY | BY | TO FIND |
|---|---|---|
| Miles | 1.6093 | kilometers |
| Miles/hour | .8684 | knots |
| Miles/hour | 1.6093 | kilometers/hour |
| Miles/hour | .447 | meters/second |
| Ounces | 28.3495 | grams |
| Ounces | $2.8349 \times 10^2$ | kilograms |
| Pounds | 453.5924 | grams |
| Pounds | .4536 | kilograms |
| Quarts | .946 | liters |
| Quarts (dry) | 67.2 | cubic inches |
| Quarts (liquid) | 57.75 | cubic inches |
| Sq. centimeters | .0011 | square feet |
| Sq. kilometers | .3861 | square miles |
| Sq. kilometers | $1.196 \times 10^6$ | square yards |
| Sq. meters | 10.7639 | square feet |
| Sq. meters | 1.196 | square yards |
| Sq. miles | 2.59 | square kilometers |
| Sq. yards | .8361 | square meters |
| Yards | 91.44 | centimeters |
| Yards | .9144 | meters |

 =

## HOW FAST?

Speed is the measure of motion. You can find it by dividing the distance covered by the time it takes to travel it.

*Speed of Light*
Light travels through space at 186,000 miles per second.

*Light-Year*
A light ray travels 5.88 trillion miles a year in space.

*Star Distance*
The star Sirius is 9 light-years away from the solar system.

*More Earthly Speeds*

Cheetah: 70 mph

White-tailed deer: 32 mph

Human being: 27.89 mph

Garden snail: 0.03 mph

Fastest automobile: 205 mph

Fastest train: 252 mph

Fastest helicopter: 249.10 mph

Fastest jet: 2,193.167 mph

*If a star is 10 light-years away, it is about 60 trillion miles distant.*

# People Pamphlet

*From VIPs to VOPs*

HUMAN BEINGS ARE ENDLESSLY
fascinating and unique.
Who are we? Where do
we come from? How are
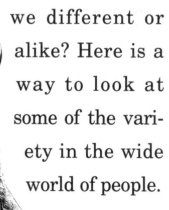
we different or
alike? Here is a
way to look at
some of the vari-
ety in the wide
world of people.

## PEOPLE AT A GLANCE

- People have lived in the world for millions of years. Today, 5 billion people live on the earth.

- The world's population grows by 100 million each year. Some 950 million people in the world are malnourished.

- There are 106 boys born for every 100 girls. The average male adult is 5'9" tall and weighs 155 pounds. The average female adult is 5'3" tall and weighs 125 pounds.

## People in Groups

*Gerontocracy:* A society or group of people in which older people are the most powerful.

## People in Families

A *nuclear family* is made up of parents and their children.

An *extended family* includes parents, children, grandparents, and/or aunts and uncles in the same household.

A *blended family* is formed when one single parent (divorced or widowed) marries another single parent.

*Matriarchy:* A society or group of people in which women are the most powerful.

*Patriarchy:* A society or group of people in which men are the most powerful.

*Timocracy:* A society or group of people in which the rich are the most powerful.

## GENERIC PEOPLE

A generic person is the name for a type of person, not a real one. The names below are often used to describe different kinds of people. Do you know any of them?

### Famous Couples

*Jane and John Doe*
The Does have been around since the 1300s and are still going strong. British lawyers used the most common first names of the time—John and Jane—whenever a person's true identity was unknown, when a person wished to remain anonymous, or when the person could be almost anyone. You can find these names today on legal documents, death certificates, and hospital records.

*Mr. and Mrs. Buttinski*
This couple is always minding other people's business. They interrupt conversation rudely and offer opinions whether or not they are wanted. Mr. and Mrs. Buttinski are not well liked.

*Mr. and Mrs. Jones*
Whatever you have, the Joneses always have more. They are the envy of their neighbors, who compete with them but can never quite "keep up."

*Mr. and Mrs. X*
People like to gossip about this couple, although they are nothing special. In fact, like their neighbors the Does, they are the perfect example of an average couple. Compared to the other generic couples, Mr. and Mrs. X are rather plain.

## Just Joe
Joe is one of the many nicknames used when one man greets another. Mac, Jack, Bud, and Buster are others. However, Joe is the most popular, and he has many different personalities.

*The Average Joe*
These Joes all represent your everyday man-in-the-street: Average Joe, Joe Blow, Joe Bunker, Joe Schmo.

*Special Joes*
Some Joes aren't just ordinary guys.

Joe Bag: This Joe is stingy. He never leaves a tip (known as "bagging the tip" in hotels all over the world).

Joe College: This American college man loves fraternities, football games, girls, and, of course, his studies.

Joe Cool: This Joe thinks he's a big shot and has everybody else convinced as well. He wears the "right" clothes, goes to the "right" parties, and is usually seen hiding behind an expensive pair of sunglasses.

Joe Soap: No one wants to be this Joe, a slow, stupid fellow who is often the object of ridicule.

G.I. Joe: This Joe was a symbol of the U.S. Army

during World War II. The soldiers relied completely on government issue (G.I.) goods, so they became known as G.I.'s.

## WHOSE FACE IS ON YOUR MONEY?

| COINS | PORTRAIT |
|---|---|
| CENT | ABRAHAM LINCOLN |
| NICKEL | THOMAS JEFFERSON |
| DIME | FRANKLIN ROOSEVELT |
| QUARTER | GEORGE WASHINGTON |
| HALF DOLLAR | JOHN F. KENNEDY |
| DOLLAR | DWIGHT EISENHOWER |
| DOLLAR | SUSAN B. ANTHONY |

| CURRENCY | PORTRAIT |
|---|---|
| $ 1 | GEORGE WASHINGTON |
| $ 2 | THOMAS JEFFERSON |
| $ 5 | ABRAHAM LINCOLN |
| $ 10 | ALEXANDER HAMILTON |
| $ 20 | ANDREW JACKSON |
| $ 50 | ULYSSES S. GRANT |
| $ 100 | BENJAMIN FRANKLIN |
| $ 500 | WILLIAM McKINLEY |
| $ 1,000 | GROVER CLEVELAND |
| $ 5,000 | JAMES MADISON |
| $ 10,000 | SALMON P. CHASE |
| $ 100,000 | WOODROW WILSON |

# COLLECTING PEOPLE

People who collect things are called by many names. Some of their names are as unusual as the items they collect.

| COLLECTOR | COLLECTION |
| --- | --- |
| ARCHTOPHILIST | TEDDY BEARS |
| BESTIARIST | MEDIEVAL BOOKS ON ANIMALS |
| BIBLIOPHILIST | BOOKS |
| BRANDOPHILIST | CIGAR BANDS |
| CONCHOLOGIST | SHELLS |
| COPOCLEPHILIST | KEY RINGS |
| DELTIOLOGIST | POSTCARDS |
| DOLOGIST | BIRD'S EGGS |
| LEPIDOPTERIST | BUTTERFLIES |
| NUMISMATIST | COINS |
| PHILATELIST | STAMPS |
| PHILOGRAPHIST | AUTOGRAPHS |
| PHONOPHILE | PHONOGRAPH RECORDS |
| PLANGONOLOGIST | DOLLS |
| RECEPTARIST | RECIPES |
| VECTURIST | SUBWAY TOKENS |
| VEXILLOLOGIST | BANNERS OR FLAGS |

## WHAT'S IN A NAME?

*The Ninja Turtles* are Donatello, Michelangelo, Raphael, and Leonardo.

*The Seven Dwarfs* are Doc, Dopey, Grumpy, Happy, Sleepy, Sneezy, and Bashful.

*The Three Musketeers* are Athos, Aramis, and Porthos.

The children in *Peter Pan* are John, Michael, and Wendy Darling.

*The Marx Brothers* are Chico (Leonard), Harpo (Adolph), Groucho (Julius), Zeppo (Herbert), and Gummo (Milton).

| Pseudonyms of Unreal People (HIDDEN IDENTITIES) | |
| --- | --- |
| Captain Marvel | Bill Batson |
| Batman | Bruce Wayne |
| Tarzan | Lord Greystoke |
| Robin Hood | Earl of Huntington |
| Lone Ranger | John Reid |
| Superman | Clark Kent |
| Spiderman | Peter Parker |
| Wonderwoman | Diana Prince |

## Name Calling in the U.S.

*Beaneaters:* People from Boston. (Boston is famous for baked beans.)

*Buckeyes:* People from Ohio. The buckeye tree that grows there was used by early settlers to make items as varied as soap, hats, and spoons.

*Chicanos:* Americans of Mexican descent whose name is short for the Spanish word *Mexicanos.*

*Conchs:* People from the Florida Keys, who eat the conch and make horns from conch shells.

*Crackers:* People from the South. In the past, crackers were eaten as a meal by backwoods settlers.

*Dixie-ites:* People who live in the southeastern U.S. The region was called Dixie after the Mason-Dixon Line, which divided it from the North.

*Downeasters:* People from Maine, named for the winds that moved commercial sailing boats from Maine to Boston in the 1800s.

*Goobers:* People from Georgia and Alabama, where peanuts are grown. Peanuts were brought to the U.S. by African slaves, and *nguba* is an African word for "peanut."

*Gothamite:* People from New York City. Gotham is a nickname for New York City, after the English town of Gotham.

*Hoosier:* People from Indiana. The word is of uncertain origin but is thought to be a fighting word.

*Jayhawker:* People from Kansas, named for the mythical bird the jayhawk (part blue jay, part hawk), which is the state's mascot.

*Nutmegger:* People from Connecticut. Early residents played a trick by selling sawdust as nutmeg.

*Rednecks:* People from the rural South. Working in the fields gave them red necks.

*Sagebrushers:* People from the western states, named for the common sagebrush plant.

*Sooners:* People from Oklahoma. They claimed their land sooner than they were supposed to, before the Oklahoma Territory was officially opened for settlement.

*Tarheels:* People from North Carolina. The area produced tar and pitch, which the settlers sold and shipped to England in the 1700s.

*Yankees:* People from New England. The early settlers were called Yanks first by the colonial Dutch in New York and then by the British during the Revolution.

# PEOPLE IN THE WORLD

"When in Rome, do as the Romans do" is a famous saying about customs. But what exactly do the Romans and other people do that is so different? Where do women wear rings in their noses to show they are married, for example? Where do people greet each other with a bow rather than a handshake? Here are some other ways people behave and beautify themselves around the world.

- In Rome, Italy, adults drink coffee standing up at a coffee bar.
- Throughout Europe, people eat with the fork in the left hand and the knife in the right.
- In India, women wear rings in their noses to show they are married.
- In New Zealand, chewing gum in public is considered impolite.
- In Russia, powerful handshakes among men are often carried to extremes.
- In Brazil, kids do not have sleepovers.
- In most parts of Asia, it is taboo to touch people's heads, especially those of children.
- In the Philippines, it is impolite to be on time for social affairs.
- In Taiwan, belching after a meal is considered a compliment to the cook.
- In Australia, pancakes are served at dinner rather than breakfast.
- In Thailand, people do not step on their doorsills. It is believed that a spirit lives in the threshold of every home.
- In many North African countries, children ride to school on donkeys.

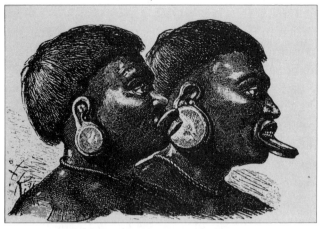

- In Ethiopia, both males and females of the Surma tribes shave their heads as a mark of beauty. The women wear lip plates; their lower lips are pierced and stretched as ever-larger plates are inserted over time. The larger the plate, the more appealing the woman.
- In Japanese homes, a hot bath is prepared for the whole family at once. Members take turns soaping, scrubbing, and rinsing off outside the tub before soaking in it.
- In France, children celebrate their name day (a saint's feast day) rather than their birthday.
- In Bangladesh, people use their right hand when they eat or hand things to other people. They consider their left hand unclean.
- In the Himalaya Mountains of Asia, the Apa Tanis tribal people wear black wooden nose plugs and tattoos on their chins.
- In Taiwan, eating or drinking in the streets is considered crude.
- In South Korea, pushing is normal and acceptable in crowded streets and stores. On the other

hand, people remove their eyeglasses when talking to an elder to show respect.

- In India, people do not wear shoes in the kitchen because some food is prepared on the floor.
- In Pakistan, a bridegroom wears garlands of money given to him by his relatives on his wedding day.
- On many Greek islands, women bake their food in a communal village oven.

## PEOPLE: RANK AND FILE

From the pecking order of chickens to the size of children, groups have a way of lining up. Here, in order of importance, are some titles of people in government, religion, and royalty.

### U.S. Government (IN ORDER OF PRESIDENTIAL SUCCESSION)

1. PRESIDENT

2. VICE PRESIDENT

3. SPEAKER OF THE HOUSE OF REPRESENTATIVES

4. PRESIDENT PRO TEMPORE OF THE SENATE

5. SECRETARY OF STATE

6. SECRETARY OF THE TREASURY

7. SECRETARY OF DEFENSE

8. ATTORNEY GENERAL

9. SECRETARY OF THE INTERIOR

10. SECRETARY OF AGRICULTURE

11. SECRETARY OF COMMERCE

## U.S. Army

GENERAL OF THE ARMY, 5 STARS

GENERAL, 4 STARS

LIEUTENANT GENERAL, 3 STARS

MAJOR GENERAL, 2 STARS

BRIGADIER GENERAL, 1 STAR

COLONEL, SILVER EAGLE PIN

LIEUTENANT COLONEL, SILVER OAK LEAF PIN

MAJOR, GOLD OAK LEAF PIN

CAPTAIN, 2 SILVER BARS

1ST LIEUTENANT, 1 SILVER BAR

2ND LIEUTENANT, 1 GOLD BAR

## U.S. Navy

FLEET ADMIRAL, 5 STRIPES

ADMIRAL, 4 STRIPES

VICE ADMIRAL, 3 STRIPES

REAR ADMIRAL, 2 STRIPES

COMMODORE, 1 STRIPE

CAPTAIN

COMMANDER

LIEUTENANT COMMANDER

LIEUTENANT JUNIOR GRADE

| World Religious Population |
| :--- |
| 1.7 BILLION CHRISTIANS |
| 935 MILLION MUSLIMS |
| 705 MILLION HINDUS |
| 303 MILLION BUDDHISTS |
| 17 MILLION JEWS |

*The Dalai Lama is the religious (Buddhist) and worldly leader of the people of Tibet.*

- Buddhists have no order of authority in their religion. A Buddhist monk who follows the religion strictly lives alone or in a monastery with these few possessions: a robe, an alms bowl (to beg for food), a needle, a string of 108 beads (to count while meditating), a razor (to shave his head), and a filter (to strain insects from his drinking water).

- Hindus have no hierarchy of religious authority. Instead, they divide their society by a caste system (from top to bottom): brahmins (priests), warriors, merchants, laborers, and outcasts, also known as untouchables.

| The Roman Catholic Church |
| :--- |
| *Pope* |
| *Cardinal* |
| *Archbishop* |
| *Bishop* |
| *Monsignor* |
| *Priest* |
| *Deacon* |

- Judaism has no one person as its spiritual leader. Each congregation chooses its own rabbi, who is a leader, teacher, and interpreter of Jewish law.

## Religious Founders and Leaders

BUDDHISM: SIDDHARTHA GAUTAMA

CHRISTIANITY: JESUS CHRIST

HINDUISM: NO FOUNDER

ISLAM: MOHAMMED

JUDAISM: MOSES

## Native American Religious Leaders

*Shamans:* Also called medicine men, shamans have contact with the world of spirits, which they call upon to help cure the sick.

*Priests:* After a long training period, priests perform public ceremonies for Indian groups.

*Prophets:* These religious leaders who predict the future arose after the Europeans arrived in America. Prophets urged their people to keep the old ways and to live separately from the Europeans.

## Native American Leaders

*Chiefs:* Each tribe has a permanent leader or chief; some have more than one. In addition, there may be a warrior chief.

*Tribal Council:* A group of old and wise tribe members who advise the chief.

# U.S. PRESIDENTIAL FAMILIES

Who's on top in America? It's the president, the highest elected official. President's wives are known as first ladies. (To date, all the presidents have been men, so we're not sure what a female president's husband would be called.) Americans have long been fascinated by the presidents, first ladies, and their families. Here they are in historical order.

*Martha Washington, the first of the first ladies, never lived in the White House. During Washington's time in office, the capital was in New York and Philadelphia.*

| PRESIDENT | WIFE | CHILDREN |
|---|---|---|
| 1. George Washington | Martha Dandridge Custis Washington | None |
| 2. John Adams | Abigail Smith Adams | Abigail, John Quincy, Susanna, Charles, Thomas |
| 3. Thomas Jefferson | Martha Wayles Skelton Jefferson | Martha, John, Lucy E., Jane, Lucy E.,* Maria |
| 4. James Madison | Dorothea (Dolley) Payne Todd Madison | None |
| 5. James Monroe | Elizabeth Kortright Monroe | Eliza, James, Maria |
| 6. John Quincy Adams | Louisa Catherine Johnson Adams | George, John, Charles, Louisa |
| 7. Andrew Jackson | Rachel Donelson Jackson | None |
| 8. Martin Van Buren | Hannah Hoes Van Buren | Abraham, John, Martin, Smith |
| 9. William Henry Harrison | Anna Tuthill Symmes Harrison | Elizabeth, John Cleves, Lucy, William, John Scott, Benjamin, Mary, Carter, Anna, James |
| 10. John Tyler | Letitia Christian Tyler | Mary, Robert, John, Letitia, Elizabeth, Alice, Tazewell |
| | Julia Gardiner Tyler | David, John Alexander, Julia, Lachlan, Lyon, Robert, Pearl |

GEORGE WASHINGTON

*After the first infant Lucy E. died, a second baby was named Lucy E.*

| PRESIDENT | WIFE | CHILDREN |
|---|---|---|
| 11. James K. Polk | Sarah Childress Polk | None |
| 12. Zachary Taylor | Margaret Mackall Smith Taylor | Ann, Sarah, Octavia, Margaret, Mary Elizabeth, Richard |
| 13. Millard Fillmore | Abigail Powers Fillmore | Millard, Mary |
| 14. Franklin Pierce | Jane Means Appleton Pierce | Frank Robert, Benjamin |
| 15. James Buchanan | None | None |
| 16. Abraham Lincoln | Mary Todd Lincoln | Robert, Edward, William, Thomas |
| 17. Andrew Johnson | Eliza McCardle Johnson | Martha, Charles, Mary, Robert, Andrew |
| 18. Ulysses S. Grant | Julia Boggs Dent Grant | Frederick, Ulysses, Ellen, Jesse |
| 19. Rutherford B. Hayes | Lucy Ware Webb Hayes | Birchard, James, Rutherford, Joseph, George, Fanny, Scott, Manning |
| 20. James A. Garfield | Lucretia Rudolph Garfield | Eliza, Harry, James, Mary, Irvin, Abram, Edward |
| 21. Chester A. Arthur | Ellen Lewis Herndon Arthur | William, Chester, Ellen |
| 22. & 24. Grover Cleveland | Frances Folsom Cleveland | Ruth, Esther, Marion, Richard, Francis |
| 23. Benjamin Harrison | Caroline Lavinia Scott Harrison | Russell, Mary |
| 25. William McKinley | Ida Saxton McKinley | Katherine, Ida |
| 26. Theodore Roosevelt | Alice Hathaway Roosevelt | Alice |
| | Edith Kermit Carow Roosevelt | Theodore, Kermit, Ethel, Archibald, Quentin |

ANDREW
JOHNSON

| PRESIDENT | WIFE | CHILDREN |
|---|---|---|
| 27. William Howard Taft | Helen Herron Taft | Robert, Helen, Charles |
| 28. Woodrow Wilson | Ellen Louise Axson Wilson | Margaret, Jessie, Eleanor |
| | Edith Bolling Galt Wilson | None |
| 29. Warren G. Harding | Florence Kling DeWolfe Harding | None |
| 30. Calvin Coolidge | Grace Anna Goodhue Coolidge | John, Calvin |
| 31. Herbert C. Hoover | Lou Henry Hoover | Herbert, Allan |
| 32. Franklin D. Roosevelt | Anna Eleanor Roosevelt Roosevelt | Anna, James, Franklin, Elliott, Franklin Delano, John |
| 33. Harry S. Truman | Elizabeth Virginia (Bess) Wallace Truman | Margaret |
| 34. Dwight D. Eisenhower | Marie (Mamie) Geneva Doud Eisenhower | Doud, John |
| 35. John F. Kennedy | Jacqueline Lee Bouvier Kennedy | Caroline, John |
| 36. Lyndon B. Johnson | Claudia (Lady Bird) Alta Taylor Johnson | Lynda, Luci |
| 37. Richard M. Nixon | Thelma Catherine (Pat) Ryan Nixon | Patricia, Julie |
| 38. Gerald R. Ford | Elizabeth Bloomer Warren Ford | Michael, Jack, Steven, Susan |
| 39. Jimmy Carter | Rosalynn Smith Carter | John, James, Donnel, Amy |
| 40. Ronald W. Reagan | Jane Wyman Reagan | Maureen, Michael |
| | Nancy Davis Reagan | Patricia, Ronald |
| 41. George H. W. Bush | Barbara Pierce Bush | George, Robin, John, Neil, Marvin, Dorothy |

FRANKLIN D.
ROOSEVELT

*Bachelor or widower presidents asked relatives (daughters, sisters, nieces) to serve as first ladies. Buchanan was a bachelor; Jefferson, Jackson, Van Buren, and Arthur were widowers.*

## KNIGHTS IN SHINING ARMOR

The knights of medieval times were warriors. Any man who trained to fight could become a knight.

*Page*

At age 7 a boy would leave his home to live with a knight and learn to use hand weapons.

*Squire*

At age 15, a page became a squire. He served a knight in his home, trained to fight on a horse, and rode to battle with the knight.

*Knight*

Knighthood was bestowed on a squire after about 5 years of service. Any knight could bestow knight-

hood. During the ceremony, the man who was doing the knighting was called the *parrain*. The tap and the words "I dub thee knight" were called the *accolade*.

## Knighthood Today
In Great Britain, the queen bestows knighthood on men and women who are accomplished or have served England in an outstanding way. Men are called "sir"; women are called "dame."

## ROYALTY
Kings and queens are not just characters in fairy tales. There are more than four dozen reigning monarchs in the world today. Spain, Morocco, Lesotho, Nepal, and the Netherlands are a few countries that still have royalty. These people of royal blood are the children of the children (and back and back) of former kings.

### British Royalty

*Kings and Queens*
They are the descendants of royal parents. A reigning king makes his wife a queen. A reigning queen makes her husband a prince.

*Princes and Princesses*
These titles are reserved for the children of kings and queens and for the grandchildren who are descended through the sons of kings or queens.

*Nobility*
These are the descendants of powerful and wealthy landowners who passed their titles on to their children and grandchildren. From top to bottom, here

*The children of nobility are called lords and ladies.*

is the order of British nobility as well as the terms of address. (Note that counts are European but not British.)

| RANK | TERM OF ADDRESS |
| --- | --- |
| KING | "YOUR MAJESTY" |
| QUEEN | "YOUR ROYAL HIGHNESS" |
| PRINCE | "YOUR ROYAL HIGHNESS" |
| DUKE AND DUCHESS | "YOUR GRACE" |
| MARQUESS | "MY LORD" |
| MARCHIONESS | "MADAM" |
| EARL | "MY LORD" |
| COUNTESS | "MADAM" |
| VISCOUNT | "MY LORD" |
| VISCOUNTESS | "MADAM" |
| BARON | "MY LORD" |
| BARONESS | "MADAM" |

## What Was So Great About Catherine the Great?

Catherine II, or Catherine the Great, was the empress of Russia from 1762 to 1796. During her reign, she built schools and hospitals, promoted the education of women, and allowed religious tolerance. She extended the borders of Russia by acquiring much of Poland. Many artists, teachers, and scientists moved to Russia because of the freedom of ideas she promoted.

## Who Was the Victoria of Victorian?

Queen Victoria ruled the British Empire for 64 years, longer than any other monarch. She became queen in 1837, when her uncle King William IV died without an heir. During her reign, the British colonial empire was the richest in the world, owning one-fourth of the world's land and ruling more than one-fourth of the world's people.

## The Six Wives of Henry VIII
Henry VIII was the 16th-century king of England who is remembered for his shocking treatment of his many wives. Here is what happened to his six wives:

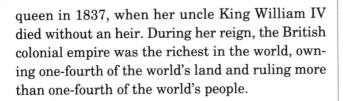

| | |
|---|---|
| *Catherine of Aragon* | Married 1509, annulled 1533; mother of Mary Tudor |
| *Ann Boleyn* | Married 1533, beheaded 1536; mother of Elizabeth I |
| *Jane Seymour* | Married 1536, died in childbirth 1537; mother of Edward VI |
| *Anne of Cleves* | Married and divorced 1540 |
| *Catherine Howard* | Married 1540, beheaded 1542 |
| *Catherine Parr* | Married 1543, survived him |

**HENRY VIII**

## More Royal Titles Around the World
*Czar / Czarina:* The ruler of Russia until 1917.

*Emir:* The native ruler in parts of Asia and Africa.

*Emperor / Empress:* The supreme head of an empire. The ancient Romans had emperors; the Japanese still do.

*Pharaoh:* A ruler of ancient Egypt.

*Rajah:* An Indian prince.

*Shah:* A sovereign of Iran.

*Sultan:* A head of a Muslim state.

*The sultan of Brunei rides in a golden chariot for important events.*

## WHAT DO THESE PEOPLE DO?

Geisha, gaffer, guru—what do they do? Do cow-punchers jab cows? Do stockbrokers break things? Here's what these people really do.

*Bellhop:* A hotel employee who escorts guests to their rooms, carries their luggage, and familiarizes them with their surroundings

*Best boy:* An assistant to a *gaffer* in TV and movie productions

*Cabin boy:* A boy who acts as a servant on a ship, especially to the captain

*Caddie:* A golf course worker who carries clubs and assists golfers

*Cowpuncher:* A ranch worker who tends cattle and horses

*Diva:* The principal female singer in an opera

*Engineer:* A person who uses the principles of math and science to plan structures such as bridges, engines, roads, and canals

*Extra:* A person with a nonspeaking part in a movie

*Gaffer:* An electrician in charge of lighting on a movie or TV set

*Geisha:* A Japanese woman who plays classical Japanese music and performs traditional dances at private parties in Japan

*Guru:* A Hindu religious teacher and spiritual guide

*Hermit:* A person who retires from society and lives alone, often for religious reasons

*Intellectual:* Someone who studies and thinks about ideas

*Intelligence agent:* Also called a spy

*Maître d':* The person who shows diners to their tables and supervises the waiters in a restaurant

*Medicine man:* A healer or sorcerer in a Native American tribe

*Page:* One who delivers messages and serves as a guide

*Patron:* A person who uses wealth and influence to help a person or a cause

*Pirate:* A person who robs ships on the high seas (outside territorial waters). Today's pirates use speedboats and carry guns.

*Spy:* One who collects and analyzes secret information about armies and battle plans

*Spycatcher:* One who tries to discover spies, also called a counterintelligence agent

*Stand-up comedian:* A person who tells jokes alone on a stage, usually in a nightclub

*Stockbroker:* A person who acts for others in buying and selling stocks or shares in a business

*Undercover agent:* Someone, usually a law enforcement agent, who pretends to be someone else in order to gain information

*Valet:* A personal servant who takes care of one's clothes, or a hotel employee who cares for clothes and does other personal services

*Mary Read and Anne Barney were female pirates in the early 1700s. Disguised as men, they served as pirates on the same ship.*

## WHO ARE THESE PEOPLE, ANYWAY?

People who have a common language, race, religion, or cultural background are considered to be an *ethnic group.*

### Aborigines
The native hunters and food gatherers of Australia are called aborigines, though the word refers to the first inhabitants of any region.

### Afrikaners
White people in South Africa who are descended from the Dutch and German settlers are Afrikaners. Many Afrikaners believe in apartheid, which is the separation of society by race.

### Aleut
These people live between Alaska and Siberia on the Aleutian Islands. They are fishermen and hunters related to the Eskimos.

### Amish
The Amish are groups of people in the rural U.S. They live simply, according to a strict religious code, without electricity or motors. They travel by horse and wagon.

### Arabs
Arabs originated in the Arabian Peninsula. Today, an Arab is anyone who speaks the Arabic language—some 150 million people in Africa and the Middle East.

### Basques
Basques live in the Pyrenees Mountains, between Spain and France. Their language is unrelated to any other in the world.

*Aborigines have lived in Australia for 40,000 years. Today most of them are of mixed descent. There are about 50,000 full-blooded aborigines left.*

### Bedouins
Bedouins are nomads; that is, they move from place to place as they herd sheep and cattle in the Arabian Desert.

### Cajun
Cajuns settled in Louisiana, far from their original home in Nova Scotia, Canada. Their music, dialect, and style of cooking remain distinctive.

### Celts
The Celts date from the Iron Age. Though today their descendants are spread throughout Ireland, Scotland, and Wales, their common Celtic language, such as Gaelic in Ireland, makes them an ethnic group.

### Creoles
Creoles include people born in the islands of the West Indies to European parents, people born in the U.S. Gulf states to French or Spanish parents, and people of mixed French or Spanish and African American descent.

### Gypsies
Originally from India, these nomadic people are found in various parts of Asia, Europe, and North America. They speak the language of Romany.

### Kurds
The Kurds have never had their own government. Their homeland, Kurdistan, extends through Iran, Syria, and Turkey. Kurds speak Kurdish and make their living by farming.

### Lapps
Lapps are nomadic people who used to follow the

reindeer herds of northern Scandinavia and are known for their colorful clothing. Their territory is called Sennoscundia.

*Mestizos*
Mestizos are Latin American people who are usually a mixture of European and Native American descent.

**Tribal People**
A tribe is a group of families with a common way of life. Despite the customs of the countries in which they live, tribes resist cultural change, preferring to keep their own traditions.

*Bushmen*
A primitive nomadic people who live on the edges of the Kalahari Desert in Namibia, Botswana, and South Africa, bushmen roam the desert in search of berries, roots, and animals. The average bushman is just over 4 feet tall.

*Inuits*
Eskimo is the European name for Inuits, who live

*Barbarians were known to the Romans as anyone living outside the Roman Empire, A.D. 400–1000.*

on the coasts in the northern parts of North America and Siberia. Their summer homes are tents; their winter homes are sod, wood, or stone huts. They rarely live in ice igloos. Eskimo-Aleut peoples, as they are also known, have their own language.

### Maoris

*Maoris greet each other by pressing their noses together.*

The first inhabitants of New Zealand, Maoris may have traveled there by canoe from Polynesia. They are tall, broad-faced, brown-eyed people who speak the Maori language.

### Masai

Masai are East African nomads who live by herding sheep and cattle. Teenage boys leave their families to train for war in a group; they may not marry until they have served as warriors. The tall and slender Masai live in mud houses.

### Pygmies

The Pygmy tribe of Zaire, Africa, is a peaceful, nomadic group that hunts and gathers its food. Pygmies' skin is a light yellow-brown. Adult male Pygmies are less than 5 feet tall. Pygmy tribes also live in the rain forests of India and the Philippines.

### Watusis

People who raise cattle in Burundi, Africa. They are among the tallest people in the world. Many of the adult males are more than 7 feet tall.

## VOPS (VERY OLD PEOPLE)

You can't get much older than 6 million years. That is when the first human beings, known as *Hominidae*, evolved. They were not like apes; they had bigger brains, different teeth, and walked upright. Would you like an introduction to some of your ancestors?

*Australopithecus,* also called "southern ape," lived in Africa in 3 million B.C. Some were the size of modern people; others were as small as chimpanzees. Their heads were apelike with low foreheads, flat noses, and jutting jaws. "Lucy" was a complete australopithecus found in Ethiopia in 1974. (She was named for the Beatles' song "Lucy in the Sky with Diamonds," which was playing in the camp when she was excavated.) Lucy was 20 years old when she died.

*Homo habilis,* or "Handyman," lived 2 million years ago and used tools. Their brain was half the size of the human brain today. Their heads were rounder and faces smaller than those of australopithecus. *Homo habilis* was the first to build huts

for shelter. "Piltdown Man" was long accepted as a skeleton of *Homo habilis*. In 1953 he was shown to be a hoax made from a human skull, ape's jaw, and the bones of extinct animals.

*Homo erectus,* the "stand-up people," lived 1 million years ago and were the first people to use fire. Their skulls were thick, their faces flat, and they had a sloping forehead with no chin. They lived in China, Japan, Africa, Europe, and Southeast Asia.

*Neanderthals* lived in Europe about 150,000 years ago and were the first to wear clothes. They looked much like modern people except that their skulls bulged more at the back and they had receding chins, larger cheeks, and more pronounced eyebrow ridges. They were also smaller and stockier and had heavier features. They cared for their sick and buried their dead. Less than half their infants reached the age of 20.

*Homo sapiens* means "wise humans." We are *Homo sapiens* and first lived on earth about 100,000 years ago. By 33,000 B.C. we were the dominant species, living everywhere but in North and South America. We look different from our ancestors because of our smaller teeth, flat foreheads, straight faces, and rounded heads. We were the first of the earth's inhabitants to communicate through art, the spoken word, and religion.

Cro-Magnon people were named after the Cro-Magnon caves near Dordogne, France, where their remains were discovered. They were early *Homo sapiens,* quite tall and erect.

# DIFFERENT GROUPS OF PEOPLE

*Army:* A collection of men and women trained to fight in battle

*Cabal:* A small group involved in secret schemes

*Caravan:* A number of people traveling together, usually in a long line

*Cast:* A group acting in a play or movie

*Choir:* A group of singers who perform together

*Class:* A group of students at the same grade level: a third-grade class

*Crowd:* A large group of people in one place

*Folk:* A people, a tribe, an ethnic group, or a nation

*Gang:* A group of people who band together

*Guild:* An association of persons of the same trade who all have the same job interests

*Huddle:* In football, players gathered briefly in a circle to plan the next play

*Mob:* An excited or angry massing of people

*Orchestra:* A group of musicians who play together, using a variety of instruments that include strings, brass, woodwind, and percussion

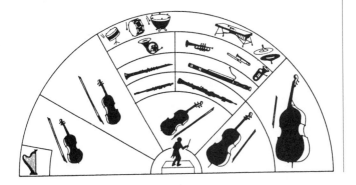

*Procession:* A group of people moving in an orderly manner

*Retinue:* A body of followers or servants of an important person; e.g., bodyguards, secretaries, or trainers

*Staff:* A group of people who work together

*Team:* A group of people who work or play together

*Throng:* A large number of people

*Troop:* A group of military people or scouts

*Troupe:* A group of actors, dancers, or acrobats who travel and perform together

# Sports Section

*Games for All Seasons*

PEOPLE HAVE ENJOYED SPORTS throughout history. For the an-  cient Greeks, though, sport was not very different from war. In fact, sports such as archery, darts, and target shooting developed from warfare or preparation for war. Today, sports are a part of our daily lives. Is your sport here?

## WHICH SPORT IS IT?

Is it baseball or softball? You've got a bat, a ball, and you're hoping for a home run, but which sport is it? So far you don't know because these sports are similar but they're not the same. A number of sports look alike. How many of them can you tell apart?

### Baseball and Softball

*Similarities*

These popular sports both use a ball, bat, and three bases on a diamond-shaped field. The object is to hit the ball and score a run. The team with the most runs wins.

*Differences*

| BASEBALL | SOFTBALL |
|---|---|
| 1. Small, hard ball | 1. Large, soft ball |
| 2. 90-foot basepath | 2. 60-foot basepath |
| 3. 9 players per team | 3. 10 players per team (slow pitch) |
| 4. Overhand pitch | 4. Underhand pitch |

### Bobsledding and Tobogganing

*Similarities*

Both are snow sports using sleds.

*Differences*

| BOBSLEDDING | TOBOGGANING |
|---|---|
| 1. Team with fastest time wins | 1. Not competitive |
| 2. Sled mounted on runners to gain speed | 2. Long, flat sled curved in front |
| 3. 2–4 men race | 3. 2–4 people coast down a hill |

# Calisthenics and Gymnastics

*Similarities*

Both require an agile, flexible body.

*Differences*

| CALISTHENICS | GYMNASTICS |
|---|---|
| Exercises to promote physical fitness such as: pull-ups, jumping jacks, sit-ups | Artistic gymnastics: vault, symmetric bars, balance beams, floor exercises, rings, high bar |

# Field Hockey and Ice Hockey

*Similarities*

Both are team sports played with a stick. To score, an object must be hit into the opposing goal.

*Differences*

| FIELD HOCKEY | ICE HOCKEY |
|---|---|
| 1. Played on a large, rectangular field | 1. Played on ice |
| 2. 11 players per team | 2. 6 players per team |
| 3. Players wear cleats | 3. Players wear ice skates |
| 4. Stick with curved end used to hit ball | 4. Long-bladed stick used to hit rubber puck |

## Horseshoes and Quoits

*Similarities*

The object of both games is to encircle a short metal pole in the ground called a stake—or get closer than your opponent.

*Differences*

| HORSESHOES | QUOITS |
| --- | --- |
| 1. 2–4 players | 1. Any number can play |
| 2. 2 horseshoes | 2. 1 iron, rubber, or heavy rope ring |

## Motocross and Cyclocross

*Similarities*

Both sports require a bike and race to the finish.

*Differences*

| MOTOCROSS | CYCLOCROSS |
| --- | --- |
| 1. BMX track: smooth, sandy soil | 1. Race course ⅓ road, ⅔ plowed land, woods, streams |
| 2. Racers jump over mounds | 2. Racers ride or carry their bikes |

## Paddleball and Racquetball

*Similarities*

These sports take place on a court with up to four walls for play. To win points, the opposing player must fail to return the ball to the front wall before its second bounce.

*Differences*

| PADDLEBALL | RACQUETBALL |
|---|---|
| Uses a perforated paddle with a short handle | Uses a strung racquet with a short handle |

*People often think table tennis and Ping-Pong are different sports, but they are the same. Ping-Pong is the company's trademark for table tennis (as Kleenex is for tissues).*

## Pool and Billiards

*Similarities*

Both games are played on a green felt table with a long stick or cue.

*Differences*

| POOL | BILLIARDS |
|---|---|
| 1. 2–4 players | 1. 2 players |
| 2. 1 white (cue) ball, 15 colored and numbered balls | 2. 1 white (cue) ball, 2 red balls |
| 3. Cue ball knocks colored balls into 6 holes, or pockets, on side and in corners | 3. Ball must hit bank to win |
| 4. Points scored when all balls in pockets | 4. 21 points win |

## Skiing, Nordic and Alpine

*Similarities*

Both require skis, poles, and snow.

*Differences*

| NORDIC CROSS-COUNTRY | ALPINE DOWNHILL SKIING |
|---|---|
| 1. Relatively flat surface: fields or trails in woods | 1. Steep mountain or hill slope |
| 2. Quick strides | 2. Fast descent from top to bottom |

*Snowboarding, part surfing and part skiing, is a fairly new winter sport. It requires a board, bindings, and boots.*

## Skittles and Tenpin Bowling

*Similarities*

A ball is rolled down an alley, trying to knock down pins.

*Differences*

| SKITTLES | TENPIN BOWLING |
|---|---|
| 1. Even number of players, 2–24 | 1. 1–5 players; 5 on a team |
| 2. Ball or thick, flat disk | 2. Ball |
| 3. 9 pins | 3. 10 pins |

# CALLING ALL ATHLETES

Do you have a nickname? How did you get it? Many athletes' nicknames have nothing to do with their sports. Here are some famous nicknames and their origins.

*Nicolai "Old One Leg" Andrianov*
This Russian gymnast could keep his legs straight and together during extremely difficult exercises, making it look as if he had only one leg.

*Steve "The Kid" Cauthen*
As a 17-year-old, Steve was already a successful jockey.

*"Joltin'" Joe DiMaggio*
Joe received this name because he hit the baseball very hard.

*Bernie "Boom-Boom" Geoffrion*
Bernie invented the slapshot in ice hockey. The stick hits the puck so hard, it makes a *boom* sound.

*Maureen "Goldfinger" Flowers*
Maureen was an excellent dart thrower. At one time, she was the best in the world.

*Julius "Dr. J" Irving*
When Julius Irving was in high school, a teammate began calling him "the doctor" as a joke. The name remained with him throughout his professional basketball career.

*Thomas "Pepper" Johnson*
This New York Giants football player received his nickname from his grandmother. He loved pepper so much, he put it on everything he ate.

### Florence "Flo Jo" Joyner

This Olympic track star's catchy nickname comes from the first letters of her first and last names.

### Sonny "The Drummer Boy" Liston

As a boxer, Sonny gave his opponents a bongo beating in the ring.

### Willie "The Say Hey Kid" Mays

Willie Mays was one of the most famous baseball players of all time. As a rookie, he would often shout "Say hey over there" to people whose names he did not know.

### Bill "The Owl Without a Vowel" Mlkvy

Bill played forward for the Temple University Owls basketball team. Since his last name does not contain a vowel, he became "the owl without a vowel."

### Helen Wills "Little Miss Poker Face" Moody

When playing the card game of poker, players cannot show any emotion so that their opponents can't guess what they're thinking. On the tennis court in the 1920s, Helen Wills Moody maintained her poise under any circumstances.

### Jack "The Golden Bear" Nicklaus

Jack has blond hair and a large, powerful body. He is considered one of the best golf players of all time.

### Leroy "Satchel" Paige

His feet looked about the size of a small suitcase, or satchel, which is where this baseball player got his nickname.

*William "The Refrigerator" Perry*
This football player astonished his teammates on the Chicago Bears with the amounts he could eat. He weighs a hefty 330 pounds.

*George Herman "Babe" Ruth*
The New York Yankees' Babe Ruth is one of baseball's all-time legends. As a young boy, he wanted to play baseball with the older neighborhood children. When they wouldn't let him, he'd cry—and was called a baby.

*Tom "Terrific" Seaver*
The media gave this New York Mets baseball player his nickname because of his terrific pitching arm. *Tom Terrific* used to be a children's cartoon show.

*O. J. "The Juice" Simpson*
Orenthal James is this football player's given name. His teammates originally believed that his initials stood for "orange juice."

*Ted "The Splendid Splinter" Williams*
Tall and thin like a splinter, with a splendid swing, Williams came to be known as "The Splendid Splinter."

*Willie "Mookie" Wilson*
His family gave this baseball player his name because of the funny way he said "milk" when he was a child.

*Mildred "Babe" Didrickson Zaharias*
An outstanding golfer and tennis player, Babe was often compared to baseball's Babe Ruth.

## SUPERSTITIONS

We all hear popular superstitions when Friday the 13th appears on the calendar. And no player wants to wear the number 13. Is it a belief in sports lore that affected them? It is said that superstitions have been a part of sports since their beginning. Players and fans alike have their ways of avoiding bad luck. Here are some of them.

*Baseball*
- Spitting into your hand before picking up the bat is said to bring good luck.
- A wad of gum stuck on a player's hat brings good luck.
- It is bad luck if a dog walks across the diamond before the first pitch.
- Some players believe it is good luck to step on one of the bases before running off the field at the end of an inning.
- Lending a bat to a fellow player is a serious jinx.

*Basketball*
- The last person to shoot a basket during the warm-up will have a good game.
- Wipe the soles of your sneakers for good luck.
- Bounce the ball before taking a foul shot for good luck.

*Bowling*
- To continue a winning streak, wear the same clothes.
- The number 300, a perfect score, on your license plate will increase your score.
- Carry charms on your bowling bag, in your pockets, or around your neck for good luck.

### Fishing

- Fish may not bite if a barefoot woman passes you on the way to the dock.
- Spit on your bait before casting your rod to make fish bite.
- Throw back your first catch for good luck.
- It is bad luck to change rods while fishing.
- Don't tell anyone how many fish you've caught until you're done or you won't catch another.

### Football

- Double numbers on a player's uniform brings good luck.
- It's bad luck for a professional football player to take a new number when he is traded to another team.
- A mascot is an important good luck symbol.

### Golf

- Start only with odd-numbered clubs.
- Balls with a number higher than 4 are bad luck.
- Carry coins in your pockets for good luck.

### Ice Hockey

- It is bad luck for hockey sticks to lie crossed.
- It is bad luck to say "shutout" in the locker room before a game.
- Players believe they'll win the game if they tap the goalie on his shin pads before a game.

### Tennis

- It's bad luck to hold more than two balls at a time when serving.
- Avoid wearing the color yellow.
- Walk around the outside of the court when switching sides for good luck.

## THE MARTIAL ARTS:
## A BELT FROM THE EAST

The martial arts have a long history. "Martial" comes from Mars, the Roman god of war, and the planet Mars received its name because of its red color, which was thought to resemble the heat and fire of battle. The martial arts were once used only for self-defense and were not even known in the U.S. when

### Where Are They From?

| CHINA | JAPAN | KOREA |
|-------|-------|-------|
| Kung fu | Karate | Tae kwon do |
| Northern and southern Shaolin boxing | Judo | T'ang su do |
| | Aikido | Hwarang do |
| | Kendo | |
| | Jiu jitsu | |
| Tai chi | Ninjutsu | |

your grandparents were children. It wasn't until 1964 that judo was accepted as an Olympic sport. Today we know karate, aikido, kung fu, and many others as rigorous sports that demand great skill and many years of training. Here are some of the most popular martial arts in the U.S.

### Aikido

Aikido, "the way of all harmony," is a purely defensive art. The defender, or *tori,* attempts to divert harm from him- or herself without causing injury to his or her opponent, or *uke.* Working at arm's length, using a series of arm and wrist holds and getting momentum from the hips and legs, the *tori* attempts to throw the *uke* to the ground. The *tori* must try to "blend" with the *uke* to redirect momentum, much like taking control of a runaway vehicle. To do this, the *tori* steers away oncoming strikes from his opponent. Aikido unites the mind, the body, and a source of energy from the mind called *ki* to accomplish its aim.

## Jiu Jitsu
Jiu jitsu is the Japanese samurai's unarmed system of fighting. It's practiced by the military as a means of self-defense. A combination of strength, balance, leverage, timing, and speed are used to defeat one's opponent. By using one's power or leverage on an elbow or wrist joint, the opponent can be held in a painful position and may give up.

## Judo
Judo, "the gentle way," was the first martial art accepted at the Olympic games. In this sport, the object is to throw and pin one's opponent. Using a series of throws and choke holds, the *judokas,* or judo players, try to get each other down on the mat.

One player must hold the other on the mat for 30 seconds to be declared the winner.

### Karate

*In karate contests, opponents are not allowed to actually strike each other. They must stop just short of making contact.*

Karate, "empty hands," is Japan's most popular martial art. Intense concentration is used to focus as much strength as possible on the object of impact. The feet, legs, elbows, head, and fists are used for kicking, punching, defensive blocking, and other techniques. Two types of contest are popular in sport karate. In *kata,* judges award points for techniques and timing. *Kumite* are sporting contests in which judges award points for well-timed attacking blows.

### Kung Fu

Kung fu is the name given by Westerners to a range of Chinese fighting styles. The object of kung fu is to halt one's opponent using a variety of moves. Originally, there were five styles, which were based on animal movements. Now there are hundreds of different styles. The five most popular styles are tiger, crane, leopard, snake, and dragon, which, combined, are called "the five animals fist."

### Ninjutsu

Ninjutsu, the Japanese art of the Ninja, was an art of stealth, meaning secret procedures. Ninjas had to be able to sneak around, as many of them were involved in espionage, or spying. Their training included instruction in unarmed combat, the use of traditional and specialized weapons, climbing devices, signals, codes, and disguises. Ninjas were ruthless fighters and would do anything to reach their goals. This art was banned in Japan in the

17th century, but it has gained popularity in the U.S. in the late 20th century. At the present time, there are only a few trained instructors in the U.S., and all are part of a Ninja family.

## Belt Ranking System

Students of both karate and judo have the honor of wearing colored belts to indicate their ability. As they pass increasingly difficult tests, they are promoted to the next *kyu,* or grade.

| LEVEL | KARATE | JUDO |
|---|---|---|
| NOVICE (BEGINNER) | RED | WHITE |
| 9TH KYU | —— | YELLOW |
| 8TH KYU | WHITE | ORANGE |
| 7TH KYU | YELLOW | ORANGE |
| 6TH KYU | ORANGE | GREEN |
| 5TH KYU | GREEN | GREEN |
| 4TH KYU | PURPLE | BLUE |
| 3RD KYU | BROWN | BLUE |
| 2ND KYU | BROWN | BROWN |
| 1ST KYU | BROWN | BROWN |

*Dan, or advanced grades, receive black belts, which are ranked from 1st to 10th dan. Some display their level by wearing one or more red tabs on their belt. For example, the 2nd level gets two red tabs.*

## OFF THE BEATEN SPORTS TRACK

Everyone has heard of basketball, baseball, and tennis, but what about snow-snake or kite-fighting? These are two of the many exotic sports that are played around the world. Try one!

### Foot Tennis

In Malaysia, this game is often played between two teams of two players each. A net is stretched at no particular height across the middle of a playing area, and a wicker ball about the size of a soccer ball is used. Players try to pass the ball back and forth over the net using only their feet, knees, and thighs. Each time the ball drops, the other team gets a point.

*Kite-Fighting*

Kite-fighting is a highly competitive sport played in India, Thailand, and South America. Each player hopes to get his or her kite to fly highest. The players try to cut their opponents' kite strings with sharp objects imbedded in their kites. The kite that flies highest and longest wins.

*Octopush*

This underwater hockey game was first played in South Africa in the 1960s. The players wear skin-diving equipment, such as masks, flippers, and snorkels, in a swimming pool. With miniature hockey sticks and an ice hockey puck, the players follow all the rules of ice hockey—on the floor of the pool.

*Snow-Snake*

This age-old Native American sport is still played today. The "snake" is a polished wooden rod whose front end is shaped like a snake's head. It slides at speeds of up to 100 mph down a long, curved trail in the snow. Each team gets four chances to throw the snake. The team whose snake goes the farthest wins.

## ANIMAL ATHLETES

Some sports depend on animals more than on people.

*Pigeon Racing*

This was once a popular sport in the U.S. Homing

pigeons were transported to a designated place, then released to fly home. Several pigeons would compete at a time, and the first pigeon to reach home won.

*Sled Dog Racing*

This sport is very popular in Alaska. Each dog team harnessed to a sled is controlled by a driver, called a musher. The teams are timed from start to finish, and the fastest team wins. The most famous annual sled dog race is the 1,200-mile Iditarod, from Anchorage to Nome.

*Polo*

Polo is played on horseback by two teams of four players each. The players carry long-handled clubs, called mallets, and try to knock a wooden ball on the ground through their opponents' goal posts. The mallet must be held in the right hand, forcing a player to control the horse with the left. The match is divided into chukkars, periods of play. The team with the most goals at the end wins.

*The first organized sport in the U.S. was horse racing. The first official race took place in 1665 on Long Island, New York. It was hoped that this sport would produce a better breed of horses in the colonies.*

# SPORTING NUMBERS

The score isn't the only number in a sport—any statistics or trivia fan will tell you that! Here are a few sporting numbers to crunch.

## Official Numbers of Players on a Team

| SPORT | NUMBER |
|---|---|
| BASEBALL | 9 |
| BASKETBALL | 5 |
| FIELD HOCKEY | 11 |
| FOOTBALL (AMERICAN) | 11 |
| FOOTBALL (AUSTRALIAN) | 18 |
| ICE HOCKEY | 6 |
| LACROSSE (MEN'S) | 10 |
| LACROSSE (WOMEN'S) | 12 |
| POLO | 4 |
| RUGBY UNION | 15 |
| SOCCER | 11 |
| SOFTBALL (FAST PITCH) | 9 |
| SOFTBALL (SLOW PITCH) | 10 |
| ULTIMATE FRISBEE | 7 |
| VOLLEYBALL | 6 |

*Three sports were invented in the U.S.: basketball (1891), volleyball (1895), and baseball (1839).*

## The Most Popular U.S. Spectator Sports

1. Professional football
2. Baseball
3. College football
4. Bowling
5. Professional basketball
6. Professional boxing

## The Least Popular U.S. Spectator Sports

1. Professional wrestling
2. LPGA golf
3. PGA senior golf
4. Professional boxing
5. College wrestling
6. PGA golf

## #1 Sport Worldwide

Soccer is the world's most popular sport. It is played by more than 20 million people in more than 140 countries.

| COUNTRY | MOST POPULAR SPORT |
| --- | --- |
| CANADA | ICE HOCKEY |
| GERMANY | SOCCER |
| JAPAN | BASEBALL |
| THE NETHERLANDS | ICE SKATING |
| NORWAY | SKIING |
| PHILIPPINES | BASKETBALL |
| SCOTLAND | GOLF |
| THAILAND | KITE FLYING |
| U.S. | BASEBALL |

## College Code for Football Numbers

| 80–89 | 70–79 | 60–69 | 50–59 | 60–69 | 70–79 | 80–89 |
| --- | --- | --- | --- | --- | --- | --- |
| LEFT ● | ● | ● | ● | ● | ● | ● RIGHT |
| END | TACKLE | GUARD | CENTER | GUARD | TACKLE | END |

●

QUARTERBACK

| ● | | ● |
| --- | --- | --- |
| HALFBACK | BACKS 1–49 | HALFBACK |

●

FULLBACK

## Back Numbers
Famous players and their numbers.

*The first baseball team to wear numbers was the New York Yankees, in 1929. The numbers represented their batting order.*

| PLAYER | NUMBER | SPORT | TEAM |
|---|---|---|---|
| Hank Aaron | 44 | Baseball | Atlanta Braves |
| Edson "Pelé" Arantes | 10 | Soccer | New York Cosmos do Nascimento |
| Yogi Berra | 8 | Baseball | New York Yankees |
| Larry Bird | 33 | Basketball | Boston Celtics |
| Jim Brown | 32 | Football | Cleveland Browns |
| Wilt Chamberlain | 13 | Basketball | Los Angeles Lakers |
| Roberto Clemente | 21 | Baseball | Pittsburgh Pirates |
| Joe DiMaggio | 5 | Baseball | New York Yankees |
| Phil Esposito | 77 | Ice hockey | New York Rangers |
| Wayne Gretzky | 99 | Ice hockey | Los Angeles Kings |
| Gordie Howe | 9 | Ice hockey | Detroit Red Wings |
| Julius "Dr. J" Irving | 6 | Basketball | Philadelphia '76ers |
| Michael Jordan | 23 | Basketball | Chicago Bulls |
| Mario Lemieux | 66 | Ice hockey | Pittsburgh Penguins |
| Mickey Mantle | 7 | Baseball | New York Yankees |
| Pete Maravich | 44 | Basketball | Atlanta Hawks |
| Billy Martin | 1 | Baseball | New York Yankees |
| Willie Mays | 24 | Baseball | San Francisco Giants |
| Joe Montana | 16 | Football | San Francisco '49ers |
| Thurman Munson | 15 | Baseball | New York Yankees |
| Stan Musial | 6 | Baseball | St. Louis Cardinals |
| Joe Namath | 12 | Football | New York Jets |
| Bobby Orr | 4 | Ice hockey | Boston Bruins |
| Jackie Robinson | 42 | Baseball | Brooklyn Dodgers |
| Bill Russell | 6 | Basketball | Boston Celtics |
| Herman "Babe" Ruth | 3 | Baseball | New York Yankees |
| Tom Seaver | 41 | Baseball | New York Mets |
| Casey Stengel | 37 | Baseball | New York Yankees |
| Ted Williams | 9 | Baseball | Boston Red Sox |

# Record-Breaking Numbers

**4** Susan Butcher, from Alaska, won the Iditarod 4 times. The Iditarod is a 1,200-mile dog sled race over ice and snow from Anchorage to Nome, Alaska.

**4** Roger Bannister ran a 3:59:4-minute mile, the first under 4 minutes, in England, on May 6, 1954.

**6** Jack Nicklaus, from Ohio, was the first golfer to win the Masters Tournament 6 times.

**7** Mark Spitz won 7 gold medals in swimming for the U.S. in the 1972 Olympics, the most ever won by a single competitor in one Olympic competition.

**8** Helen Wills Moody of the U.S. was the first to win the women's singles tennis title at Wimbledon 8 times. Martina Navratilova tied this record in 1987.

**10** Nadia Comaneci of Romania was the first gymnast to score a perfect 10 in Olympic competition, in 1976, at the age of 15. She had a perfect score 7 times.

**15** Larisa Latynina from the USSR is the only gymnast to win 15 world gold medals: 10 individual and 5 team.

**24** John Riggins, a running back for the Washington Redskins, holds the record for the most touchdowns in a season: 24 in 1983.

**56** Joe DiMaggio, of the New York Yankees, had at least one hit in 56 consecutive games in 1941.

**61** Roger Maris hit 61 home runs for the New York Yankees in 1961, breaking Babe Ruth's 1927 record of 60.

*In hockey, the number 1 has been given to the goalie since the 1930s.*

**92** Wayne Gretzky, then of the Edmonton Oilers, scored 92 goals during the 1981–82 hockey season.

**755** Hank Aaron, of the Atlanta Braves, hit 755 home runs during his baseball career.

**1,000** Jan Suffolk Todd of the U.S. was the first woman to lift 1,000 pounds in 3 power lifts. She is considered the world's strongest woman.

### SO YOU WANNA BE A PRO . . .

OK, you're the best athlete your school has ever seen, and you want to get right out there and play for the pros. But wait a minute! Look at what else you have to do before you sign up for the big time . . .

*Baseball:* Must be a high school graduate.

*Basketball:* Must be a high school graduate who either gives up college eligibility by written notice to the NBA at least 45 days before the draft or plays college basketball and is drafted from there.

*Football:* Must be a high school graduate who either plays for 4 years of college or waits 4 years after high school.

*Golf:* No age limit. Player must have a 2 handicap or better.

*Ice hockey:* Must have played high school hockey for 3 years or college hockey for 1 year. Must be 18 years old by September 15 of year drafted.

*Tennis:* No age limit. A player must state an intent to play as a professional on the official entry form or in writing before the first match of a tournament.

# Universal Knowledge

*From Galaxy to Galaxy*

THE PLANETS! THE STARS! THE

 moons! The distances! The temperatures! And the scientists, explorers, technology, equipment, astronauts, and folklore that all help make up our understanding of the universe we live in.

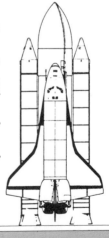

# THE UNIVERSE . . . IT'S MIND-BOGGLING!

We're getting so used to hearing gigantic numbers that a million begins to seem like no big deal. But try counting to a million sometime, and you'll realize how much it takes to make only one! When it comes to our universe, the numbers involved are truly phenomenal. Get your mind around these facts.

- The universe is all light, matter, and energy that exist in time and space.
- The sun is only one of the more than 200 billion stars in our galaxy, the Milky Way.
- The sun is 30,000 light-years from the center of our galaxy.
- The sun is 93 million miles from Earth, yet it is 270,000 times closer than the next nearest star.
- The Milky Way is one of billions of galaxies in the universe. There are as many galaxies as there are stars in the Milky Way.
- The two nearest galaxies are Andromeda and the Magellanic Clouds.
- Galaxies are grouped in clusters.
- Some clusters are grouped in superclusters.

Globular clusters *are stars grouped together in the shape of a ball.*

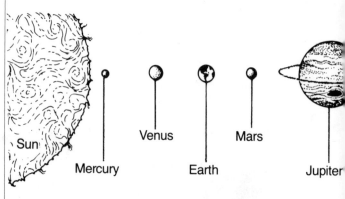

Sun

Mercury

Venus

Earth

Mars

Jupiter

## FROM ANOTHER PLANET

There are eight planets in our solar system besides Earth. So far, no life as we know it exists on any of these planets. Let's see why.

### Mercury

Mercury is a dead, nearly airless planet. The planet closest to the sun, this rocky sphere was named for the Roman god Mercury, a swift messenger. In fact, the planet Mercury travels around the sun faster than any other planet.

| | |
|---|---|
| *Size:* | A third the size of Earth |
| *Surface:* | Covered by a dusty layer of minerals (silicates), the surface is made up of plains, cliffs, and craters |
| *Atmosphere:* | A thin mixture of helium, hydrogen, and neon |
| *Temperature:* | −279°–801°F (−173°–427°C) |
| *Day:* | 176 days on Earth |
| *Year:* | 88 days on Earth |
| *Your weight:* | If you weigh 100 pounds on Earth, you would weigh 38 pounds on Mercury. |
| *Distance from Earth:* | 57 million miles, at the closest point in its orbit |

*What do Mercury, Venus, Earth, and Mars have in common? They are all solid spheres. All were alive, in times past, with volcanoes and earthquakes.*

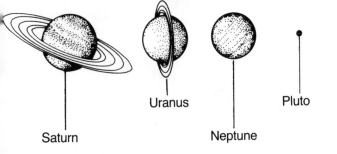

Saturn

Uranus

Neptune

Pluto

## Venus

Venus is often called Earth's twin because the two planets are close in size, but that's the only similarity. The dense atmosphere that covers Venus creates a greenhouse effect that keeps it sizzling at 864°F. Venus, named after the Roman goddess of love and beauty, is also known as the "morning star" and "evening star" since it is visible at these times to the unaided eye.

*Size:* About 650 miles smaller in diameter than Earth

*Surface:* A rocky, dusty, waterless expanse of mountains, canyons, and plains, with a 200-mile river of hardened lava

*Atmosphere:* Carbon dioxide, nitrogen, and sulfuric acid

*Temperature:* 864°F at the surface

*Day:* 243 days on Earth

*Year:* 225 days on Earth

*Your weight:* If you weigh 100 pounds on Earth, you would weigh 88 pounds on Venus.

*Distance from Earth:* At its closest, Venus is 25,700,000 miles away.

## Mars

Because of its blood-red color (which comes from iron-rich dust), this planet was named for Mars, the Roman god of war. Mars is the fourth planet from the sun, making it farther than Earth from the sun.

*Size:* About half the size of Earth

*Surface:* Canyons, dunes, volcanoes, and polar caps of water ice and carbon dioxide ice

*Atmosphere:* 97% carbon dioxide

*Temperature:* −225°– 163°F (−143°– 17°C)

*Day:* 24 hours and 37 minutes on Earth

*Year:* 687 days on Earth

*Your weight:* If you weigh 100 pounds on Earth, you would weigh 38 pounds on Mars.

*Distance from Earth:* 34,600,000 miles at the closest point in its orbit

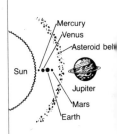

## Jupiter

Jupiter, the largest planet, was named for the most important Roman god because of its size. About 1,300 Earths would fit into it.

*Size:* 11 times the diameter of Earth

*Surface:* A hot ball of gas and liquid

*Atmosphere:* Whirling clouds of colored dust, hydrogen, helium, methane, and ammonia. The Great Red Spot is an intense windstorm 3 times larger than Earth.

*Temperature:* −234°F (−148°C) average

*Day:* 9 hours and 55 minutes on Earth

*Year:* 12 years on Earth

*Your weight:* If you weigh 100 pounds on Earth, you would weigh 265 pounds on Jupiter.

*Distance from Earth:* At its closest, 391 million miles

*A belt of asteroids (fragments of rock and iron) between Mars and Jupiter separate the four inner planets from the five outer planets.*

## Saturn

Saturn, the second-largest planet, has majestic rings surrounding it. Named for the Roman god of farming, Saturn was the farthest planet known by the ancients.

*Saturn's seven rings are flat and lie inside one another. They are made of billions of ice particles.*

| | |
|---|---|
| *Size:* About 10 times larger than Earth | |
| *Surface:* Liquid and gas | |
| *Atmosphere:* Hydrogen and helium | |
| *Temperature:* −288°F (−178°C) | |
| *Day:* 10 hours, 39 minutes on Earth | |
| *Year:* 29½ years on Earth | |
| *Your weight:* If you weigh 100 pounds on Earth, you would weigh 107 pounds on Saturn. | |
| *Distance from Earth:* 762,700,000 miles at the closest point | |

## Uranus

Uranus is a greenish-blue planet, rotating on its axis at 98° (most planets are at a 90° angle). Uranus was discovered in 1781 and named after an ancient Roman sky god.

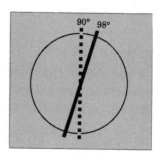

| | |
|---|---|
| *Size:* 4 times larger than Earth | |
| *Surface:* Little is known | |
| *Atmosphere:* Hydrogen, helium, and methane | |
| *Temperature:* Estimated −357°F (−216°C) | |
| *Day:* 17 hours on Earth | |
| *Year:* 30,685 days or 84 years on Earth | |
| *Your weight:* Not known | |
| *Distance from Earth:* At the closest point, 1,607,000 miles | |

## Neptune

Neptune, named for an ancient Roman sea god, is a stormy blue planet about 30 times farther from the sun than Earth. Neptune was "discovered" by mathematical calculation before 1846, when it was seen through a telescope.

| | |
|---|---|
| *Size:* | About 4 times the size of Earth |
| *Surface:* | A liquid layer covered with thick clouds |
| *Atmosphere:* | Hydrogen, helium, methane, and ammonia |
| *Temperature:* | $-353°F$ ($-214°C$) |
| *Day:* | 16 hours and 7 minutes on Earth |
| *Year:* | 165 years on Earth |
| *Your weight:* | Not known |
| *Distance from Earth:* | 2,680,000,000 miles at closest point |

## Pluto

Pluto, named after the Roman and Greek god of the underworld, is the coldest, smallest, and outermost planet in our solar system. Pluto and its moon, Charon, are called a double planet. Pluto was predicted to exist in 1905 and discovered in 1930.

| | |
|---|---|
| *Size:* | Less than one-fifth the size of Earth |
| *Surface:* | A giant snowball of methane and water mixed with rock |
| *Atmosphere:* | Methane |
| *Temperature:* | $-369°-387°F$ ($-223°-233°C$) |
| *Day:* | 6 days on Earth |
| *Year:* | 248 years on Earth |
| *Your weight:* | Not known |
| *Distance from Earth:* | At the closest point, 2.67 billion miles |

*During each revolution around the sun, Pluto passes inside Neptune's orbit for 20 years, making Neptune the outermost planet for that time. Pluto passed inside Neptune's orbit in 1979 and will stay there until 1999.*

## COLORS OF THE UNIVERSE
It's not all black and white.

*Blue Planets*
Earth, Neptune, and Uranus are all blue because of gases in their atmosphere.

*Blue Stars*
These are the hottest stars, with a surface temperature of more than 37,000°F.

### Stars Grouped by Size

 *Supergiants* may be 330 times the diameter of the sun.

 *Giants* have diameters 10 to 100 times as large as the sun.

 *Medium-size* or *dwarf* stars are about as large as the sun.

 *White dwarfs* are small stars (smaller than the distance across Asia).

 *Neutron stars* are the tiniest (some are only 12 miles in diameter).

*Yellow Stars*
These are warm stars, such as the sun. Their temperature is about 10,000°F.

*Red Stars*
The coolest stars are red. Their surface temperature is less than 5,500°F.

*Red Shift*
When light coming from a distant star is seen through a spectroscope (an instrument that separates light into its different colors), the light we receive continues to shift toward the red area of the spectrum, which is the least powerful. This means that, since the light is becoming weaker and weaker, the stars must be traveling away from us. This makes scientists believe that our universe is expanding.

*Red Spot*
A swirling cloud on the planet Jupiter is a whirlpool of gases, mainly red phosphorus.

## Black Holes

When a massive star burns out, it collapses on itself. The resulting densely compacted mass is known as a black hole because no light can escape its intense gravitational field.

## White Dwarfs

These are extremely dense objects in the universe that radiate energy and matter.

*In Africa, some people believe that the stars are hanging candles or small doorways into the sky.*

Quasars *are extremely bright, shining objects at the center of some distant galaxies. Most quasars are the size of the solar system yet can be a trillion times brighter than the sun.*

Nebulae *are huge clouds of dust and gas where stars may have been born. Some nebulae are the remains of stars that have exploded. The California Nebula is named for its shape, which resembles that of the state of California.*

*In the Southern Hemisphere, the moon appears upside down from the way people see it in the Northern Hemisphere. There people see "the man in the moon." In the Southern Hemisphere people see an old woman with a bundle of twigs.*

## MANY MOONS

Earth's moon is just one of many in the solar system.

*Earth's moon* is a small ball of gray rock revolving 239,000 miles around Earth. It has no air and no water. It is about ¼ as large as Earth.

*Moonshine* is the sun's reflection off the moon. It arrives on Earth in little more than a second after leaving the moon.

*"The man in the moon"* is the name for the dark shadow of craters and lowlands that appear to us as a face.

*Full moon* and *no moon* describe two phases of the moon as it orbits Earth. When the moon is between the sun and the earth, its sunlight side is turned away from the earth and we say there is no moon. When the earth is between the sun and moon, we can see the entire sunlit side of the moon and call it a full moon.

*The far side of the moon* is always facing away from Earth because of the force of gravity. So when we look at the moon, we always see the same side.

*Moonwalkers:* Twelve American astronauts have walked on the moon. They explored highlands and craters, took photographs, and gathered soil and rocks for study.

*The moons of Uranus:* Uranus has 15 moons. Astronomers detected 5 of them between 1787 and 1948. The space probe *Voyager* discovered 10 more in 1985 and 1986. The names of these moons are like the characters from a play by Shakespeare. They are: Oberon, Titania, Umbriel, Ariel, Miranda, Puck, Portia, Juliet, Cressida, Rosalind, Belinda, Desdemona, Cordelia, Ophelia, and Bianca. Miranda, with its deep scars and jumbled surface, is one of the strangest objects in the solar system. It seems to have been shattered by a collision, then pulled back together by gravity!

*The moons of Neptune:* Neptune has 8 moons, with Triton the largest. It is covered with a frosty crust, where active volcanoes shoot crystals of nitrogen that look like geysers. The surface temperature of Triton is –390°F, making it the coldest object in the solar system.

*The moon of Pluto:* Pluto has 1 moon, Charon. It was discovered in 1978.

*On July 20, 1969, when the American astronaut Neil Armstrong became the first person to set foot on the moon, he said, "That's one small step for a man, one giant leap for mankind."*

## SPACEWALKERS

- The Soviet cosmonaut Alexei Leonov was the first person to walk in space. On March 18, 1965, he floated outside his *Voskhod 2* spacecraft for more than 10 minutes. Even though his lifeline extended only 17½ feet, he was able to turn somersaults, perform headstands, and lie perfectly still as he and the ship sailed around Earth.

*The Stars and Stripes are painted on every American spacecraft.*

- Ed White became the first spacewalking American on June 3, 1965. His craft was *Gemini 4.*
- Svetlana Savitskava, a Russian cosmonaut, became the first woman to walk in space on July 25, 1984. Her spacecraft was *Soyuz T-12.*
- Story Musgrave and Don Peterson were the first to spacewalk from the shuttle, on April 7, 1983. They were on the shuttle mission STS-6.
- The first person to walk in space without a tether (like a leash) was Bruce McCandless, on February 7, 1984. He was part of the shuttle mission STS-418.

### The First Astronauts

*The original American astronauts were Walter Schirra, Jr., Donald K. Slayton, John H. Glenn, Jr., M. Scott Carpenter, Jr., Alan B. Shepard, Jr., Virgil I. "Gus" Grissom, and L. Gordon Cooper, Jr.*

## SPACE LETTERS

NASA uses a lot of abbreviations. Here are a few of them.

| | |
|---|---|
| EVA | Extravehicular activity (a spacewalk) |
| KSC | Kennedy Space Center (the site of NASA's shuttle launches) |
| MMU | Manned maneuvering unit (the jet backpack that astronauts wear in orbit) |
| NASA | National Aeronautics and Space Administration |
| SRB | Solid rocket booster (one of the two big rockets on either side of the shuttle at launch) |

*Skylab, a laboratory for scientists, is a U.S. space station in which many people can live and work in orbit for weeks.*

## BODIES IN SPACE

Have you ever wondered what happens to the human body after spending prolonged periods of time in space? The astronauts who spent weeks in Skylab learned that their bodies behaved differently in space than on Earth.

*Birdlegs*
Legs become thinner and thinner as time passes. The muscles of the legs push fluids and blood upward, which decrease the size of the thighs and calves.

*Wasp Waist*
The waist becomes smaller by 3 to 5 inches due to an upward shift of the internal organs.

*Height and Posture*
The body grows 1½ to 2¼ inches taller because the spine lengthens and straightens. Relaxed body posture is head tilted backward, shoulders up (like a

shrug) and arms afloat, up and forward with hands chest high.

*Face*
Loose flesh rises, giving the face a high-cheek-boned look. Bags appear under the eyes, veins in the forehead are swollen, and the whole face looks puffy.

*Feelings*
At first the body feels lightheaded and nauseated, or sick to the stomach. After a few days these feelings go away, but a full-headed feeling (like hanging upside-down) remains.

## SKY SCIENCES

*Astrology*
A pseudo-science meaning "star wisdom," astrology attempts to link human characteristics and destinies with the position of the planets. Astrologers use a horoscope chart, which literally means "hour of observation." It is a forecast of the future based on the positions of heavenly bodies at a person's precise time of birth.

*Astrometry*
This branch of astronomy studies the movements and positions of celestial bodies. It is also called positional astronomy.

*Astronautics*
This is the science of space research.

*Astronomy*
Meaning "star distribution," astronomy is the scientific study of the heavens. Astronomers study

the stars, the planets, and everything else in our universe.

*Astrophysics*
This branch of astronomy deals with the physics and chemistry of the stars.

*Cosmogony*
The study of the origin as well as the development of the universe.

*Cosmology*
The study of the physical and philosophical principles of the universe.

*Ethnoastronomy*
The study of astronomical concepts and traditions across cultures.

*Uranography*
The science of charting the skies. (*Uranos* is Greek for heaven.)

# FAMOUS STAR GAZERS

*Newton's theory of universal gravitation states that every particle of matter (anything that takes up space) attracts every other particle of matter. The force becomes weaker as the distance between particles is increased.*

*Eratosthenes, 276–195 B.C.*
This Greek astronomer was the first to measure the size of the earth accurately. He determined that the earth's polar diameter was about 7,850 miles. (In fact, the distance is actually 7,900.)

*Claudius Ptolemaeus (Ptolemy) A.D. 120–189*
Called "the Prince of Astronomers," Ptolemy observed 1,022 stars and grouped them into 48 constellations, basically the ones we know today. His book *Almagest* included stars visible from Alexandria, Egypt, his home. His work went unchallenged until the 16th century, when Europeans explored the Southern Hemisphere and saw new constellations.

*Copernicus, Nicolaus, 1473–1543*
Copernicus was the first to theorize, or suggest, that the earth orbits the sun.

*Galilei, Galileo, 1564–1642*
Galileo is considered the first astronomer to use the telescope. He discovered four of Jupiter's satellites and the craters on Earth's moon.

*Newton, Sir Isaac, 1643–1727*
This British astronomer is best remembered for discovering the principle of gravity. Legend has it that, seeing an apple fall from a tree, Newton concluded that a force, gravity, pulled it to the ground. He then used his theory of gravity to explain how the moon is held in its orbit around the earth.

*Halley, Edmond, 1656–1742*
This British astronomer predicted the orbit of the

comet that bears his name. (A comet is a glowing ball of matter that travels around the sun and often develops a long, bright tail that points away from it.) Halley's comet passes close enough to the earth to be seen about

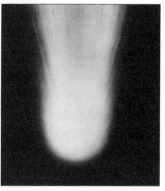

every 76 years. It was last seen in 1986 and should return in 2061.

*Herschel, Sir John, 1792–1871*
This Englishman is considered the first observer to have carefully studied the entire heavens. He traveled to Capetown, South Africa, where he discovered more than 1,250 nebulae and clusters.

*Lowell, Percival, 1855–1916*
Lowell, a wealthy American astronomer, built the Lowell Observatory in Flagstaff, Arizona, for the

*The famous writer Mark Twain was born on November 30, 1835, and died on April 21, 1910. Halley's comet was seen on Earth on both dates.*

*The Hubble space telescope, which was carried aboard the space shuttle in 1990, is named in honor of Edwin Hubble, an American astronomer. It is the most expensive telescope ever built, costing $1.5 million; its mirrors and cameras are the best ever made. NASA has had many problems with the telescope. Its mirrors curve the wrong way, and one of its antennas was wired incorrectly, causing it to shut itself down. NASA is working to correct the problems.*

purpose of observing the surface of Mars. He became famous for his discovery of the large "canals" on Mars.

*Mitchell, Maria, 1818–89*
Mitchell was America's first woman astronomer and worked with her father, also an astronomer, in their observatory. She discovered a new comet in 1847, which was later named for her, and is also known for her studies of sun spots and the satellites of planets.

## SPACE PLACES: A KIDS' GUIDE TO SPACE MUSEUMS

*Neil Armstrong Air and Space Museum*
1500 Bellefontaine Rd.
Wapakoneta, Ohio 45895
*Features:* Neil Armstrong's *Gemini 8* spacecraft, space suits, and historic aircraft as well as an exhibition of the model airplanes Armstrong collected as a boy.

*Astronaut Memorial Space Science Center*
Brevard Community College
1519 Clearlake Rd.
Cocoa, Fla. 32922
*Features:* John Glenn's training capsule and early launch vehicles as well as a planetarium and observatory.

*Percival Lowell is credited with discovering the planet Uranus, but he never saw it. His calculations led later astronomers to find Uranus, the seventh planet in our solar system.*

*Cernan Earth and Space Center*
Triton College
2000 Fifth Ave.
River Grove, Ill. 60171

*Features:* This museum honors Gene Cernan, who flew three space missions. His space suit as well as other space objects are on display.

*Henry Crown Space Center*
Chicago Museum of Science and Industry
57th St. and Lake Shore Dr.
Chicago, Ill. 60637

*Features:* There's a simulated space shuttle ride, the *Aurora 7* Mercury spacecraft, and a full-scale model of a Gemini spacecraft for NASA's proposed space station.

*Kansas Cosmosphere and Discovery Center*
1100 N. Plum St.
Hutchinson, Kans. 67501

*Features:* This center has many exhibitions, including more than 25 space suits, a lunar module, several spacecraft, a moon rock, and a planetarium and theater.

*National Air and Space Museum*
Smithsonian Institution
Independence Ave. between 4th and 7th Sts., SW
Washington, D.C. 20560

*Features:* This is the largest collection of space memorabilia. It contains the *Apollo 11* command module, John Glenn's Mercury capsule, *Friendship 7,* the first manned American spacecraft to orbit Earth, and the *Gemini 4* capsule from which Ed White became the first American to walk in space.

*The Keck telescope, the largest in the world, contains 36 hexagonal mirrors fitted together to produce a 393.7-inch mirror. It sits 14,000 feet high on Mauna Kea in Hawaii.*

## STAR LEGENDS

The constellations have been called mankind's oldest picture book. For 5,000 and more years, people have looked into a clear night sky and seen the same stars we see today. They isolated groups of stars and connected them to each other with imaginary lines, much as we play connect-the-dots.

In the past, people had an excellent knowledge of the night sky. They were able to tell when to plant and when to harvest, and later they navigated the seas with the stars' help. Characters of myth and legend were used to name and tell the stories of the stars. Here are a few.

The group of stars that looked like a man with a sword was named Orion, for the famous hunter in Greek mythology. The pattern that looked like twin boys they called Gemini, the Twins. The large, bright group of stars in the shape of a lion is known as Leo. According to Greek mythology, Leo was the fierce lion killed by Hercules.

*There are millions of stars, but only 5,780 are visible to the naked eye. The largest constellation is Hydra, the Sea Serpent. The smallest constellation is Crux, the Southern Cross.*

Twelve constellations, together called the Zodiac, form a belt around the earth. As the earth revolves around the sun, a different part of the sky becomes visible until, after a year, the earth has completed one trip and starts again. Each month, one of the 12 constellations appears above the horizon in the east to begin its march across the sky. Night after night, the constellation appears to move across our sky until it disappears below the horizon in the west and the next constellation appears in the east.

*Aries (The Ram)*
*March 21–April 19*
In Greek mythology, Aries was a winged ram with golden wool. His hide became the much-desired golden fleece.

*Taurus (The Bull)*
*April 20–May 20*
Jupiter, the supreme Roman god, turned himself into a bull when he swam from Phoenicia to Crete.

*Gemini (The Twins)*
*May 21–June 20*
This constellation reminded the Greeks of Castor and Pollux, the mythological twin sons of Zeus. It was thought to bring good luck to sailors since it appeared at the end of the winter storm season.

*Cancer (The Crab)*
*June 21–July 22*
Cancer represents the crab that Juno, queen of the gods, sent to rescue Hydra. But Hercules stepped on the crab, crushing it to death. To reward the crab for its heroic attempt, Juno chose it to represent this constellation.

*The word Zodiac comes from both Greek and Latin. It means "circle of figures" or "circle of life." According to the ancients, the year began with Aries.*

*Leo (The Lion)*
*July 23–August 22*
This large constellation honors the strength and bravery of the lion.

*Virgo (The Virgin)*
*August 23–September 22*
According to one fable, the Greek goddess Astraea believed that men were wicked and withdrew to the heavens.

*Libra (The Scales)*
*September 23–October 22*
Libra is the symbol of balance. This constellation appears at the time of the autumnal equinox, when days and nights are equal.

*Scorpio (The Scorpion)*
*September 23–November 21*
In mythology, Scorpio (or Scorpius) was the scorpion that attacked and killed the hunter Orion.

*Sagittarius (The Archer)*
*November 22–December 21*
This constellation is usually pictured as Chiron the archer, who is a centaur (half man, half horse). Chiron is said to be aiming his arrow at Scorpio to avenge the death of Orion.

*Capricorn (The Sea Goat)*
*December 22–January 19*
In many cultures, Capricorn has the head of a goat and the tail of a fish. The goat, an expert climber, represents the sun's climb from its lowest position in the sky. After December 22, the shortest day, the sun's time in the sky increases daily.

*Aquarius (The Water Bearer)*
*January 20–February 18*
The Babylonians believed that this group of stars represented an old man pouring water from a jar. The Greeks saw Ganymede, the cup bearer of the gods, who poured the water of life.

*Pisces (The Fishes)*
*February 19–March 20*
Pisces represents Venus, the Roman goddess of love and beauty, and her son Cupid. To escape from a monster, they turned into fish and jumped into a river.

## Your Astrological Profile

| ZODIAC SIGN | PERSONALITY |
| --- | --- |
| Aries | Loves new projects |
| Taurus | Stubborn and determined |
| Gemini | Changeable; double personalities |
| Cancer | Shy and hard to get to know |
| Leo | Likes authority |
| Virgo | Takes very good care of self |
| Libra | Natural peacemaker |
| Scorpio | Shrewd |
| Sagittarius | Independent and loves sports |
| Capricorn | Serious and practical |
| Aquarius | Generous and lover of the arts |
| Pisces | Sensitive and compassionate |

By 270 B.C., people knew 44 constellations by specific names and 2 more that were unnamed. In 1930 the International Astronomical Union (IAU) declared that no more constellations could be named; it would recognize only the names and boundaries of the 88 constellations known at the time. Astronomers still use this system for charting the constellations. The hemisphere you live in and the time of year determine which star legends you will see. Here are the 88 constellations.

| NAME | SYMBOL |
|------|--------|
| ANDROMEDA | Princess of Ethiopia |
| ANTLIA | The Air Pump |
| APUS | The Bird of Paradise |
| AQUARIUS | The Water Bearer |
| AQUILA | The Eagle |
| ARA | The Altar |
| ARIES | The Ram |
| AURIGA | The Charioteer |
| BOOTES | The Herdsman |
| CAELUM | The Sculptor's Chisel |
| CAMELOPARDALIS | The Giraffe |
| CANCER | The Crab |
| CANES VENATICI | The Hunting Dogs |
| CANIS MAJOR | The Greater Dog |
| CANIS MINOR | The Lesser Dog |
| CAPRICORN | The Sea Goat |
| CARINA | The Keel |
| CASSIOPEIA | The Seated Lady |
| CENTAURUS | The Centaur |
| CEPHEUS | King of Ethiopia |
| CETUS | The Sea Monster |
| CHAMELEON | The Chameleon |

| NAME | SYMBOL |
|------|--------|
| CIRCINUS | The Compass |
| COLUMBIA | The Dove |
| COMA BERENCIES | Bernice's Hair |
| CORONA AUSTRINA | The Southern Crown |
| CORONA BOREALIS | The Northern Crown |
| CORVUS | The Crow |
| CRATER | The Cup |
| CRUX | The Southern Cross |
| CYGNUS | The Swan |
| DELPHINUS | The Dolphin |
| DORADO | The Swordfish |
| DRACO | The Dragon |
| EQUULEUS | The Colt |
| ERIDANUS | The River |
| FORNAX | The Laboratory Furnace |
| GEMINI | The Twins |
| GRUS | The Crane |
| HERCULES | Hercules |
| HOROLOGIUM | The Clock |
| HYDRA | The Sea Serpent |
| HYDRUS | The Water Snake |
| INDUS | The American Indian |
| LACERTA | The Lizard |
| LEO | The Lion |
| LEO MINOR | The Lion Cub |
| LEPUS | The Hare |
| LIBRA | The Balance (Scales) |
| LUPUS | The Wolf |
| LYNX | The Lynx |
| LYRA | The Lyre |
| MENSA | The Table Mountain |
| MICROSCOPIUM | The Microscope |
| MONOCEROS | The Unicorn |

| NAME | SYMBOL |
|------|--------|
| MUSCA | The Fly |
| NORMA | The Carpenter's Square |
| OCTANS | The Octant |
| OPHIUCHUS | The Serpent Holder |
| ORION | The Great Hunter |
| PAVO | The Peacock |
| PEGASUS | The Winged Horse |
| PERSEUS | The Hero |
| PHOENIX | The Phoenix |
| PICTOR | The Painter's Easel |
| PISCES | The Fishes |
| PISCIS AUSTRINUS | The Southern Fishes |
| PUPPIS | The Stern |
| PYXIS | The Mariner's Compass |
| RETICULUM | The Net |
| SAGITTA | The Arrow |
| SAGITTARIUS | The Archer |
| SCORPIO | The Scorpion |
| SCULPTOR | The Sculptor |
| SCUTUM | The Shield |
| SERPENS | The Serpent |
| SEXTANS | The Sextant |
| TAURUS | The Bull |
| TELESCOPIUM | The Telescope |
| TRIANGULUM | The Triangle |
| TRIANGULUM AUSTRALE | The Southern Triangle |
| TUCANA | The Toucan |
| URSA MAJOR | The Large Bear |
| URSA MINOR | The Small Bear |
| VELA | The Sail |
| VIRGO | The Virgin |
| VOLANS | The Flying Fish |
| VULPECULA | The Little Fox |

# The Wide World of War

*What's All the Fighting For?*

FROM THE EARLIEST DAYS, people have fought among themselves for one reason or another. Clans, tribes, states, and nations all seem to have found war necessary. Many people today have made their life's work a search for ways to *prevent* war. We're on their side.

## BATTLE REPORT

Some battles were turning points, not only in war, but in history itself, and we still talk about them today. You may have heard of marathons, Gettysburg, or someone who has "met his or her Waterloo." Like these, the battles below changed the course of history.

| BATTLE | WHERE/WHEN | OPPONENTS |
|--------|------------|-----------|
| Zama | Zama, an ancient town in N. Africa southwest of Carthage / 202 B.C. | Romans / Carthaginians |

This battle marked the downfall of Hannibal, one of history's most famous and daring generals. For more than 60 years, the Carthaginians and the Romans fought for world power. For 16 of those years Hannibal, the Carthaginian leader, was able to hold off the Romans—until the battle of Zama. Though the Carthaginians had 15,000 fewer warriors, Hannibal thought he had solved the problem. He had 80 elephants, which he would use to send the Roman army fleeing in terror and confusion. But when Hannibal set the elephants free in the Roman ranks, the animals took the easier route and ran the other way! Hannibal and his army lost 11 elephants, the battle, and the war.

| BATTLE | WHERE/WHEN | OPPONENTS |
|--------|------------|-----------|
| Marathon | Greece / 490 B.C. | Persia / Greece |

The battle of Marathon is famous, not only because the underdog won, but also because of a legend of courage and sacrifice. Darius, the leader of Persia, Egypt, Babylon, and India, decided to become the ruler of Greece as well. But the Greeks, armed only with javelins and swords, defeated the much larger and better armed Persian army. What we remember today is the story of the messenger who brought the good news to Athens, the capital of Greece. Upon completing his 26-mile run, legend says he delivered his message, collapsed, and died. Today, the word *marathon* means a footrace of exactly 26 miles, 385 yards.

| BATTLE | WHERE/WHEN | OPPONENTS |
|--------|-----------|-----------|
| Hastings | England / 1066 | British / Normans (French from Normandy) |

This battle resulted in the Norman conquest of England. Edward the Confessor, the king of England,

*The Trojan horse won the war for Greece against Troy in classical mythology. The horse was a wooden decoy filled with soldiers, who used it to enter the city of Troy.*

had no sons and promised that when he died his throne would go to his cousin William, duke of Normandy. On his deathbed, however, the king chose Harold, the powerful earl of Wessex, as king. An enraged William rushed into battle to claim the English throne. At the battle's height, the Normans pretended to flee. When the English ran after them, the Normans turned and attacked them again. Harold was shot in the face with an arrow and died on the battlefield, leaving the throne to William. To this day, the English royal family can be traced back to William the Conqueror.

*The Hundred Years' War between England and France lasted from 1337 to 1453, more than 100 years. It ended when the English were driven out of France.*

| BATTLE | WHERE/WHEN | OPPONENTS |
|--------|-----------|-----------|
| Agincourt | France / 1415 | England / France |

This famous battle was part of the Hundred Years' War between the French and the English. English archers with their longbows were able to keep the French with their crossbows too far away to shoot. The French decided to charge. The ground was wet and muddy, causing the heavily armored troops to slip and fall. The French lost at least 5,000 men; another 1,000 were captured. The English losses totaled only 140.

| BATTLE | WHERE/WHEN | OPPONENTS |
|--------|-----------|-----------|
| Lexington and Concord | Massachusetts / 1775 | American colonists / British |

This was the opening battle of the American Revolution. British troops led by General Thomas Gage were moving from Boston toward Lexington and Concord to capture the rebel leaders Samuel

Adams and John Hancock and destroy their military supplies. The colonists were warned when Paul Revere made his famous midnight ride, shouting, "The British are coming!" At Concord, armed colonists called Minutemen resisted the British. Ralph Waldo Emerson later wrote a poem describing this conflict as "the shot heard round the world." The fighting ended almost a year later, when the British evacuated Boston. On July 4, 1776, representatives from the 13 colonies signed the Declaration of Independence to gain their freedom from Great Britain.

| BATTLE | WHERE / WHEN | OPPONENTS |
|--------|--------------|-----------|
| Waterloo | Belgium / 1815 | England & European allies / France |

This battle ended not only Napoleon's Hundred Days' War but also 23 years of almost constant war between France and the rest of Europe. France and England had been enemies for hundreds of years. The battle of Waterloo was fought by the English forces and their allies, some 68,000 men under Arthur Wellesley (later the duke of Wellington), with 45,000 Prussians under Gebhard von Blücher against the French emperor Napoleon, with almost 72,000 men. Casualties of 25,000 men destroyed the French army. Soon after this crushing defeat, Napoleon was exiled on the island of Saint Helena, where he died 6 years later. Waterloo has since come to mean a disastrous defeat of any nature.

NAPOLEON
BONAPARTE

| BATTLE | WHERE / WHEN | OPPONENTS |
| --- | --- | --- |
| Gettysburg | Pennsylvania / 1863 | Union / Confederacy |

The greatest battle of the American Civil War, Gettysburg marked the northernmost advance of the Confederate forces and is considered the war's turning point. Three bloody days of fighting ended in the failure of the Confederate army, led by General Robert E. Lee, to invade the North. Though his army outnumbered the Union forces under Major General George G. Meade, the North expected the Confederates to charge and try to break the center of its line. Cut down by enemy fire, the Confederates were quickly overwhelmed; only 150 out of 15,000 Southerners reached the Union lines. This decisive victory for the North was the beginning of the end of the Confederacy.

The battle of Britain was a series of air battles fought between the German air force, or Luftwaffe, and the British Royal Air Force, or RAF. It was the first time during World War II that Adolf Hitler's Nazi forces were thwarted. Following the fall of France, only Great Britain held out against Germany. With ground forces stopped by the English Channel, Hitler launched a heavy air attack on England. When several daytime attacks proved unsuccessful, the Germans executed a nighttime *Blitzkrieg,* or "lightning war," on London, England. This attack, begun on September 7, continued for 57 nights. During this time an average of 200 planes each night blasted the city with high-explosive bombs. The relentless raids killed more than 43,000 British and wounded five times that number. Only the outstanding performance of the RAF kept the Germans from forcing Britain to surrender. As a result, Germany abandoned its plan for invasion.

| BATTLE | WHERE / WHEN | OPPONENTS |
| --- | --- | --- |
| Guadalcanal | SW Pacific / 1942–43 | Japanese / U.S. |

This World War II battle was unique in many ways. The U.S. victory meant that Japan experienced its first setback in the Pacific islands. Also for the first time during the war, America was on the offensive. The ferocious 6-month battle for control of this tiny island 1,000 miles off the coast of Australia was fought on land, on sea, and in the

air. Although many bitter battles were still to be fought before the end in August 1945, the battle of Guadalcanal opened the way for U.S. victory in the South Pacific.

| BATTLE | WHERE / WHEN | OPPONENTS |
|---|---|---|
| Tet Offensive | S. Vietnam / 1968 | Vietnam / U.S. |

The Tet Offensive was the turning point in the Vietnam War. The North surprised the South Vietnamese and American forces in simultaneous attacks in many parts of Vietnam during the Vietnamese New Year, or Tet. Many of the attackers disguised themselves as Tet holiday celebrators. Although American troops weren't withdrawn from Vietnam until 1973, the Tet Offensive was the beginning of the end of the U.S. presence there. It was the first time the United States was unable to gain victory in war (since the War of 1812). Communist forces gained control of South Vietnam in 1975.

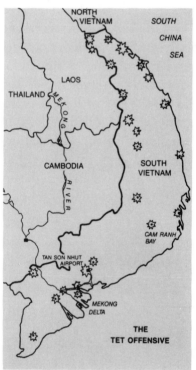

THE TET OFFENSIVE

# THE UNITED STATES AT WAR

From the American Revolution to Desert Storm, the U.S. has fought in *ten* major wars. Do you know their names, where they were fought and why, and who won? Here's a quick look. (Casualties means dead or wounded; it does not include captured or missing.)

## Revolutionary War

1775–83

American casualties: 33,769

- The 13 American colonies fought for independence from British rule to become the United States.
- Treaty of Paris

## The War of 1812

1812–15

American casualties: 6,765

- The U.S. declared war on Great Britain during its war with France.
- Treaty of Ghent

## Mexican War

1846–48

American casualties: 17,435

- The U.S. fought against Mexico over Texas and California.
- Treaty of Guadalupe Hidalgo, 1848. Mexico gave up the territory.

## Civil War

1861–65

Union casualties: 646,392

Confederate casualties: 133,821 (only an estimate; 26,000 to 31,000 soldiers may have died in prison)

*"Don't one of you fire until you see the whites of their eyes."* William Prescott at the battle of Bunker Hill, American Revolution

- The northern states fought against the southern states over slavery and states' rights.
- The South surrendered at Appomattox, Virginia, in 1865.

## Spanish-American War
1898
American casualties: 4,108

- Spain declared war on the U.S., which supported Cuba's wish to be independent of Spanish rule.
- Treaty of Paris, 1898; Cuba was freed. The U.S. obtained the Philippines for $20 million, and Puerto Rico and Guam were ceded to the U.S.

## World War I
1914–18 (U.S. involved, 1917–18)
American battle deaths: 320,710

- The U.S. joined the Allies (Britain, France, Russia, Italy, and Japan), who were at war with the Central Powers (Germany, Austria-Hungary, and Turkey), after German submarines began sinking unarmed ships—notably the *Lusitania*.
- Treaty of Versailles, after the Central Powers surrendered to the Allies.

| Nicknames for U.S. Soldiers | |
|---|---|
| World War I | *"Doughboy"* |
| World War II and Korea | *"Dogface"* |
| Vietnam | *"Grunt"* |

## World War II
1939–45 (U.S. involved, 1941–46)
American battle deaths: 1,078,162

- The U.S. joined the Allies (Britain, France, and the USSR) to fight the Axis Powers (Germany, Italy, and Japan) after the U.S. forces were at-

tacked by the Japanese at Pearl Harbor.
- Italy surrendered in 1943 and joined the Allies, Germany in 1945, and Japan later that same year, after the atomic bomb was dropped on Hiroshima and Nagasaki.

*"I have seen war. I hate war."*
*President Franklin D. Roosevelt, World War II*

## Korean War
1950–53
American casualties: 157,530
- North Korea's communist forces fought against South Korea's noncommunist forces supported by U.N. forces, principally made up of U.S. troops.
- Truce at Panmunjom, North Korea. North and South Korea remained separate, as before the war.

## Vietnam War
1954–75 (U.S. involved, 1961–75)
American casualties: 211,324
- The U.S. helped noncommunist South Vietnam fight communist North Vietnam's invasion.
- Ceasefire signed in Paris, 1973. North Vietnam's victory ended the war in 1975.

## Desert Storm
1991
Allied casualties: 287
- U.S., Britain, France, Saudi Arabia, Egypt, Syria, and Italy went to war against Iraq on January 16, 1991, in response to Iraq's August 1, 1990, invasion of Kuwait.
- Iraq withdrew from Kuwait on February 28, 1991.

## Cold War

*The longest war in U.S. history involved not weapons and warfare but words and ideas. Beginning in 1945, this war was a struggle between the U.S. and the Soviet Union. The U.S. wanted to contain the spread of communist control. The Cold War ended in 1990 with the collapse of communism in the USSR.*

## THE RULES OF WAR

If it seems to you that there are always rules to follow, no matter what you do, you won't be surprised that international law sets out strict rules of behavior for countries during wartime. The first modern international rules of war, known as the Geneva Convention, or Treaty, were made in Geneva, Switzerland, in 1864. This treaty was accepted by all the European countries, by the U.S., and by some countries in Asia and South America. New rules are added as they are needed.

*Rule 1:* Warring nations cannot use chemical weapons against each other.

*Rule 2:* The use of expanding bullets or materials calculated to cause unnecessary suffering is prohibited.

*Rule 3:* The discharge of projectiles (such as bullets or rockets) from balloons is prohibited.

*Rule 4:* Prisoners of war must be humanely treated and protected from violence. Prisoners cannot be beaten or used for propaganda purposes (to try to change the way people think about something).

*Rule 5:* Prisoners of war must give their true name and rank or they will lose their prisoner of war protection.

*Rule 6:* Nations must follow procedures to identify the dead and wounded and to send information to their families.

*Rule 7:* Killing anyone who has surrendered is prohibited.

*Rule 8:* Zones must be set up in fighting areas to

*An expanding bullet, upon impact, explodes within the body.*

which the sick and injured can be taken for treatment.

*Rule 9:* Special protection from attack is granted to civilian hospitals marked with the Red Cross.

*Rule 10:* The free passage of medical supplies is allowed.

*Rule 11:* Shipwrecked members of the armed forces at sea should be taken ashore to safety.

*Rule 12:* Any army that takes control of another country must provide food to the people in that country.

*Rule 13:* Attacks on civilians and undefended towns are prohibited.

*Rule 14:* Enemy submarines cannot sink merchant or business ships before passengers and crews have been saved.

*Rule 15:* A prisoner can be visited by a representative from his or her country and they have the right to talk privately without observers.

MIA *stands for Missing in Action.* POW *stands for Prisoner of War.*

## FOOD FOR FIGHTING

"An army lives on its stomach" goes an old saying. Today, many foods that were first designed for soldiers' stomachs have found their way into ours. Did you know that granola bars, instant noodle soup, and freeze-dried coffee are all military creations? Here are more foods for fighting.

### Candy

- M&M's, a familiar candy-coated chocolate, were made for the military in 1940.

- "Ration D" was a bar of concentrated chocolate soldiers carried in World War II.
- The Desert Bar was made by Hershey for the soldiers in Desert Storm. It is a chocolate bar designed to withstand heat up to 140°F.

### Rations

- K Rations, named after A. B. Keyes, an American physiobiologist, were carried by Americans in World War II. These lightweight packages included biscuits, canned meat, instant coffee, fruit bars, chewing gum, and powdered lemon juice. Sugar tablets and cigarettes were also included.
- M.R.E.'s (Meals Ready to Eat) are brown plastic pouches that contain prepared meals, such as barbecued meatballs or corned beef hash, and are meant to last 3 years before spoiling. They were served in the 1990–91 Persian Gulf War, where they were called "airwing Alpo."

## PRIZES OF WAR

People who win awards like those listed below are very special. They are people whose achievements have been outstanding due to their bravery, courage, or daring. The U.S. military gives 28 decorations, or awards, for outstanding achievement. Those listed here are considered the highest honors one can receive.

### Congressional Medal of Honor

*Who's eligible?* Any person involved in enemy conflict, not necessarily a member of the military. The medal is occasionally awarded in peacetime for

*The Congressional Medal of Honor is the only decoration worn around the neck. All other honors are worn on the uniform.*

extraordinary achievement.

*Achievement:* One must risk one's own life "above and beyond the call of duty" for the benefit of others. This means doing something no one could expect of you, out of your own desire to help others.

## Distinguished Service Cross

*Who's eligible?* People in or working with the armed forces during battle.

*Achievement:* This medal is the second highest honor for valor or bravery. The act of courage must be performed during a military operation and must include the risk of life so unusual that it sets one apart from one's peers, or equals.

*The head-hunters of Borneo decapitate their enemies and preserve their heads as trophies.*

## Purple Heart

*Who's eligible?* Anyone serving in the armed forces.

*Achievement:* Established by George Washington, this is the oldest American military decoration. One has to be wounded in combat.

## Distinguished Flying Cross

*Who's eligible?* All military personnel. It can also be awarded by Congress to outstanding pioneers of aviation.

*Achievement:* A person must show outstanding heroism during aerial flight.

## A WHO'S WHO OF WARRIORS

Amazons, Vandals, Vikings — what do they have in common? Do you know they were all warriors? Add guerrillas, kamikazes, and conquistadors and you have quite a group. Who were they? When and where did they fight?

*Amazons*

These female warriors of classical mythology were tall, strong, and fierce. They disfigured their bodies to perfect their skills with bows and arrows.

*Conquistadors*

Spanish soldiers who tried to conquer the people of the Americas, especially Mexico and Peru, in the 1500s were conquistadors. In their search for gold, they wanted to conquer and subjugate the native people.

*The Amazon River and Amazon Jungle of South America were so named because tribes of female warriors were thought to live along the riverbanks.*

## Cossacks

These skilled cavalrymen from the southern part of Russia fought for the Russian Empire as a tax payment in the 16th and 17th centuries. They also fought the Bolsheviks in 1918–21 and served in World War II.

## Crusaders

Crusaders were Europeans who went to the Holy Land (parts of modern Israel, Jordan, and Egypt) from the 11th to the 13th century to recover Christian holy places from the Muslims. Among them was Richard the Lion-Hearted of England, who was the absent king during the days of the legendary Robin Hood.

## Foreign Legion

In 1831, King Louis-Philippe of France formed the

*During the Children's Crusade in 1212, thousands of children were sent to Egypt to fight. Many were sold into slavery; most died of starvation and disease.*

French Foreign Legion in order to keep his colonies under control. The legion was made up of mercenary (paid) soldiers from different countries. The French Foreign Legion fought in both World Wars I and II. Today there are about 8,000 soldiers in the legion throughout the world.

### Guerrillas

Irregular troops of soldiers who ambush and sabotage their enemies are called guerrillas. Unlike ordinary soldiers, guerrillas do not fight openly with their enemy. The first known guerrillas fought in the American Revolution, although the word *guerrilla* was not coined until 1809 during the Napoleonic Peninsula Wars.

### Kamikazes

Japanese airplane pilots who truly fought to the death during World War II were kamikazes, diving

*Gladiators were trained fighters in ancient Rome. They fought each other, usually to the death, for public entertainment.*

their planes into enemy (U.S.) aircraft carriers at sea. Some 1,200 kamikaze pilots died while sinking 34 American ships.

### Rough Riders
During the Spanish-American War, a voluntary cavalry regiment from the U.S. led by Teddy Roosevelt became known as the Rough Riders. A rough rider is one who can ride an untrained horse. This regiment, made up of cowboys, miners, and law enforcement officials as well as upper-class equestrians, became famous for its victory charge at the battle of San Juan Hill in Cuba.

### Samurai
From 1100 to 1800, the samurai (Japanese for "guard") served as the warrior aristocracy of Japan. They wore two swords as a sign of distinction.

### Swiss Guard
This mercenary group was formed in the 15th century to guard the pope and continues this function in Vatican City, part of Rome, Italy.

### Vandals
The Vandals, originally Europeans, occupied a kingdom in North Africa. In the 5th century, they invaded the Roman Empire and sacked Rome. Today, *vandal* refers to someone who destroys things without reason.

### Vikings
From the 8th to the 11th century, Viking warriors from Scandinavia raided and plundered the coast of Europe. They also explored in their sturdy ships, traveling as far as Greenland and Newfoundland.

*The Vikings' favorite weapons were catapults and battering rams.*

## ANIMALS IN UNIFORM

For centuries, animals have been used to help fight wars. Before there were tanks, soldiers rode their horses into battle. Pack animals such as camels, mules, and horses carried ammunition and supplies. Many other animals have been called upon to do their duty. Here's a salute to animals in war.

### Elephants

- Battle elephants were used by Hannibal of Carthage when he crossed the Alps to fight the Romans. Elephants with carriages on their backs were able to hold four soldiers. Hannibal's elephant, Surus, was said to be extremely brave.
- Alexander the Great conquered India with the help of elephants.
- The Greek king Pyrrhus and his men rode elephants into battle against the Romans. Although the Greeks won, many men and el-

ephants died. Today "Pyrrhic victory" means a victory won at great cost.

- In the 16th century, Emperor Akbar of India used elephants in battle. The elephants were hung with bells in order to sound frightening, and their trunks were bound to straighten them so that poisoned daggers could be attached to their ends.

## Dogs

- The ancient Romans and Gauls used dogs trained to fight in battle.
- In the 15th century, the Spanish used dog warriors, which wore quilted overcoats into battle.
- Christopher Columbus used dogs to fight Native Americans.

## Cats, Canaries, and Mice

These animals didn't fight, but they were very useful in World Wars I and II.

- Cats lived with soldiers in trenches, where they killed mice during World War I.
- Canaries and mice were used during World War II when soldiers sent them into the tunnels being dug behind enemy lines to detect bad air and poison gas.

## Pigeons

- During World War I, before radiotelephones were used, carrier pigeons took messages between ships at sea.
- In 19th-century Europe, messenger pigeons were sent out two at a time because falcons were trained to attack them, thereby intercepting the message.

## WACKY WARS!

Wars can start over the stupidest things! Entire countries have lost their sense of what is worth fighting for in some of the cases below. We hope you wouldn't let a soccer game, pigs, or a bucket do the same to you.

### The War of the Oaken Bucket (Italy) 1325–37

This ridiculous war started over a stolen bucket. When a group of soldiers from Modena invaded Bologna to steal a brown oak bucket, thousands of citizens were killed. Bologna became angry and went to war with Modena to take back their bucket and restore their pride. The two cities fought for 12 years and thousands of lives were lost. Modena won the war; the people of Bologna never got their bucket back.

### The War of Jenkins' Ear (Great Britain vs. Spain) 1739–43

War was immediately declared after Captain Robert Jenkins appeared in Parliament, the governing body of Great Britain, holding the remains of his ear in his hand. He claimed that the Spanish had cut it off after boarding his ship in the West Indies, for they did not want English traders doing business in their American colonies. The war went on for 4 years, because of Jenkins and his ear. There was no clear winner; it ended in a draw.

### The War of the Fleeing Wife (Africa vs. Great Britain) 1879

Husbands and wives often disagree. In this case, a marital disagreement resulted in war. Umblana, the wife of the Zulu chief Sitlay, left him and hid in British territory. When the Zulus found her, they shot her. England declared war on the Zulus for crossing into their territory. The Zulu forces were crushed by the British.

### The Pig War (Austria-Hungary vs. Serbia) 1906–9

We know that pigs can make a big mess, but in this case they caused a war. Pigs wᵉre not allowed to be sold by Serbia to Austria-Hungary. Serbia wanted to become less dependent on goods from Austria-Hungary and started trading their pigs for French goods. As a result, Austria-Hungary got angry with Serbia and forced Serbia to find new markets for their pigs.

### The War of the Stray Dog (Greece vs. Bulgaria) 1925

Dogs are always straying from their owners, and that's just how this war began. When the dog of a Greek soldier wandered across the border into

*Among the more unusual armaments of war are the boomerang of the Austra- lian aborigi- nes, the yo yo of the Filipi- nos, and the slingshots of European armies before the 16th century.*

Macedonia, the soldier ran after it and was shot by a Bulgarian guard. The Greek troops became so angry that they invaded Bulgaria. More than 50 men were killed before the League of Nations intervened and stopped the war.

*The Soccer War (El Salvador vs. Honduras)*
*July 14–30, 1969*

If these soccer fans had practiced good sportsmanship, this war may never have begun. Tensions from a soccer match between the national teams of El Salvador and Honduras, exacerbated by the economic disparities between the two countries, escalated into fighting. Salvadoran immigrants were then expelled from Honduras and the countries went to war. Some 2,000 people were killed in 16 days. The Organization of American States intervened to end the fighting.

# The World

*From Afghanistan to Zimbabwe
with Stops in Between*

SOME SAY IT'S A SMALL WORLD,  but there's so much to know about it, including our own  country, that you could say it's really very big. We suggest you "pack a lunch" for your trip through this world.

## THE WORLD IN MOTION

Our world is moving constantly, spinning at a rate of 1,000 miles per hour. We are whirling around the sun at 20 miles per second. We, and our whole galaxy, are racing through space at more than a million miles an hour. The surface of our world is moving and changing, too. How has the face of the earth changed over time? Look at some of these extraordinary facts.

*Millions of years from now, Los Angeles will be close to Alaska.*

**Fact:** 200 million years ago most of the earth's land was one huge continent named *Pangaea,* meaning "all lands." All the seas were one huge ocean called *Panthalassa,* meaning "all seas."

**Fact:** Millions of years ago, the place that is now New York City was on the equator.

**Fact:** Millions of years ago, Antarctica was a rain forest.

**Fact:** Millions of years ago, India broke away from Africa, slammed into Eurasia, and rumpled up the Himalaya Mountains.

**Fact:** The Atlantic Ocean grows wider by an inch a year while the Pacific Ocean shrinks.

**Fact:** The coastline of the Atlantic Ocean sinks about 4 inches every 100 years.

**Fact:** France is slowly tilting northward, rising in the southern part and sinking along the channel coast.

**Fact:** Africa is slowly tearing itself apart in a place called the Rift Valley, between Zaire and East Africa.

**Fact:** The Andes Mountains of South America are growing higher.

**Fact:** A new island was born in 1963. It is a volcanic island off the coast of Iceland called Surtsey.

## FAMILIES
You're not the only one with relatives; countries have them, too. Families of countries exist for several reasons: location, trade, or politics, for example. Like any family, countries that are related don't always agree with one another.

### The Low Countries
Much of the land of this geographical family of European countries is located at or below sea level: the Netherlands, Belgium, and Luxembourg.

### NATO Countries
The North Atlantic Treaty Organization (NATO), formed in 1949, has one goal: to protect the political belief of democracy. Today, the member countries are: Belgium, Canada, Denmark, France, Germany, Greece, Iceland, Italy, Luxembourg, the Netherlands, Norway, Portugal, Spain, Turkey, the United Kingdom, and the U.S.

*Although Holland is a popular name for the Netherlands, North and South Holland are actually two provinces in the Netherlands.*

## Polynesia
Polynesia, "many islands," is a collective term for the islands of the east-central Pacific Ocean, which include Cook, Easter, Pitcairn, Samoa, Tahiti, and Tuvalu as well as the Hawaiian islands.

## Scandinavia
This family has many ties: geographical, cultural, political, and historical. These countries occupy a region of northern Europe: Denmark (sometimes includes Finland, Iceland, and the Faeroe Islands), Norway, and Sweden.

## The Far East
These countries of the Eastern Hemisphere are connected geographically: China, Japan, North Ko-

*Latin America refers to all countries south of the U.S.*

rea, South Korea, Mongolia, the Philippines, and Taiwan.

*The Middle East*
These countries of western Asia, northern Africa, and the Arabian Peninsula are related geographically: Bahrain, Egypt, Iran, Iraq, Israel, Jordan, Katar, Kuwait, Lebanon, Oman, Saudi Arabia, Syria, Turkey, the United Arab Emirates, and Yemen.

*Central America*
Central America refers to the seven countries of North America between Mexico and South America: Belize, Costa Rica, El Salvador, Guatemala, Honduras, Nicaragua, and Panama.

*The Union of Soviet Socialist Republics (USSR)*
The USSR, 15 republics in eastern Europe and northern Asia, was formed in 1922, after the Russian Revolution. Until 1991 it was the world's largest country, covering one-sixth of the land area of the world. Many people thought that the USSR was Russia. But Russia was really only one of its republics. Since December 31, 1991, the USSR no longer exists as a country. The republics of the USSR were: Armenia, Azerbaijan, Belorus (Byelorussia), Estonia, Georgia, Kazakhistan, Kirghizia, Latvia, Lithuania, Moldavia, Russia, Tadzhikstan, Turkmenistan, Ukraine, and Uzbekistan.

*The United Arab Emirates*
This group of seven kingdoms, created in 1971, is ruled by sheiks on the Persian Gulf coast of the Arabian Peninsula. In the Muslim world, an emir is a ruler or prince; an emirate is his state. The

kingdoms are: Abu Dhabi, Ajman, Dubai, Fujairah, Ras al-Khaimah, Sharjah, and Umm al-Qaiwain.

## The United Kingdom of Great Britain and Northern Ireland

These countries are ruled by the British royal family and Parliament: England, Northern Ireland, Scotland, and Wales.

## The Warsaw Pact Countries

This political family was composed of communist countries that were united in 1955 to keep communism alive. Since the collapse of communism, they have been struggling to find their way: Albania (withdrew in 1968), Bulgaria, Czechoslovakia, East Germany (now united with West Germany), Hungary, Poland, Romania, and the USSR.

*Great Britain includes England, Scotland, and Wales. The British Isles include Great Britain, Ireland, the Isle of Man, and the Channel Islands.*

## The Southeast Asian Countries

These countries in Southeast Asia are bound by geography: Brunei, Indonesia, Kampuchea (Cambodia), Laos, Malaysia, Myanmar (Burma), North Vietnam, Singapore, South Vietnam, and Thailand.

# WORLD CHAMPIONS FROM
# TOP TO BOTTOM

**HIGHEST POINT ON LAND:**
Mount Everest, Himalayan Mountains, Nepal-Tibet, 29,028 feet
above sea level

**LOWEST POINT ON LAND:**
The Dead Sea, Israel-Jordan, water surface 1,302 feet below sea
level

**HIGHEST UNDERWATER PEAK:**
Mount Pico of the Azores Islands, 7,613 feet above sea surface,
20,000 feet below sea surface to sea floor

**DEEPEST UNDERWATER TRENCH:**
Mariana Trench, 200 miles southwest of Guam in the Pacific
Ocean, 36,198 feet below the ocean surface

**TALLEST MOUNTAIN:**
Mauna Kea, Hawaii, rises 33,476 feet from Pacific Ocean floor,
13,796 feet are above sea surface

**HIGHEST LAKE:**
The highest navigable lake is Lake Titicaca in Peru, 12,506 feet
above sea level

**LOWEST LAKE:**
The Dead Sea, Israel-Jordan, surface of water 1,302 feet below sea
level

**DEEPEST OCEAN:**
Pacific Ocean, average depth 14,000 feet

**LARGEST CONTINENT:**
Asia, 17,300,000 square miles

**SMALLEST CONTINENT:**
Australia, 2,966,000 square miles

**LARGEST OCEAN:**
Pacific Ocean, 64,186,300 square miles

**SMALLEST OCEAN:**
Arctic Ocean, 5,400,000 square miles

**LARGEST GULF:**
Gulf of Mexico, 580,000 square miles

**LARGEST BAY:**
The Bay of Bengal, 839,000 square miles

**LARGEST SEA:**
The South China Sea, 1,148,500 square miles

**LARGEST SALTWATER LAKE:**
The Caspian Sea, Europe-Asia, 143,550 square miles

**LARGEST FRESHWATER LAKE:**
Lake Superior, U.S.-Canada, 31,700 square miles

*An* atoll *is a coral island that encircles a lagoon. An* archipelago *is a string of islands.*

**DEEPEST LAKE:**
Lake Baikal, USSR, 5,315 feet deep

**LARGEST ISLAND:**
Greenland, 840,000 square miles

**LARGEST PENINSULA:**
Arabia, 1,250,000 square miles

**LARGEST ATOLL (LAND AREA):**
Christmas Island (Kiritimati since 1980), Pacific Ocean, 94 square miles

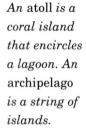

**LARGEST ARCHIPELAGO:**
Indonesia, 3,500-mile stretch of 13,000 islands

**LARGEST GORGE:**
Grand Canyon, Colorado River, Arizona, U.S., 277 miles long, 1–18 miles wide, 1 mile deep

**DEEPEST GORGE:**
Hells Canyon, Snake River, Idaho, 7,900 feet

**LONGEST MOUNTAIN RANGE:**
The Andes of South America, 5,000 miles

**LONGEST RIVER:**
The Nile, Africa, 4,145 miles

**SHORTEST RIVER:**
The Roe, Montana, U.S., 201 feet long

**LARGEST RIVER:**
The Amazon, South America, basin of 2,720,000 square miles

**LONGEST ESTUARY:**
Ob River, USSR, 550 miles up to 50 miles wide

**LARGEST LAGOON:**
Lagoa dos Patos, Brazil, 158 miles long, 4,110 square miles

## WHAT'S MISSING ON THIS CONTINENT?

We always talk about what each continent has—which is the biggest, which has the longest river, which has the most people. Now let's see what each continent doesn't have. Here are some things that entire continents do without.

*Asia* and *Europe* are not separate landmasses. They are divided by the Ural Mountains.

*Antarctica* has no country. The U.S. and other countries have science stations here, but no nation owns the land.

*Europe* has no desert.

*Africa,* the world's hottest landmass, has no cold climate.

*Australia* has no active volcanoes.

*Australia* has only one country, Australia.

| Continents are the great landmasses of the earth. In order of size they are: | |
| --- | --- |
| ASIA | 17,128,500 SQUARE MILES |
| AFRICA | 11,707,000 SQUARE MILES |
| NORTH AMERICA | 9,363,000 SQUARE MILES |
| SOUTH AMERICA | 6,875,000 SQUARE MILES |
| ANTARCTICA | 5,500,000 SQUARE MILES |
| EUROPE | 4,057,000 SQUARE MILES |
| AUSTRALIA | 2,966,100 SQUARE MILES |

# WHERE THE NAME FITS THE PLACE—OR DOES IT?

*Is Greenland Green?*
No. Much of Greenland is covered with a thick blanket of ice. The Viking explorers called it Greenland in order to lure settlers!

*Is the Dead Sea Dead?*
Yes. There is no life in this sea between Israel and Jordan. It is a dead end for the Jordan River. With no place to go, the water evaporates and leaves heavy deposits of minerals, which makes the sea uninhabitable and much saltier than the oceans.

*Is It Chilly in Chile?*
Yes and no. The southern region of Chile is cold and humid, with snow-covered mountains and glaciers. The northern region is warm and dry. The middle region is warm and balmy, much like the Mediterranean in climate.

*Some claim you can see 40 shades of green in the Irish countryside.*

*Is the Red Sea Red?*
Yes. Red algae frequently appear in this sea, coloring it red. The Red Sea is in the Middle East between Africa and the Arabian Peninsula.

*Are There Emeralds in the Emerald Isle?*
No. Ireland is called the Emerald Isle because of its green countryside, not because of gemstones. The green landscape is the result of underlying limestone and frequent rains and mists.

*Is Iceland Icy?*
Not very. Natural hot springs warm the buildings and pools of this island. The harbors never freeze because of the warm waters of the Gulf Stream,

which flows around the island. The only ice is in Iceland's high central area, which is covered with snow.

*Are There Canaries in the Canary Islands?*
Yes. Wild canaries were first discovered on these islands. But the name Canary comes from the wild dogs found here by the Romans. (*Canis* is Latin for "dog.") The Canary Islands are in the Atlantic Ocean off the northwest coast of Africa.

*Is the Yellow River Yellow?*
Yes. The Yellow River (or Huang Ho) is a 3,000-mile-long river in China. It carries tons of yellow silt (soil), which gives the river its color.

*Is Red Square Red?*
No. Red Square in Moscow is so named because Red means "beautiful" in Russian.

*Are There Spices in the Spice Islands?*
Yes. The Spice Islands, in Indonesia, are now called the Moluccas. They are rich in spices such as nutmeg and cloves.

*Is There Ivory on the Ivory Coast?*
Yes. The Ivory Coast of Africa was once the center of the ivory trade for Europeans, who slaughtered elephants to obtain their valuable ivory tusks.

## WHAT COUNTRIES CALL THEMSELVES
Most of our maps and encyclopedias list the English names for the countries of the world. Here are a few of the names countries have for themselves.

*People from New Zealand call themselves Kiwis, after their rare kiwi bird.*

| | |
|---|---|
| BELGIUM | BELGIQUE |
| CAMBODIA | KAMPUCHEA |
| CZECHOSLOVAKIA | CESKOSLOVENSKO |
| GERMANY | DEUTSCHLAND |
| GREECE | HELLAS (ANCIENT); ELLAS |
| GREENLAND | KALATDLIT-NUNAT |
| ISRAEL | YISRAEL |
| JAPAN | NIPPON |
| THE NETHERLANDS | NEDERLAND |
| POLAND | POLSKA |
| SPAIN | ESPAÑA |

## WHATEVER HAPPENED TO CONSTANTINOPLE?

Like people, countries sometimes change their names or disappear altogether. Have you ever wondered what happened to these places?

- *Abyssinia,* an ancient African kingdom, became *Ethiopia.*

- *Angora,* the home of angora goats, became *Ankara,* the capital of Turkey.

- *Bohemia* was a European kingdom, the homeland of Gypsies. After World War I, the Czech people of Bohemia and Moravia joined the Slovaks of Slovakia to form the country of *Czechoslovakia.*

> ### Where was the Roman Empire?
>
> *It once covered North Africa, Spain, France, Germany, Great Britain, Greece, Italy, the Middle East, and parts of eastern Europe.*

- *Ceylon* became a republic in 1972 and changed its name to *Sri Lanka,* which means "splendid thing."

- *Constantinople* was named after the Roman emperor Constantine. When the Turks captured the city, they renamed it *Istanbul.* Many people still called it Constantinople until 1930, when it officially became Istanbul.

- *Peking,* China, is now *Beijing.*

- The kingdom of *Persia* is now *Iran.*

- *Prussia* no longer exists. After World War II, it was divided among Poland, Germany, and the USSR.

- *Rhodesia* in Africa was named after Cecil Rhodes, an Englishman who encouraged Euro-

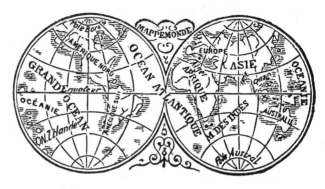

pean whites to settle Africa. Today, Southern Rhodesia is *Zimbabwe*; Northern Rhodesia is *Zambia*.

- *Saigon,* the capital of South Vietnam, became *Ho Chi Minh City* when the communists took over the country. Ho Chi Minh was a communist leader.

- *St. Petersburg,* Russia, was built by the Russian czar Peter the Great. Its name was changed to *Petrograd* and then to *Leningrad*. Lenin was the leader of the revolution that overthrew the Russian czars. In 1991 it was renamed St. Petersburg!

- *Siam* is now *Thailand.*

- *Tanganyika* and *Zanzibar,* in Africa, united to become one country, *Tanzania.*

## WHERE IN THE WORLD ...

*is Count Dracula's castle?*
In the Transylvania region of *Romania*. The castle where Dracula was born still stands in the town of *Sighisoara.*

*is a whole country a desert?*
There is a saying that *Djibouti,* in *Africa,* is "too hot for the devil." It's a hot, dry, desert country where less than 1 square mile is farmland.

*can you find the Temple of the Tooth?*
In *Kandy, Sri Lanka,* where Buddhists built a temple to honor Buddha's tooth. Every year great festivals are held here.

*does a country's government know who owns which trees?*
In *Oman,* in the Mideast. Its date palms are so valuable, the country keeps a list of who owns which trees.

*Where would you go for a safari?*
*To* Nairobi, Africa, *the world's center for tourist safaris.*

329

*can you ride with gauchos?*
In *South America,* cowboys are known as gauchos. *Argentina* is one of the countries where gauchos herd sheep and cattle.

*was pizza first made?*
*Naples, Italy,* is the home of the pizza. Neapolitan women first created pizza pies about 200 years ago.

*are there baby palaces?*
In *North Korea,* nursery schools run by the government are called palaces.

*are the streets "paved" with water?*
In *Venice, Italy,* the streets are canals, and the people move about on boats called gondolas.

*can you lead a double life?*
*Andorra,* a country sandwiched between *Spain* and *France,* is ruled by co-princes, one Spanish, one French. There are two post offices, school systems, courts, and currencies (the franc and the peseta).

*are the streets of the board game Monopoly?*
You'll find Boardwalk, Park Place, Baltic Avenue, and all the rest in *Atlantic City, New Jersey.*

*would you go for a Nobel Prize?*
*Stockholm, Sweden,* is the home of the Nobel Prize, which is awarded yearly to people who have made extraordinary contributions to world peace, the sciences, literature, and medicine.

*is London Bridge?*
The old granite bridge that was always falling down was taken apart in London, shipped to the U.S., and rebuilt in *Arizona.* A new concrete bridge was built in London.

would you find the queen of Sheba's kingdom?
*Yemen,* in the Middle East, was once the kingdom of the queen of Sheba.

*is a shaky country?*
*New Zealanders* call their country "shaky country" because about 400 earthquakes rock it yearly.

*can you throw snowballs across the equator?*
In *Ecuador, South America,* a country named after the equator. It is the only country where both the temperature and the latitude reach zero. There are glaciers in the high mountains of this equatorial country.

*is King Arthur buried?*
An ancient monastery in *Glastonbury, England,* is said to be the burial place of King Arthur and the Excalibur sword.

*is Sherwood Forest?*
In *Nottinghamshire, England.* At one time it was the royal hunting grounds for the king of England; now it is under the protection of the British Forestry Commission.

*is the home of the yodel?*
In the *Swiss Alps,* where cow herders first yodeled to call from the mountains to the meadows. Yodelerfests are held yearly in *Engelberg, Switzerland.*

*are Dorothy's ruby slippers?*
The slippers worn by Judy Garland in the movie *The Wizard of Oz* are in the Smithsonian Institution in *Washington, D.C.*

*Where is the home of bullfights?*
Seville, Spain, *is known as the bullfighting capital of the world.*

## MONUMENTAL PLACES

These famous landmarks are stunning examples of both the power of nature and the strength and ingenuity of people.

*The Acropolis*

This ancient marble ruin is high in the center of Athens, Greece. The Parthenon, a temple built to the goddess Athena Parthenos, was built there 2,000 years ago. Its ruins can still be seen today.

*The Alhambra*

This fortress and palace in Granada, Spain, was built by North African people called Moors, who once ruled there. King Ferdinand and Queen Isabella sent an army to capture Alhambra and drive the Moors out of Spain.

*Angkor Wat*

This ancient temple and palace built by the Khmers is in Cambodia. For hundreds of years it

*You can take an elevator, ascending on a curve, to the top of the Eiffel Tower and buy a hot dog!*

was hidden, swallowed up by the jungle. Once uncovered, massive temples, gates, and canals with picture carvings told much about life in the Khmer Empire. Why this complex was abandoned is still a mystery.

*Australian Fence*
The world's longest fence, at 6,000 miles, was built in the Australian outback by sheepherders to keep dingos (wild dogs) away from their sheep.

*Ayers Rock*
This gigantic red sandstone boulder, which rises 1,143 feet above the Australian desert, is a mile and a half long. Its colors change from pink at dawn to orange at midday, red at sunset, and lavender at night.

*Colosseum*
This ancient open theater in Rome, Italy, held fights in which gladiators and wild beasts fought to

*Today the Colosseum, in partial ruins, is the home of thousands of stray cats.*

## The Seven Wonders of the Ancient World

| WONDER | LOCATION |
| --- | --- |
| Hanging Gardens of Babylon | South of Baghdad, Iraq |
| Colossus of Rhodes | Greek island of Rhodes in the Aegean Sea |
| Great Temple of Diana | Ephesus, Turkey |
| Great Pyramids | Giza, Egypt |
| Statue of Zeus | Olympia, Greece |
| Pharos of Alexandria | Pharos, an island off Alexandria, Egypt (lighthouse) |
| Mausoleum of Halicarnassus | Bodium, Turkey |

*Easter Island belongs to Chile, although it is some 2,000 miles away in the Pacific Ocean.*

the death before cheering audiences of thousands.

### Easter Island Statues
These mysterious carved stone statues stand on the shore of Easter Island facing inland. No one knows who made them or why.

### Eiffel Tower
This open, ironwork structure is a symbol of France. Built in 1889 for the Centennial Exposition in Paris, its 984-foot height made it the world's first skyscraper. The tower was named for its designer, the engineer Alexandre Gustave Eiffel.

### The Great Wall of China
This wall is so big and long, it can be seen from the moon! It was built more than 2,000 years ago to protect China from invaders. The walls, 12 feet thick and 25 feet high, stretch 1,500 miles across China.

### The Kremlin

Kremlin means "fortress" in Russian. Moscow's Kremlin is a walled fortress surrounding palaces, cathedrals, and government buildings. The throne of Czar Ivan the Terrible is in the Armory Palace in the Kremlin.

### The Leaning Tower of Pisa

This 184.5-foot marble bell tower was built in Pisa, Italy, about 700 years ago. It began to lean during its construction and now tilts more than 17 feet from the perpendicular. Stairs lead to the top, where the bells remain silent. It's thought that the clanging will make the tower lean more.

### The Pan-American Highway

The longest highway in the world, it starts in northwest Alaska and stretches all the way to Chile. It then crosses South America to end in Brasilia, Brazil.

### Stonehenge

This ring of huge stones set in place 4,000 years ago is in the countryside of southern England. No one knows how or why they are there.

## The Taj Mahal

This white marble tomb was built in the 17th century by an emperor of India in memory of his beloved wife, Mumtaz-i-Mahal. (*Taj* means "crown.") The emperor had to create an entire town for the 20,000 men who needed 20 years to build the structure. It is still considered one of the most gracious and beautiful buildings in the world.

## The White Cliffs of Dover

The Strait of Dover separates France from England. On the English side near the town of Dover, graceful white cliffs made of chalk line the coast.

## Zimbabwe

A ruined city with thick stone walls sits mysteriously in the bush of Africa. Since stones are rare in that region, people think they were once part of a great empire. The African country of Zimbabwe was named for these ruins.

## OFF THE BEATEN PATH

If you went from here to Timbuktu, where exactly would you go? Is it really a long way to Tipperary? It depends on where you are. Here are some of those places famous for being remote.

*Badlands:* The Badlands is a rugged and barren region in southwestern South Dakota and northwestern Nebraska. The soil there is too poor to farm.

*Highlands:* The Highlands is a mountainous region of northern Scotland that is famous for its beautiful terrain.

*High Seas:* The high seas is the area beyond 3 miles from any nation's territory, where no country has authority. Modern pirates still sail on these waters.

*Klondike:* The entire region of gold fields in north-western Canada extending to Alaska is the Klondike. Gold was discovered there in the 1890s.

*Lapland:* Reindeer roam in this region above the Arctic Circle that extends through the northern parts of Sweden, Norway, and Finland.

*Outback:* The outback is the wild west of Australia. It is an area west of the Great Dividing Range, which is desert land, with red dust.

*Pole of Inaccessibility:* This point on Antarctica is the farthest inland from all the seas that surround the continent.

*Siberia:* This is a vast area of northern Asia. Parts of Siberia are permanently frozen, and the average winter temperature is –50°F. It has long been a place for runaways, exiles, and Russian prisoners.

*Timbuktu:* Timbuktu is a city in Mali, Africa, near the Niger River and Sahara, a trading post once thought to be a city of gold. Many adventurers died trying to reach Timbuktu.

*Tipperary:* Tipperary is an Irish county. It's not very far from many places, but it earned this reputation from the song "It's a Long Way to Tipperary," sung by soldiers during World War I.

*The Gulf Stream carries 25 million tons of warm water. It is 90 miles wide and 1 mile deep and moves at 4–6 mph.*

## WORLDWIDE ADVENTURES

### Digging to China

If you *could* dig to China, you'd have to begin in
Chile or Argentina. If you started digging in Hawaii, you'd end up in the Kalahari Desert. If you
started at the South Pole, you'd reach the North
Pole. These are *antipodes,* places opposite each
other on the globe.

### Go Fly a Kite

If you put a kite aloft in the trade winds it would
fly west, directed by the earth's rotation. The trade
winds blow just north and south of the equator.
Watch out for the doldrums, an area between the
two belts of trade winds which has long periods
with no wind.

### Send a Message in a Bottle

Throw a bottle into the Gulf Stream off the coast of
Florida. It may wash ashore in Bermuda or far
north on the shores of Iceland! (Other ocean cur-

*In 1991,
thousands of
Nike shoes
fell off a
cargo ship
northeast of
Hawaii.
Scientists
learned about
ocean cur-
rents by
locating the
shoes as they
washed
ashore on the
west coast of
the U.S.*

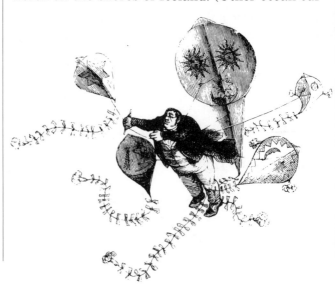

*Here is a formula for finding opposite places in the world. Find the latitude of your starting place. Change the direction. For example, if it's north make it south. Find the longitude. Subtract it from 180. Change the direction. For example, if it's east, make it west. The new latitude and longitude will be the opposite point on the globe. Where is the opposite of your home?*

rents are the Humboldt, Equatorial, Japan, and Antarctic.)

### Ride a River of Ice
Climb on the Columbia Glacier in Prince William Sound in Alaska, but don't expect a fast ride. A turtle moves faster in 10 minutes than this glacier moves in a day.

### Float on an Iceberg
The largest iceberg ever was sighted in the south Pacific Ocean in 1956. It was 208 miles long and 60 miles wide, about the size of Belgium.

### Meet Fata Morgana
Fata Morgana is the name for a mirage associated with the enchantress Morgan Le Fay, of Arthurian legend. It is caused by a layer of hot air over water or two layers of air with unequal density. (What appears to the human eye is a shape as simple as a cottage or as wondrous as a castle.) Fata Morgana occurs in the Strait of Messina, near Japan, and over the Great Lakes in the U.S.

# FIFTY STATES, FIFTY CAPITALS, AND FIFTY FUN FACTS

| STATE/CAPITAL | HOME OF |
| --- | --- |
| ALABAMA<br>Montgomery | George Washington Carver, who discovered more than 300 uses for peanuts |
| ALASKA<br>Juneau | The longest coastline in the U.S., 6,640 miles, greater than that of all other states combined |
| ARIZONA<br>Phoenix | The most telescopes in the world, in Tucson |
| ARKANSAS<br>Little Rock | The only active diamond mine in the U.S. |
| CALIFORNIA<br>Sacramento | "General Sherman," a 3,500-year-old tree, and a stand of bristlecone pines 4,000 years old are the world's oldest living things |
| COLORADO<br>Denver | The world's largest silver nugget (1,840 pounds) found in 1894 near Aspen |
| CONNECTICUT<br>Hartford | The first American cookbook, published in Hartford in 1796: *American Cookery* by Amelia Simmons |
| DELAWARE<br>Dover | The first log cabins in North America, built in 1683 by Swedish immigrants |
| FLORIDA<br>Tallahassee | U.S. spacecraft launchings from Cape Canaveral, formerly Cape Kennedy |
| GEORGIA<br>Atlanta | The Girl Scouts, founded in Savannah by Juliette Gordon Low in 1912 |
| HAWAII<br>Honolulu | The only royal palace in the U.S. (Iolani) |
| IDAHO<br>Boise | The longest main street in America, 33 miles, in Island Park |
| ILLINOIS<br>Springfield | The tallest building in the world, Sears Tower, in Chicago |
| INDIANA<br>Indianapolis | The famous car race: Indy 500 |
| IOWA<br>Des Moines | The shortest and steepest railroad in the U.S., Dubuque: 60° incline, 296 feet |
| KANSAS<br>Topeka | Helium discovered in 1905 at the University of Kansas |

| STATE/CAPITAL | HOME OF |
|---|---|
| KENTUCKY<br>Frankfort | The largest underground cave in the world: 300 miles long, the Mammoth-Flint Cave system |
| LOUISIANA<br>Baton Rouge | The most crayfish: 98% of the world's crayfish |
| MAINE<br>Augusta | The most easterly point in the U.S., West Quoddy Head |
| MARYLAND<br>Annapolis | The first umbrella factory in the U.S., 1928, Baltimore |
| MASSACHUSETTS<br>Boston | The first World Series, 1903: the Boston Pilgrims vs. the Pittsburgh Pirates |
| MICHIGAN<br>Lansing | The Cereal Bowl of America, Battle Creek, produces most cereal in the U.S. |
| MINNESOTA<br>St. Paul | The oldest rock in the world, 3.8 billion years old, found in Minnesota River valley |
| MISSISSIPPI<br>Jackson | Coca-Cola, first bottled in 1894 in Vicksburg |
| MISSOURI<br>Jefferson City | Mark Twain and some of his characters, such as Tom Sawyer and Huckleberry Finn |
| MONTANA<br>Helena | Grasshopper Glacier, named for the grasshoppers that can still be seen frozen in ice |
| NEBRASKA<br>Lincoln | The only roller skating museum in the world, in Lincoln |
| NEVADA<br>Carson City | Rare fish such as the Devils Hole pup, found only in Devils Hole, and other rare fish from prehistoric lakes; also the driest state |
| NEW HAMPSHIRE<br>Concord | Artificial rain, first used near Concord in 1947 to fight a forest fire |
| NEW JERSEY<br>Trenton | The world's first drive-in movie theater, built in 1933 near Camden |
| NEW MEXICO<br>Santa Fe | "Smokey Bear," a cub orphaned by fire in 1950, buried in Smokey Bear Historical State Park in 1976 |
| NEW YORK<br>Albany | "Uncle Sam," the symbol of the U.S., in Troy |
| NORTH CAROLINA<br>Raleigh | Virginia Dare, the first English child born in America, on Roanoke Island in 1587 |

| STATE/CAPITAL | HOME OF |
|---|---|
| NORTH DAKOTA<br>Bismarck | The geographic center of North America, in Pierce County, near Balta |
| OHIO<br>Columbus | The first electric traffic lights, invented and installed in Cleveland in 1914 |
| OKLAHOMA<br>Oklahoma City | The first parking meter, installed in Oklahoma City in 1935 |
| OREGON<br>Salem | The world's smallest park, *totaling* 452 inches, created in Portland on St. Patrick's Day for leprechauns and snail races |
| PENNSYLVANIA<br>Harrisburg | The first magazine in America: the *American Magazine,* published in Philadelphia for 3 months in 1741 |
| RHODE ISLAND<br>Providence | Rhode Island Red chickens, first bred in 1854; the start of poultry as a major American industry |
| SOUTH CAROLINA<br>Columbia | The first tea farm in the U.S., created in 1890 near Summerville |
| SOUTH DAKOTA<br>Pierre | The world's largest natural, indoor warm-water pool, Evans' Plunge in Hot Springs |
| TENNESSEE<br>Nashville | Graceland, the estate and gravesite of Elvis Presley |
| TEXAS<br>Austin | NASA, in Houston, headquarters for all manned U.S. space projects |
| UTAH<br>Salt Lake City | Rainbow Bridge, the largest natural stone bridge in the world, 290 feet high, 275 feet across |
| VERMONT<br>Montpelier | The largest production of maple syrup in the U.S. |
| VIRGINIA<br>Richmond | The only full-length statue of George Washington, placed in capitol in 1796 |
| WASHINGTON<br>Olympia | Lunar Rover, the vehicle used by astronauts on the moon; Boeing, in Seattle, makes aircraft and spacecraft |
| WEST VIRGINIA<br>Charleston | Marbles; most of the country's glass marbles made around Parkersburg |
| WISCONSIN<br>Madison | The typewriter, invented in Milwaukee in 1867 |
| WYOMING<br>Cheyenne | The "Register of the Desert," a huge granite boulder covering 27 acres with 5,000 early pioneer names carved on it |

# STATE REGIONS
These regions have similar climate, geography, traditions, and history.

**New England**
Connecticut, Maine, Massachusetts, New Hampshire, Rhode Island, Vermont

**Middle Atlantic**
New Jersey, New York, Pennsylvania

**Southern**
Alabama, Arkansas, Delaware, Florida, Georgia, Kentucky, Louisiana, Maryland, Mississippi, North Carolina, South Carolina, Tennessee, Virginia, West Virginia

**Midwest**
Illinois, Indiana, Iowa, Kansas, Michigan, Minnesota, Missouri, Nebraska, North Dakota, Ohio, South Dakota, Wisconsin

**Rocky Mountain**
Colorado, Idaho, Montana, Nevada, Utah, Wyoming

**Southwest**
Arizona, New Mexico, Oklahoma, Texas

**Pacific Coast**
California, Oregon, Washington

## Sizing Up the States

*Largest:*
Alaska, 570,833 square miles

*Smallest:*
Rhode Island, 1,212 square miles

*Most populous:*
California, 29,839,250 residents

*Least populous:*
Wyoming, 455,975 residents

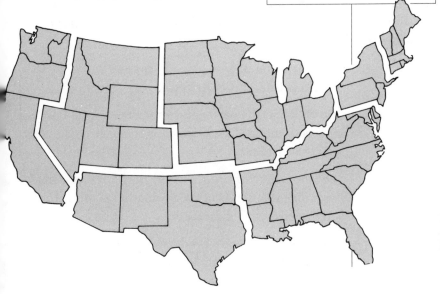

## WORLDWIDE TREASURE HUNT

There may be lost pirate treasure buried in the coves of the Caribbean Islands. There are certainly lost treasures of gold and jewels aboard early Spanish sailing ships sunk at sea. But not all treasure is lost. The earth is full of found treasures. Here are just a few of them.

*Bauxite:* This mineral is used to make aluminum. *Guinea* in Africa is rich with it.

*Cashews:* These delicious nuts grow on trees in *Mozambique,* a country in southeast Africa.

*Chewing Gum:* The sapodilla tree of *Central America* is the source of chicle, which is what puts the chew in chewing gum.

*Chocolate:* The seed of the cacao tree, which is found on many *Caribbean islands,* is used to make chocolate.

*Chromium:* This metal is used to make stainless steel. There is plenty of chromium in *Zimbabwe, Africa.*

*Copper:* One of the richest "copper belts" in the world is in *Zambia, Africa.*

*Cork:* Bulletin boards and stoppers in wine bottles are both made of cork, which is the bark of the cork oak tree in *Spain.*

*Diamonds: Namibia, Africa,* supplies the most valuable diamonds of the 18 countries in southern Africa rich with diamonds.

*Emeralds: Colombia* produces the most emeralds of any country in South America.

*The largest chocolate factory in the world is in Hershey, Pennsylvania.*

*Gold:* The world's largest gold mine is in *Juneau, Alaska.*

*Mahogany:* The trees that supply this beautiful wood grow in *Central America.*

*Nitrates:* This mineral used to preserve foods is found in the desert of *Chile.*

*Perfume:* In the south of *France,* flowers are grown for their oils, which are used in making perfumes.

*Seaweed:* Off the coast of *Japan,* seaweed is harvested to eat or to flavor foods.

*Sugar:* Sugarcane is grown in many countries in *Central America* and the *Caribbean Islands.*

*Vanilla:* There wouldn't be vanilla ice cream without the vanilla bean. More than half the world's vanilla is grown in *Madagascar.*

*Wool:* Most of the world's wool is supplied by the sheep of *Australia.*

## HOLY PLACES
Throughout the world are places of special significance to different religious groups. Here's just a sampling of the world's sacred spots.

The *Holy Land* — a collective name for Israel, Jordan, and Egypt — is a place of pilgrimage for Muslims, Jews, and Christians.

The *Ganges River* in India is sacred to Hindus. They drink its water, bathe in it, and scatter the ashes of their dead in it. *Fuji,* in Japan, is sacred to the Buddhist and Shinto religions.

*Kairouan, Tunisia, became one of Islam's holy cities when, according to legend, a spring opened up at the feet of a holy leader, revealing a golden chalice last seen in Mecca.*

The *Black Hills* of South Dakota are a holy place for Native Americans, who travel there in quest of a vision, a moment of peace and oneness with the universe. Vision quests last 4 days and 4 nights.

*Mount Fai Shan* is China's sacred mountain. It is thought to be a center of living energy — a holy place for Taoists and Buddhists.

The *Sacred Mosque in Mecca* is where Muslims the world over face 5 times a day to pray.

*Lourdes, France,* is the home of a Roman Catholic shrine where the Virgin Mary was said to appear to St. Bernadette.

## PLACES OF PAIN

There are places in the world whose names bring to mind human pain and suffering caused by other people, nature, or both. Included here are some of these places and the horrors and disasters that caused their infamy.

*Auschwitz* was only one of the Nazi concentration camps. They were built in the 1930s to exterminate Jews by killing them in gas chambers. Auschwitz, in Poland, is now called Oswiecim.

*Bangladesh,* a small country next to India, is the site of a constant battle with nature. Over the years it has suffered from floods, tidal waves, cyclones, tornados, and famine.

*Belfast,* in Northern Ireland, is the scene of frequent terrorist activities in the ongoing struggle between Catholics and Protestants.

*The Black Hole of Calcutta,* a small dungeon (18 x 14 feet) in Calcutta, India, is reputed to have held 146 British prisoners in 1756. On their first day in prison, 123 of the prisoners died from suffocation. The Black Hole of Calcutta became the name for that otherwise nameless jail.

*Hiroshima, Nagasaki:* When the U.S. dropped atom bombs on these two Japanese cities to end World War II, millions died or were maimed, and the cities were destroyed.

*Pearl Harbor:* This U.S. naval base in Hawaii was attacked by the Japanese on December 7, 1941: 18 ships were sunk, 200 planes were destroyed, and 3,700 casualties suffered. This surprise attack propelled the U.S. into World War II.

*Ring of Fire:* This is where the land plates of Asia and the Americas meet the Pacific Ocean plate. Some 60% of the world's volcanic eruptions and earthquakes occur along this line.

*Soweto* is a group of townships in South Africa where black Africans live and where severe racial violence erupts in the struggle against apartheid (racial separation).

*The Tower of London* is a fortress in London, England. Inside, the Traitor's Gate and Bloody Tower were the site of many beheadings.

*Wounded Knee* is a creek in South Dakota where, in 1890, U.S. soldiers killed 200 Sioux women, children, and warriors.

# CIRCLING THE GLOBE

You can't see them, but they're there. Points and lines on a map define not only where you are, but also when you're there. Navigators still rely on these imaginary lines to get where they are going. You can use them, too.

*The horse latitudes lie at 30° north and 30° south. They are known for lack of wind. Becalmed sailors probably named them for the many horses on board ship that died for lack of water.*

### The Antarctic Circle
The Antarctic Circle lies three-quarters of the way between the equator and the South Pole.

### The Arctic Circle
Three-quarters of the way between the equator and the North Pole lies the Arctic Circle. Above this line is the Arctic region, where nights last for 24 hours in the middle of winter. It is known as the Land of the Midnight Sun because in summer the sun never sets.

### DEW Line
The DEW (distant early warning) line is a 3,000-mile line of radar stations north of the Arctic Circle. It should notify the U.S. and Canada of the approach of enemy planes or missiles.

### The Equator
This imaginary circle goes around the middle of the earth for 24,902 miles. It divides the Northern Hemisphere from the Southern Hemisphere and is exactly between the North and South Poles.

### The International Date Line
An imaginary line where the date changes one day when passed. It is one day earlier east of the line than it is on the west.

### Latitude
Lines that run east and west on a map. The

equator's latitude is 0° and the poles are 90° south and north. One degree of latitude equals about 69 miles.

## Longitude

Lines that run north and south on a map from pole to pole. Longitude is used together with latitude to form a grid on which it is possible to locate any place on the earth.

## The Tropic of Cancer

A parallel line of latitude that is a quarter of the way from the equator to the North Pole. During the summer solstice, the sun is directly overhead.

## The Tropic of Capricorn

This line of latitude is a quarter of the way from the equator to the South Pole. During the winter solstice, the sun is directly overhead.

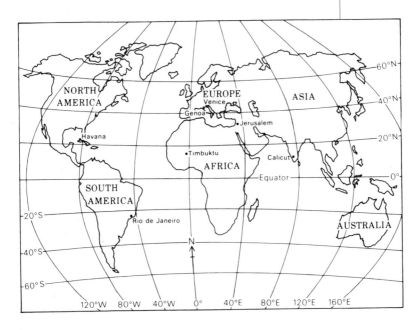

## THE WHOLE WIDE WORLD

The U.S. is just one country in our big world. Did you know that at this writing there are 183 countries? Some have states, some have territories, others have neither. Yet every country has distinct boundaries and its own name and flag, and most issue their own money. Get out your atlas—here are all the countries:

AFGHANISTAN •
ALBANIA • ALGERIA • ANDORRA •
ANGOLA • ANTIGUA/BARBUDA • ARGENTINA •
ARMENIA • AUSTRALIA • AUSTRIA • AZERBAIJAN • BAHAMAS
• BAHRAIN • BANGLADESH • BARBADOS • BELGIUM • BELIZE •
BELORUS • BENIN • BHUTAN • BIRKINA FASO • BOLIVIA • BOTSWANA •
BRAZIL • BRUNEI • BULGARIA • BURUNDI • CAMEROON • CANADA • CAPE VERDE
• CENTRAL AFRICAN REPUBLIC • CHAD • CHILE • CHINA • COLOMBIA • COMOROS
• CONGO • COSTA RICA • CUBA • CYPRUS • CZECHOSLOVAKIA • DENMARK • DJIBOUTI •
DOMINICA • DOMINICAN REPUBLIC • ECUADOR • EGYPT • EL SALVADOR • EQUATORIAL
GUINEA • ESTONIA • ETHIOPIA • FIJI • FINLAND • FRANCE • GABON • GAMBIA • GEORGIA •
GERMANY • GHANA • GREECE • GRENADA • GUATEMALA • GUINEA • GUINEA-BISSAU • GUYANA
• HAITI • HONDURAS • HUNGARY • ICELAND • INDIA • INDONESIA • IRAN • IRAQ • IRELAND •
ISRAEL • ITALY • IVORY • COAST • JAMAICA • JAPAN • JORDAN • KAMPUCHEA • KAZAKHISTAN •
KENYA • KIRGHIZIA • KIRIBATI • KOREA • NORTH KOREA • SOUTH KUWAIT • LAOS • LATVIA • LEBA-
NON • LESOTHO • LIBERIA • LIBYA • LIECHTENSTEIN • LITHUANIA • LUXEMBOURG • MADAGASCAR
• MALAWI • MALAYSIA • MALDIVES • MALI • MALTA • MAURITANIA • MAURITIUS • MEXICO •
MOLDAVIA • MONACO • MONGOLIA • MOROCCO • MOZAMBIQUE • MYANMAR (BURMA) • NAMIBIA
• NAURU • NEPAL • NETHERLANDS • NEW ZEALAND • NICARAGUA • NIGER • NIGERIA • NORWAY
• OMAN • PAKISTAN • PANAMA • PAPUA • NEW GUINEA • PARAGUAY • PERU • PHILIPPINES •
POLAND • PORTUGAL • QATAR • ROMANIA • RUSSIA • RWANDA • ST. CHRISTOPHER AND NEVIS
• ST. LUCIA • ST. VINCENT AND THE GRENADINES • SAN MARINO • SÃO TOMÉ AND PRINCIPE
• SAUDI ARABIA • SENEGAL • SEYCHELLES • SIERRA LEONE • SINGAPORE • SOLOMON
ISLANDS • SOMALIA • SOUTH AFRICA • SPAIN • SRI LANKA • SUDAN • SURINAME •
SWAZILAND • SWEDEN • SWITZERLAND • SYRIA • TADZHIKISTAN • TAIWAN • TAN-
ZANIA • THAILAND • TOGO • TONGA • TRINIDAD AND TOBAGO • TUNISIA •
TURKEY • TURKMENISTAN • TUVALU • UGANDA • UKRAINE • UNITED
ARAB EMIRATES • UNITED KINGDOM • UNITED STATES • URU-
GUAY • UZBEKISTAN • VANUATU • VATICAN CITY •
VENEZUELA • VIETNAM • WESTERN SAMOA •
YEMEN • YUGOSLAVIA • ZAIRE •
ZAMBIA • ZIMBABWE

## THE WORLD OF FASHION

The next time you put on your argyles or bikini, remember that they took their names from real places on the globe.

*Ascot,* a village in Berkshire, England, is the home of a famous annual horse race. During the 1700s, people who attended the races wore a wide, loosely tied scarf, which started a new fashion trend known as the ascot.

*Bikini,* a tiny coral island in the Pacific Marshall Islands, is where the U.S. conducted atom bomb tests in the late 1940s. Four days after the A-bomb was exploded, a French designer introduced a scanty, two-piece bathing suit and called it the bikini. He believed it would cause a fashion explosion, and indeed it did.

*Cologne* (in German spelled *Köln*), is the city in Germany where cologne was first produced. Cologne is a scented liquid made of alcohol and various fragrant oils, similar to perfume.

*Fez* is a city in Morocco. A fez is a brimless felt hat, usually red, with a black tassel hanging from its crown. It was first worn by men in Morocco and is still worn by Muslim men today.

*Guernsey* is one of the Channel Islands in the southwest-central English Channel. A guernsey is a snug, knitted wool shirt first worn by seamen in this area.

*Nîmes,* France, is the source of denim. In French it was called *serge de Nîmes,* or "fabric from Nîmes," and *de Nîmes* became "denim."

*Panama hats are woven straw hats made in Ecuador. However, they were named for Panama because they were shipped from there in the 1800s.*

351

*Rhinestone* (Bas-Rhin) is a district in France where rhinestones were first made. Rhinestones are colorless, artificial gems made of paste or glass.

*Suede* is the French pronunciation of Sweden, where this soft, velvety leather was first made.

*Tuxedo* is in Westchester County, north of New York City. The tuxedo, a black formal men's dinner suit without "tails," was first worn here.

# Index

Ninjutsu, 256–57
Nocturnal animals, 12

# O

Occupations, 82–90, 232–34
Oil spills, 144
Omnivorous animals, 12
Orion, 284
Ostriches, 27, 57
Otters, 18
Owls, 17, 21, 26
Ozone layer, 143

# P

Pain, places of, 346–47
Pan-American Highway, 335
Parakeets, 18
Parish, Peggy, 67
Peacocks, 23
Penguins, 20–21, 26
People, 211–42
  behavior of, 219–21
  groups of, 241–42
  generic names for, 213–15
  in groups, 212–13
  ethnic groups, 235–37
  titles of, 221–22
  tribal groups, 237–238
Perrault, Charles, 66
Pestilence, 124–25
Peter Pan, 217
Pet Rock, 93
Pets, 30–31
Phoenix, the, 21
pH scale, 143
Pisces (The Fish), 287
Pigs, 17, 34
Pigeons, used in battle, 311
Pinnipeds, 12
Planets, the, 267–71
Platypus, 27
Pluto, 271
Polynesian countries, 318
Portuguese man-of-war, 28
Prairie dogs, 14, 25
Predators, 12

Presidents, U.S.
  and families, 225–27
  and occupations, 90
  and pets, 30
Primates, 12
Pseudonyms, 158–59
  of unreal people, 217
Ptolemy, 280

# Q

Quadrupeds, 12

# R

Rabbit, cottontail, 27
Raccoons, 17
Rats, 17, 28
Ravens, 21
Recycling, 140–43
Reindeer, 18
Religions, 223–24
Remoras, 16
Rheas, 21
Rhinoceros, 18
Richter scale, 121
Rodents, 12
Rights, 183–86
Roman numerals, 200
Rooster, 17
Rough Riders, 309
Royalty, 229–31

# S

Sagittarius (The Archer), 286
Sailfish, 13
Samurai, 309
Sand grouse, 21
Saturn, 270
Scandinavian countries, 318
Scavengers, 16–17
Scorpio (The Scorpion), 286
Scorpion fish, 27
Scorpions, 14
Sea cucumbers, 26, 22
Seagulls, 16
Seahorses, 21
Seals, 19, 31

*oring Book* copyright © 1989 **Environmental Protection Agency Logo** EPA **Earth Photo** NASA **Dinosaur** Laurel Cook **Cousteau Society Logo** The Cousteau Society **Rainforest Alliance Logo** The Rainforest Alliance

**SPEAKING OF LANGUAGE**
**Baker's Dozen, Homonym, Blue Ribbon, Traffic Light** Sara Mintz Zwicker

**LAWS AND RIGHTS**
**Courtroom Layout** Sara Mintz Zwicker **The Constitution** The National Archives, Washington, D.C. **United Nations Seal** The United Nations **Policeman's Gear, Bullet Proof Vest** Sara Mintz Zwicker

**MEASURING UP**
**Abacus** Copyright © 1984, by the Riverside Publishing Company. Reproduced by permission of Houghton Mifflin Company. **Time Zone Map** Sara Mintz Zwicker **Thermometer** Laurel Cook **Clouds** Laurel Cook **Strawberries** Sara Mintz Zwicker **Highway Map** Sara Mintz Zwicker **Metric Rulers** Laurel Cook **Gallon of Milk** Laurel Cook

**PEOPLE PAMPHLET**
**U.S. Seal** Department of the Treasury, Bureau of Engraving and Printing **Henry VIII** Library of Congress **Neanderthal Silhouettes** *Illustrated Atlas of World History,* Copyright © 1990 by Grisewood & Dempsey, Ltd. **Orchestra** Laurel Cook

**SPORTS SECTION**
**Joe Montana** San Francisco '49ers **Gymnastics vs. Calisthenics** Sara Mintz Zwicker **Sports Jerseys** Sara Mintz Zwicker **Hockey Goalie** Sara Mintz Zwicker **NBA Logo** National Basketball Association **NFL Logo** National Football League **NHL Logo** National Hockey League

**UNIVERSAL KNOWLEDGE**
**Saturn** NASA **Planets** Laurel Cook **Asteroid Belt Diagram** Laurel Cook **Quasar** NASA **Astronaut on Moon** NASA **NASA Logo** NASA **Halley's Comet** NASA **Leo Constellation** Laurel Cook

**WIDE WORLD OF WAR**
**Trojan Horse** Bettmann Archive **Congressional Medal of Honor** Official U.S. Navy photograph **Purple Heart** Official U.S. Navy photograph

**THE WORLD**
**Latin America** Sara Mintz Zwicker **Atoll and Archipelago** Sara Mintz Zwicker